FUNDAMENTAL PRINCIPLES OF EU LAW AGAINST MONEY LAUNDERING

Fundamental Principles of EU Law Against Money Laundering

EMMANUEL IOANNIDES
Economic Crime/Compliance Expert, MICA

Routledge
Taylor & Francis Group
LONDON AND NEW YORK

First published 2014 by Ashgate Publishing

Published 2016 by Routledge
2 Park Square, Milton Park, Abingdon, Oxfordshire OX14 4RN
711 Third Avenue, New York, NY 10017, USA

First issued in paperback 2016

Routledge is an imprint of the Taylor & Francis Group, an informa business

British Library Cataloguing in Publication Data
A catalogue record for this book is available from the British Library

The Library of Congress has cataloged the printed edition as follows:
Ioannides, Emmanuel, author.
Fundamental principles of EU law against money laundering / by Emmanuel Ioannides.
pages cm
Includes bibliographical references and index.
ISBN 978-1-4724-3188-2 (hardback)
1. Money laundering--European Union countries--Prevention. 2. Money--Law and legislation--European Union countries--Criminal provisions. I. Title.
KJE7475.I57 2015
345.24'0268--dc23

2014021464

ISBN 13: 978-1-138-63754-2 (pbk)
ISBN 13: 978-1-4724-3188-2 (hbk)

Contents

Table of Cases

Hong Kong Cases

Attorney-General for Hong Kong v Hui Kin Hong [1005] HKCA Crim 351 (Court of Appeal of Hong Kong), paras 5–9.
Attorney-General for Hong Kong v Reid (1994) 1 AC 324.

Scottish Cases

Ahmed v Her Majesty's Advocate 2009 ScotHC HCJAC 60, para 30.

United Kingdom Cases

A

R v Ali [2006] WLR 316 (CA), 351, para 148.
Assets Recovery Agency v Green [2005] EWHC 3168 Admin (HC), paras 33–34.
Assets Recovery Agency v Jackson [2007] EWHC 2553 (QB).
Assets Recovery Agency v Olupitan [2007] EWHC 162 (QB).

C

R v Churchill [1967] 2 AC 224.
Crofter Hand-Woven Harris Tweed Co v Vei tch [1942] AC 435, 439.

D

R v Da Silva [2006] EWCA Crim 1654 (CA).
Director of Assets Recovery Agency v Szepietowski [2007] EWCA Civ 766 (CA).

E

R v El Kurd [2007] EWCA Crim 1888 (CA), para 64.

F

Federation of Tour Operators v HM Treasury [2008] EWCA Civ 752.

G

R v Gabriel [2006] EWCA Crim 229 (CA).

H

Hussien v Chong Fook Kam [1970] AC 948B [13].
Hogan v The Director of Public Prosecutions [2007] EWHC 978 Admin (QB), para 43.

I

R v IK [2007] EWCA Crim 491 (CA).

K

K Ltd v National Westminister Bank Plc [2006] EWCA Civ 1039 (CA) 156.

L

R v Liaquat [2005] EWCA Crim 87 (CA).

M

R v Montila [2004] UKHL 50, para 42.

N

N2J Limited v Cater Allen [2006] EWHC B10 (QB).
R v NW [2008] EWCA Crim2 (CA), paras16, 22.

P

Serious Organised Crime Agency v Pelekanos [2009] EWHC 2307 (QB), paras 6–18.

S

R v Saik [2006] UKHL 18, para 23.
R v Sakavickas [2004] EWCA Crim 2686 (CA).

Shah v HSBC Private Bank (UK) Ltd [2009] EWHC 79 (QB).
Sheldrake v DPP and Attorney-General [2004] 3 WLR 976.
Squirrell Ltd v National Westminister Bank Plc [2005] EWHC 664 (Ch).
R v South Yorkshire Police [2004] UKHL 39.

U

UMBS Online Ltd v Serious Organised Crime Agency Rev 2 [2007] EWCA Civ 406 (CA).

W

R v Whittington [2009] Crim 1641 (AC), paras 40–42.

United States of America Cases

C

California Bankers Association v Shultz 416 US 21 (1974).

U

United States v Miller 435 US 435 442 (1976).

Judgements of the European Court of Justice

Joined Cases C – 92/09 and 93/09 *Volker und Markus Schecke and Eifert* [2010] ECR I–0000.

The European Court of Human Rights

A

Asan Rushiti v Austria App no 28389/95 (ECtHR, 21 March 2000) para 31.
ASML Netherlands BV v Semiconductor Industry Services GmbH (SEMIS) App no 283/05 (ECtHR, 28 September 2006), para 26.

C

Coster v the United Kingdom App no 24876/94 (ECtHR, 28 January 2001), para 104.
Connors v the United Kingdom App no 66746/01 (ECtHR, 27 May 2004), para 82.

G

Grayson & Barnham v The United Kingdom App no 19955/05 (ECtHR, 23 September 2008), paras 9, 11, 16 and 18.

S

S and Marper v the United Kingdom App nos 30562/04 and 30566/04 (ECtHR, 4 December 2008), para 87.

List of Journal Abbreviations

BLI	*Business Law International*
Brit J Criminol	*British Journal of Criminology*
BTR	*British Tax Review*
Comp Law	*Company Lawyer*
ELJ	*European Law Journal*
ELRev	*European Law Review*
ICCLR	*International Company and Commercial Law Review*
ICLQ	*International and Comparative Law Quarterly*
IJCL	*International Journal of Constitutional Law*
JBL	*Journal of Business Law*
JFC	*Journal of Financial Crime*
JIBL	*Journal of International Banking Law*
JIBLR	*Journal of International Banking Law and Regulation*
JIFM	*Journal of International Financial Markets*
JMLC	*Journal of Money Laundering Control*
PCB	*Private Client Business*

Preface

The European Union's anti-money laundering system has been restructured to combat international economic crime and to reshape criminal finance. Today's money laundering conspiracies are more complex and are pregnant with the proceeds of transnational crime. The more criminals succeed in introducing their ill-gotten gains from the informal to the formal economies, the more financial systems and anti-money laundering systems will be exposed to the serious and immediate threats of corruption and penetration.

The reporting system and the exchange of information platforms enable competent authorities to rapidly trace, freeze and confiscate criminal and subversive assets, and to sanction wrongdoers. The harmonious operation of the reporting system and the exchange of information constitutes the central and suspicious eye of the global anti-money laundering regime. However, without the co-existence of the latter and their operational harmony, the central eye of the global anti-money laundering regime will become legally and operationally obsolete.

Against that background, not all suspects and accused persons will be found guilty, that is, subject to not failing to reasonably and truthfully explain the source of their wealth to the competent authorities applying money laundering controls. On the one hand, prosecutors shoulder the burden of proving in court the class of crime as opposed to particularising the specific offence having generated the criminal proceeds traced and attacked by the anti-money laundering system. On the other hand, defendants rightly shoulder the burden of offering, to the satisfaction of the court, reasonable and truthful explanations about the sources of their wealth.

In today's globalised financial system, the shifting of responsibility to private sector reporters to disclose alleged offences through the submission of Suspicious Activity Reports; the confidential investigation of the financial affairs of suspects on the precondition that Suspicious Activity Reports are well founded so as to constitute the starting point for financial intelligence; and the statutory imposition of the obligation on suspects and accused persons to publicly explain the sources of unexplained wealth in their possession and control, cannot but constitute the prescribed tools for the prevention and control of economic crime, illicit enrichment and terrorist financing. After all, businesses and financial institutions have become more transparent and more accountable to financial regulators and to tax authorities than ever before as a result of the responsibility shifted to them by financial regulation.

Moreover, effective money laundering controls must also be compatible with the ECHR. Compatibility is synonymous with proportionality, especially in regard to the retention and movement of the personal of unconvicted persons.

Unconvicted persons are innocent persons and their right to information privacy is inviolable under Article 8(1) of the ECHR. It is therefore the duty of legislators and financial regulators to ensure that when criminal proceedings are terminated against suspects and accused persons due to acquittal or discontinuance, the retention and movement of their sensitive personal data, such as fingerprints, cellular samples and DNA profiles, does not stigmatise them for the rest of their lives as a result of the erroneous application of Article 8(2) of the ECHR.

Prior to turning to the introduction of the book, I would like to single out for thanks Professor Barry Rider, who gave me the opportunity to research and study under him, and for having made numerous meaningful and useful suggestions during the course of my research at the Institute of Advanced Legal Studies, School of Advanced Studies, University of London. Indeed, his guidance and observations were invaluable. His work has not only inspired me, but it has also made me all the more devoted to this fascinating, challenging, and evolving area of the law. In the same spirit, I would like to also single out for thanks Dr Chizu Nakajima, Cass Business School, City University of London and Professor Andrew Campbell, School of Law, University of Leeds, for having encouraged me to take the decision for the publication of this book as a means of contributing to the academic scholarship.

I cannot but close this preface by thanking my loved ones, including my colleagues and associates, for having tolerated my social isolation all these years. I will not explicitly refer to names, relations and professions, for I have come to appreciate that, sometimes, anonymity leaves an enduring gentle touch in writings. However, I do genuinely feel the need to express my most sincere apologies to all these persons, for my conversations with them primarily concerned the law and nothing else but the law.

Introduction:
The Guide to Understanding AML Law

Conceptual Framework

In present times, one of our biggest challenges is to confront the new realities of economic crime and to redefine proportionately our anti-money laundering and counter-terrorism financing policies. This can be accomplished through deepening knowledge and understanding of the phenomenon we call money laundering and sharing that knowledge and understanding openly yet modestly with those who have similar views as well as with those who happen to have diametrically opposite opinions on the effects of anti-money laundering legislation on the financial, political and social aspects of out lives.

We Europeans, despite our being part of a pluralistic politico-economic community well founded upon the principle of a united diversity, are still part of a world vexed with problems, the solution of which requires, on the part of governments and their officials, legislators, financial regulators, judges, prosecutors, practitioners, academics and professionals handling other people's money, to work in collective partnership to ensure that money laundering controls are effective, proportionate and, where circumstances permit, cost-effective.

Of course, it should also be recognised that studies of this nature and character constitute intellectually stimulating sources for the further development of a substantial dialogue between the key players in Member States that will hopefully endeavour to enhance mutual recognition, which is based on the principles of mutual trust, criminal justice, judicial cooperation and compliance with the ECHR.

The transfer of clean money is neither illegal nor worthy of prosecution. Anomy has no place in those financial activities involving property in disposable form emanating from lawful sources. Yet the genuine need to protect national security, public safety, financial integrity and stability, and economic wellbeing as a whole, have become so compelling that today's financial regulators can discharge their enforcement responsibilities only through the application of money laundering controls on the blueprints of financial activities taking place through financial intermediaries at the national and cross-border levels.

The mandatory rules of financial regulation are highly peculiar if not socially unpleasant as they provide that suspicion can be eliminated only when two specific criteria are satisfied: the documentary evidence of the lawful sources of the funds involved and the establishment of innocent financial and commercial motives on the part of the transacting parties. In short, when suspects fail to publicly, reasonably and truthfully explain the legal sources of the property they handle, possess and control, the suspicion of criminal liability cannot be eliminated and will thus become the subject of judicial procedures.

As any jurist would confirm, the imposition of the aforementioned two obligations on natural and legal persons, not only unveils the confidentiality of financial and commercial transactions, but also consolidates the legal extroversion of two diametrically contrary forces that establish innocence or guilt in the context of anti-money laundering law: the statutorily guaranteed confidential submission of self-induced suspicion by reporters and the publicly offered reasonable and truthful explanations on the part of those who have been reported for alleged wrongdoing.

Against that background, it is important to appreciate that these two opposite forces will colourfully paint the suspect's or even the accused's picture of innocence or guilt in the following five different stages of the prevention and control of money laundering: genesis of automated or self-induced suspicion of unusual financial activities; internal processing of the findings of suspicion by financial institutions; submission of Suspicious Activity Reports as disclosures of alleged offences to financial intelligence units (triggering the investigation of the financial affairs of suspects); confidential and compatible with the ECHR financial investigations of suspects; and prosecution of suspects for money laundering, the bringing of the indictment for the offences, and trial.

With the above submissions in mind, it would be useful to recall that anti-money laundering laws are 30 years old. In these three decades, systematic legal research has sufficiently established that money laundering is criminal finance. Henceforth, the criminal liability of money laundering conspirators is strict. Despite the fact that today's financial regulation enables us to fix our eyes on evolving transparency laws, it does not always make sense to the untutored eye that the prevention and control of economically motivated serious crime concerns nothing else but human greed, self-interest and what theologians would be inclined to refer to as the propensity of the ethically weak to fall for Mammon.

Yet what makes this book all the more intellectually challenging is its quest to raise awareness of the great extent to which the international, regional and national legislators have *horizontally* linked this *vertical* lawmaking process to the promotion of global prosperity, in addition to sustainable economic and social development.

Paradoxically, the heteromorphous criminal, civil and tax laws of European Union Member States are continuously being enhanced to combat illicit enrichment in all of its different forms; while wrongdoers, organised criminals and those who become concerned in terrorist financing schemes are constantly preoccupied with discovering systemic weaknesses or inventing new techniques to bypass the controls of the anti-money laundering legislation and to corrupt those holding positions of trust in the financial system.

There are two different categories of readers that will find this book interesting and intellectually stimulating. In the first category there are those who are already convinced that financial regulation has a tremendous potential to enable societies to: deal effectively and proportionately with the immediate and serious threats posed by organised crime and terrorist financing to national security, public safety and financial stability; promote the integrity of financial systems; trace, prosecute and sanction those who engage in serious and economically motivated crimes (money laundering, corruption, fraud, market abuse, insider dealing and the peculation of public and private wealth); and enhance transparency, accountability, good central governance and tax justice at the global level. In the second category there are those who are equally convinced that anti-money laundering legislation is draconian, financially unbearable, and one of the main drivers of the surveillance–security state.

Contents Overview

The contents of this book are divided into eight chapters excluding the introduction. Part I deals with the basic principles of the law and is divided into three chapters (chapters 1–3). Part II deals with the advanced principles of the law and is divided into four chapters (chapters 4–7). With the exception of the introduction and Chapter 8, which contains the conclusions, recommendations and some prognostications, chapters 1 to 7 are identically structured. They contain an introductory section setting out the structural and methodological approaches to the legal issues addressed. At the end of each chapter, a concise recapitulation of the fundamentally important issues discussed is provided in an effort to avoid unnecessary complexity.

Chapter 1 sets out the conceptual scene of money laundering countermeasures and puts to the test the 12 conceptual objectives of anti-money laundering laws through a critical assessment of *what* European Union Member States can achieve from the reporting system and the exchange of information.

Chapter 2 examines *how* the criminal enterprise is resisted and disrupted in light of the amalgamation of international and regional anti-money laundering measures under European Union law, and emphasises the concept of internationalism for mutual benefit. The last section focuses on the legally *interactive* provisions of Directive 2005/60/EC, Regulation 1889/2005 of the European Parliament and of the Council of 26 October 2004 on control of cash entering or leaving the Community, and Regulation 1781/2006 of the European Parliament and of the Council of 15 November 2006 on information on the payer accompanying transfer of funds.

Chapter 3 examines in detail the role of anti-money laundering laws dealing with organised crime and corruption by focusing in particular on: the critical function of anti-money laundering in dealing with transnational organised crime especially from the United Nations' perspective; the role of money laundering in the context of organised crime and corruption; and the role of corruption as the internal enemy of the anti-money laundering system. The fifth and last section closes not only the chapter, but also Part I of the book, and defends the position that the previous trends were drugs, organised crime, terrorism financing and money laundering, but the current trend is corruption.

In Part II, Chapter 4 is concerned with the *economics* of the anti-money laundering strategy and equates global anti-money laundering policy with the establishment and vertical enforcement of rules of transparency from the international to the national level. The critical analysis is thus devoted to four popular topics: unaccountable wealth; taxation; transparency laws; and the *power* versus *reinvestment* issue.

Chapter 5 addresses from the common law perspective three fundamentally important issues concerning the *pragmatic* maintenance of criminal and subversive assets within the reach of the law: shifting statutory responsibility to financial institutions to disclose offences; anatomising the conspiracy charge to launder criminal proceeds; and reflecting upon the burden of proof mainly in criminal cases.

Chapter 6 *thinks* in financial intelligence law. Its areas of primary concern are mainly three: setting the scene of Suspicious Activity Reports analysis; setting out the fundamentals of the law of intelligence; and putting to the test all the hypotheses and legal observations by focusing in particular on the case of the Hellenic Financial Intelligence Unit.

Chapter 7 is equally dynamic for it addresses the following two crucial issues with a particular focus on the UK: the impact of the retention and movement of personal data on the rights of unconvicted persons; and the main effects of financial regulation on businesses. The legal arguments on the incompatibility with the ECHR are based on research findings deriving mainly from jurisprudence and authority, whereas the effects of financial regulation on businesses are presented on the notional platform that concerns the way that people structure and conduct business at the present time.

The final chapter in this book, Chapter 8, provides a synoptic assessment and modestly offers to the readers four key prognostications that look into the future of financial regulation in regard to: the security state; whether the European Union's anti-money laundering regime will become more restrictive and punitive in the future; the rise of the global transparency regime in the immediate future; and the legal changes that technological advancements can bring in the field of DNA analysis in the next decade or so.

PART I
Basic Principles

of Financial Intelligence Units assembled by the Egmont Group; and the engagement of financial institutions in the fight against money laundering.[5]

4. Make criminal wealth vulnerable upon it entering the formal economy,[6] assist in the rapid tracing of criminal assets, and promote civil recovery action domestically and abroad.[7]
5. Eradicate to the maximum possible degree unfair competition,[8] corporate and financial malpractice,[9] market abuse and insider dealing,[10] fraud[11] and tax evasion.[12]
6. Provide a new generation of smarter and more cost-effective tools for the tracing of criminal proceeds. Member States are expected to apply these tools within the framework of an adopted strategy that is based on the principles of effectiveness, proportionality and engagement of stakeholders from the public and private sectors.
7. Facilitate the extraction of information from private sector stakeholders[13] concerning the identity of those persons engaged in apparently suspicious transactions and, at the same time, provide for a system of multiple checks[14] of commercial, financial and personal data[15] by law enforcement and intelligence agencies at the national, regional and international levels.

---

5 HM Treasury, 'The Financial Challenge to Crime and Terrorism 02/2007' <http://www.hm-treasury.gov.uk/d/financialchallenge_crime_280208.pdf> accessed 28 February 2014.

6 European Union Committee, *Money Laundering and the Financing of Terrorism* (HL 2008–09, 132–I) paras 1–5 <http://www.publications.parliament.uk/pa/Id200809/Idselect/Ideucom/132/13204.htm#a2> accessed 9 November 2010.

7 Text to n 6 paras 67–95.

8 European Union Committee – Minutes of Evidence, *Money Laundering and the Financing of Terrorism* (HL 2008–09, 132–II) Question 463 of Lord Dear addressed to witness Mr Ian Pearson, Member of the House of Commons, Economic Secretary to the Treasury, <http://www.publications.parliament.uk/pa/Idselect/Ideucom/132/9042904.htm> accessed 9 November 2010.

9 Europa, 'Corporate and Financial Malpractice' (Europa website 2006) <http://europa.eu/scadplus/leg/en/lvb/133224.htm> accessed 28 February 2014.

10 European Commission, 'Consultations: Internal Market, Call for Evidence: Review of Directive 2003/6/EC on Insider Dealing and Market Manipulation 4/09' (Europa website 2009) <http://europa.eu/internal_market/consultations/docs/2009/market_abuse/call_for_evidence.pdf> accessed 28 February 2014.

11 Europa, 'Mutual Administrative Assistance in the Fight against Fraud' (Europa website 2007) <http://Europa.eu/scadplus/leg/en/lvb/110122.htm> accessed 28 February 2014.

12 Europa, 'Fiscalis 2013 (2008–2013)' (Europa website 2008) <http://europa.eu/scadplus/leg/en/lvb/111051.html> accessed 28 February 2014.

13 Text to n 6 paras 96–113.

14 Text to n 6 paras 100–123.

15 Text to n 8 Question 193 of Lord Marlesford addressed to witness Mr David Thomas, Director, UKFIU, Serious Organised Crime Agency. It is useful to note that

8. Provide a mechanism for the continuous revision and clarification of universally adopted proactive and reactive tools against the laundering of criminal proceeds; increase the level of accountability and private sector engagement;[16] and promote the sharing of knowledge and understanding of newly emerging typologies of money laundering and terrorism financing activity.[17]
9. Tighten controls on persons holding positions of trust in the public and private sectors and, more specifically, prevent corrupted political leaders from siphoning off taxpayers' money.[18] The deeper notion of this objective has to do with the prevention and control of the accumulation of unaccountable wealth in the wrong hands and the prevention and control of illicit enrichment as a whole.[19]
10. Promote and enhance good governance, best practices, transparency and corporate social responsibility.
11. Increase financial regulatory and law enforcement activity in regard to capital flight from *hot* areas through the informal value transfer system,[20] and assist in resolving the problem of how funds are actually transferred from the European Union to destinations such as North Africa without traceable money[21] transfer[22] orders.

Mr Thomas submitted that, in 2008, the 200,000 Suspicious Activity Reports submitted, accrued to the total figure of 1,500,000 Suspicious Activity Reports. Moreover, Mr Thomas underlined that the information extracted is continuously processed by different law enforcement agencies having different investigative interests at stake.

16 Text to n 8 Question 391 of Lord Richard on the role of the Financial Action Task Force and the conditions for membership to it, addressed to witness Sir James Sassoon, former President of the Financial Action Task Force.

17 Text to n 8 Question 391.

18 Text to n 8 Question 462 where Lord Marlesford stressed that one of the most substantive points of the discussion was the protection of taxpayers' money from corrupted leaders.

19 UNODC (United Nations Office on Drugs and Crime), 'Objectives for the Global Programme against Money Laundering, Proceeds of Crime and the Financing of Terrorism' (UN website 2009) <http://www.unodc.org/unodc/en/money-laundering/programme-objectives.htnl> accessed 28 February 2014.

20 Text to n 8 Question 255 of Lord Jopling addressed to witness Professor Gilles de Kerchove, European Union Counter-Terrorism Coordinator, on the Hawala system of informal remittances.

21 Text to n 8 Question 257 of Lord Jopling to which Professor de Kerchove responded by making reference to the North African communities in Europe transmitting money to North Africa without traces.

22 Text to n 8 Question 252 of Baroness Henig addressed to Professor de Kerchove.

12. Enhance the international initiatives to improve poor governance[23] and combat systemic corruption[24] in non-cooperative countries and territories.[25]

Justifications for the Extension of the Anti-Money Laundering Regime

Some Reflections on the Position before Making Drugs Illegal

In the past, gambling was banned, but in present times governments are running lotteries. In the nineteenth century, morphine and opium were not illegal in Europe and in America. Godfrey's Cordial syrup, which contained opium, was widely used to make Victorian babies quieter. Surprisingly, cocaine was the base of numerous remedies for the cold. The non-alcoholic version of French Wine Cola not only contained traces of coca, but also became the top-selling soft drink. Marijuana was used by Queen Victoria to ease the pains of menstruation. Opium was smuggled into China by British merchants in order to balance the purchase of tea for export to Britain. In 1887, America banned opium imports from the Chinese, but allowed those by Americans because the opium import tax was one of the main sources of federal revenue.[26] In other words, the main driver for changing the position of legality or illegality is moral outrage, which is usually backed by vested interests.[27]

Perhaps, the position of governments before making drugs illegal reflects Hans Kelsen's philosophical understanding of justice as social happiness. Should that be the case, then one could further construe that this social happiness is an inspiration that varies with time and place, just as human expectations vary. Dr Kris Hinterseer provided an alternative realistic explanation for the application of *relaxed* money laundering controls as he entertained the theorem that governments at times will either wittingly or unwittingly compromise money laundering controls in order to achieve their political objectives and political priorities.[28]

It is only rational not to take excessive comfort from the general philosophical presumption that drugs were made illegal due to the transformation of social happiness into moral outrage. All the more so, the inquiry into the reasons that must

23 Text to n 8 Question 391 of Lord Richard to which Sir James Sassoon stressed that the involvement of the International Monetary Fund and the World Bank in ensuring implementation of the Financial Action Task Force global standards would actually put pressure on countries whose financial governance is poor to put their houses in order.

24 Commission, 'Proposal for a Directive of the European Parliament and of the Council on the freezing and confiscation of proceeds of crime in the European Union' COM (2012) 85 final.

25 Text to n 8 Question 417 of Lord Hannay of Chiswick on the role of Non-cooperative countries and territories to which Sir James Sassoon responded by referring to the northern part of Cyprus, Uzbekistan and Iran.

26 *The Economist*, 'A Survey of Illegal Drugs' (2001) 360 (8232) 4.

27 Text to n 26.

28 Hinterseer (n 3) 40.

have led governments to wage war on drugs is of particular legal interest. It is also important to keep in mind that it actually took several decades from 1887 to the 1930s for heavy and habitual drug use to substitute medical or casual drug use, as the youth, in particular, increasingly experimented with different types of narcotic and highly addictive psychotropic substances. Drug trafficking and drug dealing evolved in parallel to the different periods of demand for people's experimentation with the herb and the resin of cannabis (1930s), heroin (1970s), cocaine (1980s), and crack cocaine and chemically synthetic drugs (1990s onwards).[29]

Perhaps, the experimentation with different types of narcotics was a fashion trend, which inevitably became a major problem of addiction and a lucrative market of the illicit economy. The phenomenon caused loss of human life, the rise of fatal and non-fatal offences against the person, and the rise of serious offences. The blending of criminal proceeds with lawful wealth[30] became the darling of drug traffickers, drug dealers and money launderers.[31]

Taken together, the above submissions raise the central issue of state intervention in the sphere of the person's sovereignty.[32]

The general principle to consider is that, in the ordinary course of life, it is only over our own bodies and minds that we are sovereign. However, it is equally important to appreciate that, in the context of drug trafficking, drug dealing and drug use, this general principle fails the penal test because our sovereignty extends to harm the physical and moral wellbeing of ourselves and of others. Consequently, it is against the particular legal background of state intervention in the interests of the protection of public interest,[33] legal goods[34] and public morals that one should notionally seek to identify the first justification for the extension[35] of the global anti-money laundering regime.[36]

---

29 *The Economist* (n 26) 5.

30 Oskar Engdahl, 'The Role of Money in Economic Crime' (2008) 48 BJC 2, 154–170.

31 Günther Kaiser, 'The Penal Control of Serious Economic Criminality' in Leonidas Kotsalis (tr), *Penal Series of University of Athens* (Ant N Sakkoulas Publishers 1983) 12–80.

32 *The Economist* (n 26) 5.

33 PC Van Dyne and Michael Levi, 'Drugs and Money: Managing the Drug Trade and Crime – Money in Europe' (2007) 47 BJC 4, 698–701.

34 DK Spirakos, *The Critical Function of the Notion of Legal Good* (Ant N Sakkoulas Publishers 1996) 17–31.

35 GOPAC – Global Organisation of Parliamentarians Against Corruption, 'GOPAC Anti-Money Laundering Initiative: A Proposal 08/06' (GOPAC website 2009) <http://www.gopacnetwork.org/Docs/Global/AML_PROPOSAL_FINAL_en.pdf> accessed 28 February 2014.

36 GN Dimitrainas, *Laundering Dirty Money: Issues of Application of Law 2331/1995* (Nomiki Bibliothiki SA 2002) 24–60; Tom Bennett, *Money Laundering Compliance* (2nd edn, Tottel Publishing 2007) 131–150; Constantin Stefanou and Helen Xanthaki, 'Greece: Money Laundering' (2009) 3 JMLC 2, 161–172; Helen Tsingou, 'Who Governs and Why? The Making of the Global Anti-money Laundering Regime' <http://www.

Justification 1: The War on Drugs

Money laundering became a major policy issue at the G7 Summit in 1989.[37] The United States invited the other Summit participants to join the fight against drugs and to cooperate to establish a task force that would deter and disrupt criminal finance, which was seeping through the banking system and the financial system as a whole.[38] The commonly held view is that, ever since, the Financial Action Task Force has been recognised as the foremost international standard setter of universal norms against money laundering.[39]

As Dr Amandine Scherrer rightly observed, the objectives of the original 1990 Recommendations of the Financial Action Task Force should be classified into three main categories: the improvement of anti-money laundering systems at the national level; the enhancement of international cooperation; and the facilitation of the financial system to effectively combat money laundering.[40]

Furthermore, Dr Scherrer envisioned the aforementioned three categories as the foundations of the *soft* law regime, which influenced the various *hard* law regimes at the national and regional (European Union) levels.[41] But, more deeply, the views and legal developments considered thus far confirm the following crucial points in regard to the evolution of global anti-money laundering standards from 1990 to 2001.

---

garnet-eu-org/fileadmin/documents/workshop_reports/JERP%205.2.4:%20Global%20 Economic%Governance%20and%market%20Regulation%Tsingou_Garnet_2006.pdf> accessed 28 February 2014.

37 Konstantin Magliveras, 'Defeating the Money Launderer – the International and European Network' (1992) JBL 3, 161–177; Johan Viogaert, 'Fighting Economic Crime – Action taken in the European Union' (2001) 9 JFC 1, 22.

38 Sub-Committee F – Home Affairs Money Laundering and the Financing of Terrorism, *Inquiry into EU and International Cooperation to Counter Money Laundering and the Financing of Terrorism: Submission of the Financial Action Task Force Secretariat E/08–09/F99 ML* (HL 2008–09, 132–II) 1 <http://www.parliament.uk/documents/uplo oad(F099)FATFwrittenevidence.pdg> accessed 28 February 2014.

39 Text to n 38 paras 38–39.

40 Amandine Scherrer, 'Explaining Compliance with International Commitments to Combat Financial Crime: The G8 and FATF' (International Studies Association website 2006) <http://www.g7.utoronto.ca/scholar/Scherrer.pdf> accessed 28 February 2014.

41 Text to n 40 para 1.

The legal weapon used in the international[42] war on drugs[43] was the criminalisation of the substantive offence of money laundering.[44] Yet it is equally essential not to fail to recognise that the United Nations Single Convention on Narcotic Drugs, 1961, its amending 1972 Protocol, and the United Nations Convention on Psychotropic Substances, 1971, remain the solid basis for concerted international efforts to control narcotic drugs and psychotropic substances.

Moreover, it may also be argued that Articles 3 (Offences and sanctions), 4 (Jurisdiction), 5 (Confiscation), 6 (Extradition), 7 (Mutual legal assistance), 8 (Transfer of proceedings) and 9 (Other forms of cooperation and training) of the United Nations Convention Against Illicit Traffic in Narcotic Drugs and Psychotropic Substances, 1988, have essentially laid down the foundations for international anti-money laundering measures.

The following examples can adequately defend this position: the 1988 Basel Capital Accord setting out the agreement among the G10 central banks to apply common minimum capital standards to their banking industries and the Basel I–II frameworks of the Bank for International Settlements; the 1990 Council of Europe Convention and Recommendation No R (80) on Measures Against the Transfer and Safekeeping of Funds of Criminal Origin; the 1995 Egmont Group; the 2000 Wolfsberg Global Anti-Money Laundering Guidelines for Private Banking; the European Bank for Reconstruction and Development; the European Central Bank; the International Monetary Fund; the World Bank; Interpol; Europol; the Inter-American Drug Abuse Control Commission; the Organisation for Economic Cooperation and Development; Counter-Terrorism Committee of the Security Council, United Nations; and the United Nations Office on Drugs and Crime.

The adoption of money laundering countermeasures to protect the financial system from money laundering and *grey* capital flight[45] in the 1990s, constituted the first stage of the extension[46] of the global anti-money laundering regime.[47] The Currency and Financial Transactions Reporting Act of 1970, passed by the

---

42 Jeffrey Simser, 'Money Laundering and Asset Cloaking Techniques' (2008) 11 JMLC 1, 15–24; Abdullahi Shehu, 'International Initiatives against Corruption and Money Laundering: An Overview' (2005) 12 JFC 13, 234; Kern Alexander, 'Multi-National Efforts to Combat Financial Crime and the Financial Action Task Force' (2000) 2 JIFM 5, 178–192.

43 Valsamis Mitsilegas, *Money Laundering Counter-Measures in the European Union: A New Paradigm of Security Governance Versus Fundamental Legal Principles* (Kluwer 2003) 44.

44 Guy Stessens, *Money Laundering: A New International Law Enforcement Model* (CUP 2000) 5.

45 Hinterseer (n 3) 39–61.

46 Scherrer (n 40) 2–3.

47 As regards the Financial Action Task Force at the time of writing this book, it has 34 members (16 G20 members are direct members); 157 jurisdictions are members of its eight FATF-Style Bodies; and its Offshore Group on Banking Supervisors comprises of

United States Congress, which has been amended over the years and is commonly described today as the Bank Secrecy Act, is the essential key to reach a better understanding of the anti-money laundering scene across the Atlantic from 1970 to 1990.

As George P. Schultz, Secretary of the Treasury of the United States from 1972 to 1974, has confirmed,[48] the constitutionality of the Bank Secrecy Act has been unsuccessfully challenged for imposing unreasonable burdens of reporting and recordkeeping on financial institutions in *California Bankers Association*.[49] Similarly, in the *Miller*[50] case, the Supreme Court of the United States rejected a similar constitutional challenge by ruling that the right to privacy under the Fourth Amendment does not apply to the maintenance of financial records by a financial institution. The Money Laundering Control Act of 1986 criminalised the offence of money laundering at the Federal level,[51] provided for civil forfeiture for Bank Secrecy Act violations, and obliged banks to comply with the reporting and recordkeeping standards of the Bank Secrecy Act.

And by 1990, the Financial Crimes Enforcement Network (FinCEN) was established as an office under the auspices of the Department of the Treasury.[52] It should therefore be underlined that the global anti-money laundering regime was, and still is, pregnant[53] with the universal norms of the soft law[54] regime.[55]

---

16 members. Therefore, a total of 161 different member jurisdictions in nine groups are committed to implementing international standards.

48 Financial Crimes Enforcement Network, 'Prepared Remarks of James Freis, Jr Director, Financial Crimes Enforcement Network US Department of the Treasury Delivered at the West Coast Anti-Money Laundering Forum' (FinCEN website, 2 May 2012) <http://www.fincen.gov/news_room/speech/pdf/20120502.pdf> accessed 19 June 2012.

49 *California Bankers Association v Shultz* 416 US 21 (1974).

50 *United States v Miller* 435 US 435 442 (1976).

51 Text to n 48 para 8.

52 In 2001, under the USA PATRIOT Act of 2001, the Financial Crimes Enforcement Network became a Bureau (Financial Intelligence Unit) and was entrusted with the responsibilities of receiving, analysing and disseminating financial intelligence.

53 EUROPOL, 'OCTA 2008: EU Organised Crime Threat Assessment' (EUROPOL website 2009) <http://www.Europol.europa.eu/publications/European_Organised_Crime_Threat_Assessment_(OCTA)/OCTA2008.pdf> accessed 28 February 2014.

54 Text to n 8 Question 401 of Lord Mawson to which the former president of the Financial Action Task Force, Sir James Sassoon, explained that the Financial Action Task Force ultimately determines money laundering policy-making.

55 Text to n 8 Questions 247–248 of Baroness Garden of Frognal to which Professor de Kerchove responded by stating that the Financial Action Task Force is where all the anti-money laundering policies are defined and refined.

Justification 2: The War on Organised Crime

The extension of the criminalisation of money laundering to cross-border serious crimes,[56] essentially, beyond drug trafficking offences, has its roots in the 1996 Financial Action Task Force Recommendations.[57] The impetus for enhanced international cooperation in the fight against transnational organised crime can be found both in European Union[58] and United Nations[59] instruments.

It is also pointed out that the academic commentators have not always spoken with one voice on the image of transnational organised crime. As Dr Scherrer has rightly observed, researchers appear to have different views on the definition of the image of organised versus disorganised criminal activity. Perhaps, the diverse fragmentation and fluidity of criminal networks operating within specific geographical areas[60] are the main reasons for the disagreement on the image of transnational organised crime.[61]

However, the epicentre of the present analysis is not the academic commentators' intellectually stimulating interpretations of the image of transnational organised crime, but rather the harm it can cause to human dignity, liberty, security, and the stability and integrity of financial institutions.[62] Why should we, therefore, be concerned with the image of transnational organised crime per se when the information publicly released by investigative authorities reveals that international

56 Recommendation 1 of the Financial Action Task Force: Assessing risks and applying a risk-based approach.

57 WC Gilmore, *Dirty Money: The Evolution of Money Laundering Counter-Measures* (2nd edn, Council of Europe Publishing 1999) 89–91.

58 Joint Action 98/733/JHA of 21 December 1998 on making it a criminal offence to participate in a criminal organisation in the Member States of the EU [1998] OJ L351/1; Council Directive 2001/97/EC of the European Parliament and of the Council of 4 December 2001 amending Council Directive 91/308/EEC on prevention of the use of the financial system for the purpose of money laundering [2001] OJ L344/76.

59 United Nations Convention Against Transnational Organised Crime (the Palermo Convention) concluded on behalf of the European Community on 6 August 2004 by Council Decision 2004/579/EC [2004] OJ L261/69.

60 Scherrer (n 40) 3.

61 Scherrer (n 40) 7–8.

62 Peter Reuter, *Disorganised Crime: The Economics of the Visible Hand* (MIT Press 1983); Panayota Vassou, *Assessing Transnational Organised Crime: Results of a Pilot Survey of 40 Selected Organised Criminal Groups in 16 Countries* (Nathanson Centre for the Study of Organised Crime and Corruption, York University, 2005); Michael Levi, 'Criminal Asset-Stripping: Confiscating the Proceeds of Crime in England and Wales' in A Edwards and P Gill (eds), *Transnational Organised Crime: Perspectives on Global Security* (Routledge 2003) 213–225.

organised crime can corrupt public officials;[63] is connected to violence;[64] generates illicit fortune; abuses positions of public trust;[65] has strong links with narcoterrorism and weapons trafficking;[66] launders proceeds of crime from the informal to the formal economy;[67] and abuses the Internet for drug trafficking?[68]

It is evident that transnational organised crime involves serious and highly profitable offences.[69] Therefore, it can be argued that it constitutes the second justification for the extension of the global anti-money laundering regime to prevent and control the illicit enrichment of those engaged in transnational organised criminal activities.[70] It is precisely for this reason that in the light of Articles 29,

---

63 US Department of Justice, 'Overview of the Law Enforcement Strategy to Combat International Organised Crime 4/08' (US Department of Justice website 2009) <http://www.usdoj.gov/criminal/icitap/press/room/2008/apr/04-23-08combat-intl-crime-overview.pdf> accessed 28 February 2014.

64 US Department of Justice (n 63) 9.

65 US Department of Justice (n 63) 6, 8.

66 US Department of Justice, 'FY 2008 Performance Budget Drug Enforcement Administration Congressional Budget Submission' <http://www.usdoj.gov/jmd/2008justification/Pdf/35_dea.pdf> accessed 28 February 2014.

67 US Department of Justice (n 66) 17.

68 US Department of Justice (n 66) 19.

69 Catherine Austin Fitts, 'Dillon Read & Co Inc And the Aristocracy of Stock Profits' (Paper published on the Internet on the RJR Nabisco Group 2006) <http://www.dunalke.com/3_RJR_Nabisco.htm> accessed 28 February 2014; The Center of Public Integrity, 'Tobacco Companies Linked to Criminal Organizations in Cigarette Smuggling' (The Center of Public Integrity website 2008) <http://www.projects.publicintegrity.org/org/Content.aspx?content=article&id=354> accessed 28 February 2014; Anthony Kennedy, 'Dead Fish across Trail: Illustrations of Money Laundering Methods' (2005) 8 JMLC 4, 305–319.

70 EUROPOL European Law Enforcement Cooperation, 'Annual Report 1998' (EUROPOL website 2009) <http://www.Europol.europa.eu/index.asp?page=publar1998> accessed 28 February 2014; EUROPOL European Law Enforcement Cooperation, 'Annual Report 1999' (EUROPOL website 2009) <http://www.Europol.europa.eu/index.asp?page=publar1999> accessed 28 February 2014; EUROPOL European Law Enforcement Cooperation, 'Annual Report 2000' (EUROPOL website 2009) <http://www.Europol.europa.eu/index.asp?page=publar2000> accessed 28 February 2014; EUROPOL European Law Enforcement Cooperation, 'Annual Report 2001' (EUROPOL website 2009) <http://www.Europol.europa.eu/index.asp?page=publar2001> accessed 28 February 2014; EUROPOL European Law Enforcement Cooperation, 'Annual Report 2002' (EUROPOL website 2009) <http://www.Europol.europa.eu/index.asp?page=publar2002> accessed 28 February 2014; EUROPOL European Law Enforcement Cooperation, 'Annual Report 2003' (EUROPOL website 2009) <http://www.Europol.europa.eu/index.asp?page=publar2003> accessed 28 February 2014; EUROPOL European Law Enforcement Cooperation, 'Annual Report 2004' (EUROPOL website 2009) <http://www.Europol.europa.eu/index.asp?page=publar2004> accessed 28 February 2014; EUROPOL European Law Enforcement Cooperation, 'Annual Report 2005' (EUROPOL website 2009) <http://www.Europol.europa.eu/index.asp?page=publar2005> accessed 28 February

31(1) and 34(2)(b) of the Treaty on European Union, the Council of the European Union has adopted a Framework Decision,[71] which not only defined transnational organised crime, but also laid down special provisions on the particulars of the offences relating to participation in a criminal organisation; the penalties to be imposed on natural and legal persons; and the measures to be taken by Member States on issues relating to jurisdiction and coordination of prosecution.[72]

Justification 3: The War on the Financing of Terrorism

Terrorism is a criminal and lethal method of obtaining political objectives, which essentially differs from organised crime in that it does not aim for profit-making. Plainly terrorism treats both lawful and unlawful funds as the same means to achieve its irrational, criminal and lethal end.

Following the tragic events of September 11, we have all witnessed the third extension of the global anti-money laundering regime to combat the financing of terrorism. Indeed, it has been rightly argued that the financing sources of terrorism are mostly legitimate[73] and that the sums involved are moderate.[74] On this issue, Professor Cameron of Uppsala University has aptly reminded us that the London bombings must have cost a maximum of £8,000.[75] It is therefore crucial to mentally process and set out the toxic triptych of the crime of the financing of terrorism.

There can be a symbiotic relationship[76] between terrorism and organised crime as the latter can finance the operational costs of terror.[77] Terrorism financing should be perceived as a conspiracy that looks into the future attack of human life,

---

2014; EUROPOL, 'OCTA 2006: EU ORGANISED CRIME THREAT ASSESSMENT 2006' (EUROPOL website 2009) <http://www.Europol.europa.eu/publications/European_Organised_Crime_Threat_Assessment_(OCTA)/OCTA2008.pdf> accessed 28 February 2014.

71 Council Framework Decision 2008/841/JHA on the fight against organised crime [2008] OJ L300/42 arts 1–7.

72 Commission, 'Communication from the Commission to the European Parliament, the Council and the National Parliaments on the review of the proposal for a Council Regulation on the establishment of the European Public Prosecutor's Office with regard to the principle of subsidiarity, in accordance with Protocol No 2' (Communication) COM (2013) 851 final.

73 Scherrer (n 40) 9.

74 Sub-Committee F – Home Affairs on Money Laundering and the Financing of Terrorism, *Written Evidence submitted 30 January 2009 by Professor Iain Cameron, Professor in Public International Law, Uppsala University E/08–09/F47 ML* (HL 2008–09, 132–II) paras 3–5 <http://www.parliament.uk/documents/upload/F047/Professor Cameron300109.pdf> accessed 28 February 2014.

75 Text to n 74 paras 4–5.

76 Text to n 66.

77 *Los Angeles Times*, 'In the News: Money Laundering' (*Los Angeles Times* website 2009) <http://www.articles.latimes.com/keyword/money-laundering> accessed 28 February 2014.

international security and legal order[78] from all possible angles.[79] The financing of terrorism, therefore, aims, among other things, to cause harm to lawful wealth and to those who protect and create wealth in the financial system.

The position that there is huge public interest in ensuring that credit and financial institutions, enterprises and certain vulnerable professions to the corruptive powers of organised crime and money laundering should not only blow the whistle upon the detection of suspicious activities, but should also become the vigilant eyes of investigative and judicial authorities,[80] is all the more convincing. On the other hand, it should also be underlined that this third extension of the global anti-money laundering regime to combat and punish the financing of terrorism has raised serious questions about the need to enhance the transparency of the anti-money laundering and counter-terrorism financing system,[81] and to make it ECHR compliant, especially in the light of the *Kadi*[82] judgment.

As this is not the proper place to enter into a detailed discussion of the compatibility of the anti-money laundering and counter-terrorism financing system with the ECHR, the important point to note is that the loosening of controls on terrorism financing is too big of a risk to take even if it has been clearly established that terrorism financing is mostly linked to lawful wealth[83] and involves smaller amounts than organised crime. It is in this last submission that one can hopefully find a convincing argument for the justification of the third extension of the global anti-money laundering regime to combat and punish the financing of terrorism[84] through the effective monitoring of financial flows.[85]

---

78 Council Framework Decision 2008/919/JHA of 28 November 2008 amending Framework Decision 2002/475/JHA on combating terrorism [2008] OJ L330/21 preamble, arts 1–4.

79 Text to n 63 paras 1–7.

80 Text to n 6 paras 97–113, 174–182.

81 Commission Directive 2005/60/EC of the European Parliament and of the Council of 26 October 2005 on the prevention of the use of the financial system for the purpose of money laundering and terrorist activity [2005] OJ L309/15.

82 Sub-Committee F – Home Affairs on Money Laundering and the Financing of Terrorism, *Inquiry into Money Laundering and the Financing of Terrorism – Memorandum by HM Treasury, Annex A: The Kadi Case and the ECJ Judgment* (HL 2008–09, 132–II) <http://www.parliament.uk/documents/upload/F047/ProfessorCameron300109.pdf> accessed 28 February 2014.

83 Text to n 74 paras 4–5.

84 Commission, 'An area of Freedom, security and justice serving the citizen' (Communication) COM (2009) 0262 final.

85 Barry Rider, 'Financial Regulation and Supervision after 11th September 2001' (2003) 10 JFC 3, 336–358.

Time Present: The War on Illicit Enrichment

According to Europol, money laundering constitutes the final phase of all the different forms of organised criminal activity.[86] All the more reason for European Union anti-money laundering policy-makers to protect the Union's integrated financial markets through the prosecution of all crimes generating illicit enrichment.[87] Henceforth, the current trend is to trace, prosecute and sanction illicit enrichment as a whole (corruption; tax evasion; private corruption; insider dealing; misappropriation of funds; market abuse; counterfeiting, and piracy),[88] including criminal infiltration of financial institutions and businesses from within.

But there is more to be said about the fight against insider dealing and piracy prior to closing the discussion on the justifications for the extension of the global anti-money laundering regime. In an effort to avoid unnecessary complexity, a distillation of core ideas on insider dealing will be presented in the first place. Thereupon, the discussion will shift to a peculiar legal aspect of Somali piracy.

Some Reflections on Insider Dealing

The problem of insider dealing is neither new[89] nor academically unexplored.[90] One of the internationally recognised leading authorities in this area of the law, Professor Barry Rider, has underlined that criminal penetration is not the main driving force behind insider activity in financial institutions.[91]

It is important to appreciate that the prevention and control of insider dealing not only aims to protect the integrity, stability and reputation of the European Union's integrated financial markets, but also to control the particular crime that generates illicit enrichment.[92]

---

86 EUROPOL, 'Financial & Property Crimes 1/06' (Europol website 2006) 1 <http://www.Europol.europa.eu/publications/Serious_Crime_Overviews/overviewFCPpdf> accessed 28 February 2014.

87 Text to n 53.

88 COM (2009) 0262 final (n 84) 21 paras 1–5.

89 Commission Directive 2003/6/EC of the European Parliament and of the Council of 28 January 2003 on insider dealing and market manipulation (market abuse) [2003] OJ L96/16; Commission Directive 2004/72/EC of 29 April 2004 implementing Directive 2003/6/EC of the European Parliament and of the Council as regards accepted market practices, the definition of inside information in relation to derivatives on commodities, the drawing up of lists of insiders, the notification of managers' transactions and the notification of suspicious transactions [2004] OJ L162/70 (articles 1–11).

90 Barry Rider, 'Inside Out' (2006) 14 JFC 3, 265–266.

91 Barry Rider, 'An Insider Paradox' (2008) 29 Comp Law 1, 1.

92 Barry Rider and others, *Market Abuse and Insider Dealing* (2nd edn, Tottel 2009) 3, paras 1.6–1.7.

This crime involves the abuse of confidential information, which is a peculiar legal good, to either make profit or avoid loss, whereas money laundering abuses the financial system to launder the proceeds of crime. With even stronger reason, criminal finance, as Professor Rider has confirmed, cannot be equated with confidential information. However, the paradox lies with the fact that the misuse of confidential information can generate criminal finance.

The misuse of confidential information by insiders such as company directors and high-ranking staff appears to entail more perplexing legal issues than money laundering. From a prosecutorial point of view, it is absolutely necessary to clearly establish how the person in a special relationship with the legal entity accessed the privileged information. However, if the suspect can establish that the information obtained derived from an external source, then it is not possible to prosecute and sanction the alleged wrongdoer for insider dealing.[93]

Henceforth, prosecutors must prove beyond any reasonable doubt that the perpetrator was not only in possession of privileged information, but also that the quality of the specific information he possessed influenced his decision to buy or sell the financial instruments in question for the purpose of making profit or avoiding loss. Indeed, this is highly complex, if not almost improvable.

In practice, the prosecutor's work of proving that the particular proprietary information influenced the mind of the alleged perpetrator who engaged in the buying or selling of intangible assets is almost the same as trying to fit a square peg into a round hole. It is not always the case that those accused of insider dealing will be found to have bought or sold intangible assets directly in their own name or will be found to have acquired part of the shares of another company in lieu of a prospective merger or acquisition deal. Another important point to appreciate is that inside information may be protected by many legal systems, but not all legal systems consider inside information to be property.[94]

Lastly, it is underlined that in the context of insider fraud, unless the Suspicious Activity Report is submitted by the enterprise concerned, the anti-money laundering mechanism cannot be triggered to investigate the financial affairs of the perpetrator with a view to bring him to justice. This view is reinforced when one takes into account that reputable financial institutions and other highly respected companies would be very hesitant to expose themselves to a scandal of insider fraud.

Scandals of insider fraud are newsworthy and can thus accelerate the devaluation of the shares of the enterprise and of its shareholders. As Professor Barry Rider rightly pointed out, the company is the legal entity owning its own assets, but the property of the shareholders constitutes the percentage of their share in the enterprise.[95] Ultimately, the value of shares will always depend on corporate reputation and performance.

---

93 Rider (n 92) 5.

94 Rider (n 92) 6.

95 Rider (n 92) 2.

Some Reflections on Somali Piracy

The payment of ransom to Somali pirates for the release of kidnapped vessels off the Horn of Africa is particularly relevant to the application of anti-money laundering provisions. Indeed, the payment of ransom is not a criminal offence under English law,[96] but as Lord Hannay of Chiswick reasoned, the act of piracy is a crime under international law.[97]

At the political level, it is ambiguous if not anecdotal, that the United Kingdom has deployed part of its naval resources to prevent piracy off the Gulf of Aden and the policy implemented thus far appears to be one of turning a blind eye to the money that British insurance firms pay as compensation to shipowners for the ransom paid to Somali pirates. The following question may be asked, shouldn't we be concerned with the potential channelling of these funds to finance terrorism and organised crime?

The general public has no idea whatsoever how much money is paid out in Lloyd's ransom policies, as insurers do not disclose any relevant information.[98] On the one hand, shipowners appear to raise money from their own resources to pay the ransom. On the other hand, there are those who support the view that since shipowners' money is not criminal finance, the issue at stake entails making arrangements to facilitate what at a certain point is about to become criminal money.[99]

Last but not least, there are also those who genuinely believe that the Financial Action Task Force does not have a role to play in resolving this issue because this is a matter to be dealt with by the competent operational authorities.[100] Perhaps, this legal issue is not too complex to resolve. It is therefore important to appreciate a number of interrelated legal points from the prosecutorial point of view.

First, once the Somali pirates are in physical possession of the lawful money that shipowners have raised to pay as ransom, the money becomes the proceeds

---

96 Sub-Committee F – Home Affairs on Money Laundering and the Financing of Terrorism, *Corrected oral evidence given by Mr Sean McGovern, General Counsel, Ms Louise Shield, Head of Communications, and Mr Andy Wragg, Senior Manager, International Regulatory Affairs Team, Lloyd's* (HL 2008–09, 132–II) 9 <http://www.publications.parliament.uk/pa/Id200809/Idselect/Ideucom/999/euf30509ev9.pdf> accessed 28 February 2014.

97 European Union Committee – Minutes of Evidence, *Money Laundering and the Financing of Terrorism* (HL 2008–09, 132–II) Question 486 addressed to witness Mr Stephen Webb, Acting Director of Policing Policy and Operations, Home Office, <http://www.publications.parliament.uk/pa/Idselect/Ideucom/132/9042905.htm> accessed 10 November 2010.

98 European Union Committee – Minutes of Evidence (n 97) Question 541.

99 European Union Committee – Minutes of Evidence (n 8) Question 479.

100 European Union Committee – Minutes of Evidence (n 8) Question 488.

of kidnapping and extortion. At that point, there is an obligation on the part of law enforcement and judicial authorities to trace the money if it is possible.[101]

Second, irrespective of whether there exists or does not exist apparent evidence that the criminal proceeds are channelled to reception points for the financing of terrorism, the fact that Somalia is a failed state should automatically activate the mechanisms of the repressive authorities of the country where the insurers are based or the country whose law is applicable in the insurance contract or the flag state of the kidnapped vessel.

Third, even if we accepted that both the Proceeds of Crime Act 2000 and the legislation on combating the financing of terrorism are inapplicable because the transaction for the compensation of the ship-owning company is a legitimate one between the insurer and the insured through the well-known and perfectly legitimate process of general average,[102] this could not suffice to prevent the automatic extension of the anti-money laundering regime to include the shipowners or to suspend temporarily their unregulated status in the public interest.

In conclusion, even in the absence of a statutory burden imposed on shipowners, they are under a legal and ethical duty to report and to seek consent from the Serious Organised Crime Agency. This obligation arises from section 328(1) of the Proceeds of Crime Act 2000 and it should not be narrowly interpreted so as to include regulated persons only. Henceforward, unregulated persons should report specific activities that apparently make a person or a group of persons suspicious and potentially dangerous.

All the more so, the same principle applies to insurers because they are part of the regulated sector and they are under an obligation to report to the Serious Organised Crime Agency their intention to pay compensation to shipowners and should also seek consent to proceed further even if the funds in question do not constitute criminal finance.

Even if some of us would be prepared to accept that a Suspicious Activity Report could be useless in the light of public information on piracy made widely known to the general public through the media, it would still remain untested if the competent authorities would excuse both the insurers and the shipowners from seeking consent when it is crystal clear that the law as it presently stands requires the exact opposite.

Indeed, all of what has been submitted herein has to do with shedding some light on certain grey areas of the obligation under the law to seek consent and to thus trigger the anti-money laundering mechanism.[103] It is therefore necessary to maintain the principle of the law[104] even in those circumstances in which it is apparent that the law as it stands needs to be amended.

101 European Union Committee – Minutes of Evidence (n 8) Question 57.

102 European Union Committee – Minutes of Evidence (n 97) Question 528.

103 European Union Committee – Minutes of Evidence (n 8) Question 482.

104 European Union Committee – Minutes of Evidence (n 8) Question 483.

The Reporting System and the Exchange of Information

Setting the Scene

In June 1995, a group of government agencies and international organisations met at the Egmont Arenberg Palace in Brussels to discuss the problem of money laundering and the possibilities to confront this global challenge. A Legal Working Group was thus established to examine how cross-border exchange of financial intelligence could be enhanced and institutionalised.

The Egmont Group's definition of a Financial Intelligence Unit[105] was adopted by the United Nations Convention Against Transnational Organised Crime (the Palermo Convention) of 2000,[106] which, among other things, urged signatory states to establish national Financial Intelligence Units that would serve as the national central agencies[107] for the collection, analysis and dissemination of information relating to the misuse of the financial system for illegal purposes.[108]

As of December 2013, the Egmont Group Financial Intelligence Units of the World comprises of 139 Operational Units, which fully meet the Egmont Financial Intelligence Unit definition.[109] The benefits of Egmont Group membership can best be summarised as follows. First, the expansion and systematisation of international cooperation in the area of reciprocal exchange of financial intelligence. Second, the continuous development of Financial Intelligence Units through training and personnel exchanges. Third, the encouragement of improved and more secure use of the expandable Egmont Secure Web through the proper application of technology. Fourth, promoting the establishment of Financial Intelligence Units

105 As of June 2004, the revised definition of a Financial Intelligence Unit is a central, national agency responsible for the receipt, analysis and dissemination to competent authorities of financial information concerning suspected criminal proceeds and potential financing of terrorism, or required by national legislation or regulation, for the purpose of combating money laundering and the financing of terrorism.

106 Article 7 of the Palermo Convention.

107 JJ Freis Jr, Director, FinCEN, US Department of Treasury, 'Global Markets and Global Vulnerabilities: Fighting Transnational Crime Through Financial Intelligence. Remarks Delivered at the Academic Session on Global Initiatives to Avoid the Mis(use) of the Financial System for Illegal Purposes' (The Committee on International Monetary Law of the International Law Association – (MOCOMILA) Salamanca, Spain, April 2008) 10 <http://www.fincen.gov/news_room/speech/pdf/20080425.pdf> accessed 28 February 2014.

108 Text to n 107.

109 The Egmont Group, The Egmont Group Financial Intelligence Units of the World, 'Operational Units Meeting the Egmont Definition Status as of June 2009 0609' (The Egmont Group website 2009) <http://www.egmontgroup.org/list_of_fius.pdf> accessed 28 February 2014.

in countries that either do not have in place anti-money laundering and counter-terrorism financing systems or are in the process of developing such systems.[110]

The Connecting Link: Private Sector Information

Neither the reporting system nor the exchange of information can operate without the systematic extraction of financial intelligence information from private sector stakeholders.

The extraction of this wealth of material is not only the starting point for financial intelligence, but also the platform upon which law enforcement and judicial authorities can effectively combat money laundering, the financing of terrorism, and corruption.[111]

Consequently, we should be consistently mindful of the following three solid notions that the reporting system encompasses. Turning private sector stakeholders into secret reporters; transforming financial institutions and enterprises into the eyes of law enforcement and prosecutorial authorities; and transplanting to reporters a sophisticated, qualitative and systemic undercover reporting culture.[112]

However, it is equally important to underline that the factual evidence[113] of successful reporting (Suspicious Activity Reports – Tactical and Strategic Analysis – Exchange of Information)[114] facilitates the application of multiple controls by law enforcement authorities, for the prosecution and sanction of different crimes, and at all levels of cooperation (national, regional and international) to combat money laundering and the financing of terrorism.[115]

Ultimately, it should also be taken into consideration that the exchange of information through the secure channels of Financial Intelligence Units, which is the smart product of intelligence gathering that is initially triggered by automated or self-induced suspicion, aims to facilitate effective assistance in cross-border criminal investigations.[116] On the one hand, the exchange of information guarantees

---

110 The Egmont Group, 'Benefits of Egmont Group Membership' (The Egmont Group website 2009) <http://www.egmontgroup.org/files/library_egmont_docs/egmont_membership_benefit.pdf> accessed 28 February 2014.

111 European Union Committee – Minutes of Evidence (n 8) Question 191 of Lord Hodgson of Astley Abbots to Mr David Thomas, Director, UKFIU, SOCA, on the subject of Politically Exposed Persons and those public servants around the world who may be involved in kleptocratic activities.

112 European Union Committee – Minutes of Evidence (n 8) Question 175 on the qualitative aspect of Suspicious Activity Reports.

113 European Union Committee – Minutes of Evidence (n 8) Questions 193, 201, 203.

114 JJ Freis Jr (n 107) 15.

115 Sir James Sassoon (n 8) Question 391 on the potential of sophisticated electronic filtering that can lead to the proper and effective extraction of financial intelligence for the efficacious implementation of anti-money laundering policy.

116 JJ Freis Jr (n 107) 16.

the protection of sensitive commercial, financial and personal information processed by Financial Intelligence Units, but on the other hand, the intelligence extracted cannot constitute admissible evidence in judicial hearings due to its highly confidential nature.[117]

Certain Areas of Weakness

So much on the special properties of the reporting system and the exchange of information in the context of applying effective money laundering controls. Unfortunately, the reporting system and the exchange of information have been linked to certain weaknesses of the reactive side of anti-money laundering policy implementation[118] for reasons that have to do mainly with the poor performance of the Member States,[119] with the exception of the United Kingdom.[120]

The same position, although more detailed as to how difficult it is to apply the existing tools to trace suspicious transactions through cooperation amongst the European Union's intelligence[121] community and the financial sector, was expressed by Professor Gilles de Kerchove, European Union Counter-Terrorism Coordinator,[122] and Mr Hans G. Nilsson, Head of JHA Counsellors,[123] during their formal discussion with the members of Sub-Committee F – Home Affairs Money Laundering and the Financing of Terrorism of the House of Lords.

At the same time, it is equally disappointing that the Council of Europe Convention on Laundering, Search, Seizure and Confiscation of the Proceeds from Crime and on the Financing of Terrorism (the Warsaw Convention)[124] has not entered into force yet; whereas due to prolonged delays, the European Union–United States of America Agreements on Extradition and Mutual Assistance in Criminal Matters are effective only as of 7 April 2009.[125]

Especially in regard to the Warsaw Convention, Mr Hans G. Nilsson, Head of JHA Counsellors, underlined that Member States are not making effective use of the Convention because there are no limits for implementation,[126] whereas the use

117 JJ Freis Jr (n 107) 17.

118 COM (2012) 85 final (n 24).

119 COM (2009) 0262 final (n 84).

120 Text to n 8 Question 252.

121 Council Decision (EC) 2000/642/JHA concerning arrangements for cooperation between financial intelligence units for the Member States in respect of exchanging information [2000] OJ L271/14, articles 1–10.

122 Text to n 8 Question 252.

123 Text to n 8 Question 253.

124 At the time of writing this book, only 18 of the 47 countries had ratified the 2001 Protocol.

125 European Commission, 'Treaties Office Database: Summary of Treaty' (Europa website 2009) <http://ec.europa.eu/world/agreements/prepareCreateTreatiesWorkspace/treatiesGeneralData.do?step=0&redirect=true&treatyId=5461> accessed 28 February 2014.

126 Text to n 20 response to Question 246.

of framework decisions is more effective because they explicitly provide for the maximum time for implementation by national legislators.[127]

However, the disappointment extends to the area of confiscation and recovery of criminal proceeds as the data of Member States are not only imprecise,[128] but they also have to show a noticeable disparity[129] between the quantity of criminal assets seized and the estimated figures that organised criminal activity generates[130] in Member States.[131] Whilst it is difficult to refer with precision to the proportion of assets held outside the United Kingdom, a significant proportion of money laundering cases involves unenforced confiscation orders of assets held or hidden abroad (86 per cent according to the Customs Prosecution Office in September 2008).[132] It is further clarified that the term, abroad, actually refers to property held in another Member State, that is, outside of the jurisdiction of the United Kingdom, but well within the European Union.

Consequently, the issue in question, as we will ascertain in the next and final subsection of this chapter, has to do with strengthening the apparently weak cooperation amongst Member States in the confiscation and recovery of criminal proceeds with a view to also minimise the trend to hide assets in other jurisdictions,[133] and to lay down the foundations for a uniform and standardised system of efficacious legal assistance in confiscation orders.[134]

This unwillingness of Member States to collectively work in partnership to prevent and control the accumulation of unaccountable wealth in criminal hands, has a negative impact on their potentiality to extract huge amounts of money from criminal asset recovery that could contribute to their budgetary needs.

---

127 Text to n 126.

128 Sub-Committee F – Home Affairs on Money Laundering and the Financing of Terrorism, *Corrected oral evidence given by The Commission: Mr Philippe Pellè Deputy Head, Company Law, Corporate Governance and Financial Crime; Mrs Agnete Philipson and Mr Mariano Fernandez Salas, Directorate General for the Internal Market and Services (DG MARKET), Mr Jakub Boratynski, Head of Unit on Organised Crime, Mr Sebastiano Tine, Head of Financial Crime Sector, and Mr Mickael Roudaut, Directorate General for Justice, Freedom and Security (DG JLS)* (HL 2008–09, 132–II) <http://www.publications.parliament.uk/pa/ld200809/ldselect/ldeucom/999/euf250309ev5.pdf> accessed 28 February 2014.

129 Text to n 128 Question 303.

130 In 2007, the figures of the report were: €140,000,000 for the United Kingdom; €83,000,000 for Spain; €60,000,000 for France; and €145,000,000 for Italy. At the same time, the annual revenues of organised crime in Italy were estimated over €140,000,000,000.

131 Text to n 128 Question 305.

132 Text to n 8 Question 131.

133 Text to n 8 Question 142 with reference to assets being hidden in Spain and France.

134 Text to n 8 Question 165.

The Future of Freezing and Confiscation of Criminal Proceeds

According to United Nations estimated figures, illicit financial flows amounted to approximately USD $2,100,000,000,000 in 2009 or almost 4 per cent of global GDP.[135] Criminal proceeds are initially hidden and then reinvested in assets in Member States that are not connected with the place where the crimes were committed. Indeed, this is how cross-border organised crime distorts competition, undermines trust in the financial system, and deprives Member States' and the Union's budget of tax revenues. Henceforward, the more our systems of seizure and confiscation of criminal assets and Asset Recovery Agencies remain underdeveloped, the more illegal enterprises will be able to generate illegal profit and negatively affect the functioning of the Internal Market.

Having the institutional setup and the financial and human resources for the rapid seizure and confiscation of criminal proceeds is absolutely necessary. But it is equally necessary to introduce measures for the preservation of the value of these assets and to ensure that all confiscation and freezing orders issued by a Member State will be effectively enforced against criminal assets located in another Member State without confronting gaps owed to lack of implementation, clarity and coherence between existing provisions.

As underlined in the previous subsection, specific weaknesses in the area of confiscation and freezing orders is a major deficiency in the performance of Member States, mainly due to slow transposition of Community instruments, incomplete and incorrect implementation of Community instruments, conflicting legal traditions, lack of efficiency in securing and maintaining assets, lack of resources and training, limited cross-agency communication, and lack of precise and comparable statistics,[136] even though there have been in place fundamental Community instruments. The existing Community provisions can best be summarised as follows:

1. Council Framework Decision 2001/500JHA[137] obliging Member States not only to enable confiscation, but to also allow value confiscation where direct criminal proceeds cannot be seized by ensuring that other Member States' requests are given the same priority as proceedings under domestic law.

135 COM (2012) 85 final (n 24) 2, para 3.

136 European Commission Directorate – General Justice, Freedom and Security 'Assessing the Effectiveness of EU Member States' Practices in the Identification, Tracing, Freezing and Confiscation of Criminal Assets' (Europa website 2009) <http://ec.europa.eu/home-affairs/news/intro/docs/20120312/final_asset_recovery_report_june_2009.pdf> accessed 28 February 2014.

137 Council Framework 2001/500/JHA of 26 June 2001 on money laundering, the identification, tracing, freezing, seizing and confiscation of instrumentalities and the proceeds of crime [2001] OJ L182/1.

2. Council Framework Decision 2005/212/JHA[138] harmonising confiscation laws; ordinary confiscation and value confiscation is obligatory for all crimes punishable by one year of imprisonment;[139] whereas extended confiscation must apply to certain serious offences committed within the framework of a criminal organisation.
3. Council Framework Decision 2003/577/JHA[140] providing for the mutual recognition of freezing orders of property or evidence.
4. Council Framework Decision 2006/783/JHA[141] providing for the mutual recognition of confiscation orders.
5. Council Decision 2007/845/JHA[142] providing for the exchange of information and cooperation between Asset Recovery Offices, obliging Member States to set up national Asset Recovery Offices as national central contact points for the facilitation of the rapid tracing of criminal assets throughout the European Union.

Of equal importance is the strategic initiative of the European Commission's Work Programme 2011 to protect the Union's formal economy from corruption[143] and fraud.[144] In the context of laying down enhanced measures for the protection of taxpayers' money, the European Commission has proposed the amendment of the legal framework of the European Anti-Fraud Office[145] and has called upon Member

---

138 Council Framework Decision 2005/212/JHA of 24 February 2005 on Confiscation of Crime-Related Proceeds, Instrumentalities and Property [2005] OJ L668/49.

139 Any criminal offence punishable by deprivation of liberty for more than one year triggers the automatic confiscation of the proceeds.

140 Council Framework Decision 2003/577/JHA of 22 July 2003 on the execution in the European Union of orders freezing property or evidence.

141 Council Framework Decision 2006/783/JHA of 6 October 2006 on the application of the principle of mutual recognition to confiscation orders [2006] OJ L328/59.

142 Council Decision 2007/845/JHA of 6 December 2007 concerning cooperation between Asset Recovery Offices of the Member States in the field of tracing and identification of proceeds from, or other property related to, crime [2007] OJ L332/103.

143 Commission, 'Establishing an EU Anti-corruption reporting mechanism for periodic assessment ("EU Anti – corruption Report")' (Communication) COM (2011) 3673 final.

144 Commission, 'Communication from the Commission to the European Parliament, the Council, the European Economic and Social Committee, and the Committee of the Regions and the Court of Auditors on the Commission Anti-Fraud Strategy' COM (2011) 376 final.

145 Commission, 'Regulation of the European Parliament and of the Council amending Regulation (EC) No 1073/1999 concerning investigations conducted by the European Anti-Fraud Office (OLAF) and repealing Regulation (EURATOM) No 1074/1999' COM (2011) 135 final.

States to employ the criminal and administrative laws in those investigations that are necessary for the protection of the financial interests of the Union.[146]

Last but not least, by Communication (2013) 45 final of 5 February 2013,[147] the European Commission has proposed to repeal Directive 2005/60/EC (the Third Anti-Money Laundering Directive) with a view to improve the comprehensibility and accessibility of the anti-money laundering legislative framework for all stakeholders and to lay the foundations for the harmonisation of criminal law for the prosecution and sanction of money laundering offences on the basis of Article 83(1) of the Treaty on the Functioning of the European Union.[148]

Furthermore, under Article 5(3) of the Treaty on the Functioning of the European Union, the Union can act if Member States cannot effectively implement all the aforementioned measures. All the more so, the European Union is in a better position than individual Member States to effectively regulate freezing and confiscation of criminal proceeds by virtue of Article 67 of the Treaty on the Functioning of the European Union.[149]

Harmonised non-conviction based confiscation measures are foreseen only for those cases involving limited choices, that is, where the defendant cannot be prosecuted due to death, illness, flight or where it is apparent that the confiscation can be barred by statutory limitations. Extended confiscation measures are foreseen for those cases that a national court ascertains that a person convicted of an offence is in possession of assets, which on the basis of probabilities, have derived from other criminal activities.[150] However, extended[151] confiscation measures cannot

146 Commission, 'Communication from the Commission to the European Parliament, the Council, the European Economic and Social Committee and the Committee of the Regions on the protection of the financial interests of the European Union by criminal law and by administrative investigations' COM (2011) 293 final.

147 Commission, 'Proposal for a Directive of the European Parliament and of the Council on the prevention of the use of the financial system for the purpose of money laundering and terrorist financing' COM (2013) 45 final.

148 Its scope covers the following offences: terrorism, trafficking in human beings and sexual exploitation of women and children, illicit drug trafficking, money laundering, corruption, counterfeiting of instruments of payment, computer crime, and organised crime. The offence of illicit arms trafficking is covered where the crime is committed in the context of organised crime.

149 An important element of the policy of maximal legislative option.

150 The ability to confiscate assets that go beyond the direct criminal proceeds. The criminal conviction may be followed after confiscation, but the courts are empowered to confiscate additional assets that may be considered to be the proceeds of similar crimes committed.

151 The confiscation of assets is obligatory for assets belonging directly or indirectly to those persons convicted of serious crimes that are closely related to organised crime and terrorism activities.

apply to those cases that the affected person has been previously acquitted in trial or where the *ne bis in idem* principle is applicable.[152]

Third party confiscation measures are foreseen for those cases involving acquiring third parties that have paid a lower amount than market value indicators and ought to have suspected that the assets were criminal proceeds. Of course, all the measures presented thus far are foreseen without prejudice to the affected person's right to be represented by a lawyer, to receive all decisions affecting the property in question, and to appeal against such decisions.[153]

Finally, the management of assets frozen in view of possible confiscation at a later stage is of paramount importance. Under Article 10(1) of COM (2012) 85 final,[154] Member States are obliged to establish national centralised offices for the purpose of adequately managing the property frozen in the light of a possible confiscation at a later stage. Of course, under the second paragraph of the aforementioned Article, Member States are empowered to sell or transfer the property seized if it is apparent that its value will decline.[155]

It therefore remains to be seen whether Member States will endeavour additional efforts not only to put their houses in order, but to also work in collective partnership to establish a more efficacious system for the freezing and confiscation of criminal proceeds in the European Union. The positive element to be remembered in this subsection is that the European Union is all the more determined and empowered to properly and adequately address these weaknesses in the area of freedom, security and justice serving the European citizen.

152 Safeguard: Article 48 of the Charter of Fundamental Rights of the European Union is of the utmost importance.

153 Safeguard: Article 47 of the Charter of Fundamental Rights of the European Union.

154 COM (2012) 85 final (n 24) 22, paras 1–2.

155 Text to n 154.

Chapter 2
How the Criminal Enterprise is Resisted and Disrupted

Internationalism

International cooperation is the product of internationalism. The latter can best be referred to as the melting pot of political ideologies and differences in the interests of promoting intergovernmental collaboration. The important point to note, however, is that without the support of general legal principles and statutes, political tactics cannot be legitimised and properly channelled.

Yet people neither recall with ease that internationalism is a 27-year-old concept, nor that its true origins can be traced back to the Report of the Twenty-second United Nations of the Next Decade Conference.[1] Substantially, internationalism, not soft law, was the main concept that united the diverse community of the rich-world coalition and the developing countries to combat economic crime and to promote healthy economic growth.

Ever since, the evolution of international standards has been notionally connected with the protection of universal legal goods such as liberty, democracy, stability, security, political accountability, and the strengthening of the rule of law. On this conceptual base, the Financial Action Task Force has continuously gained public support for vertical standard-setting in international money laundering and terrorism financing countermeasures.[2]

The conceptual base of intergovernmental cooperation for the prevention and control of economic crime is broad enough to encompass the gathering of data on judicial independence, crime reports, and quality of policing by the World Bank for the assessment of rule-of-law and governance measures implemented by sovereign states all over the world.[3]

As already pointed out, money laundering became a major policy issue in the G7 Summit in 1989,[4] where participant countries agreed to cooperate in partnership and to establish the Financial Action Task Force with a view to combat the threats

1 The Stanley Foundation, '22nd UN of the Next Decade Conference 1987: The United Nations and the Future of Internationalism 06/87' (The United Nations and the Future of Internationalism 06/87, Iowa, 1987) 3.

2 Text to n 8 in chapter 1.

3 *The Economist*, 'Order in the Jungle' (2008) 386 (8571) 85.

4 Text to n 37 in chapter 1.

posed by economic crime to the international financial system.[5] In regard to the condition of cooperation of international organisations or regimes in the 1990s, Oran Young of Cornell University rightly suggested at the time that international organisations did not operate in anarchy, but rather in a social state lacking central administration.[6]

Twenty-five years later, it is evident that the concept of internationalism united both institutions and regimes to cooperate under the auspices of international or supranational organisations such as the Financial Action Task Force, the Council of Europe, the Organisation for Economic Cooperation and Development, and the United Nations, with a view to combat economic crime in all its major forms.[7]

From a different conceptual angle, the central normative authority that states enjoyed within societies in contradistinction to the limited normative authority that international organisations enjoyed at the time at the international level, has become decentralised at present or suffers from a chronic normative atrophy.

There are two equally convincing explanations for this socio-legal phenomenon. Either the centre of normative gravity was displaced as a result of states' volition to improve justice in the world economy or the long-term strategy was to control the redistribution of wealth through a blend of political, legal and technocratic tools. If the late libertarian, Professor Ralf Dahrendorf, had second thoughts about state intervention, Adam Smith's prosperity theorem, institutions and redistribution,[8] why shouldn't we too?

As we are entitled to be concerned with wealth and those who create and protect it,[9] similarly, governments are expected to be seriously concerned with the protection of institutions that promote liberty, prosperity and the redistribution of wealth. After all, Dr Scherrer's[10] reflection on the stigmatisation of non-cooperative states, which was seen as a form of normative imperialism by Professor Valsamis Mitsilegas[11] of Queen Mary, University of London, is susceptible to the following alternative refinement.

---

5 Text to n 38 in chapter 1, paras 38–39.

6 Oran R Young, *International Cooperation: Building Regimes for Natural Resources and the Environment* (1st edn, Cornell University Press 1989) 37.

7 Text to n 44 in chapter 1.

8 *The Economist*, 'Ralf Dahrendorf Definer and Defender of Liberty' (2009) 391 (8637) 98.

9 Professor Barry AK Rider, 'The Twenty-Seventh International Symposium on Economic Crime: The Enemy Within – Internal Threats to the Stability and Integrity of Financial Institutions' (Symposium Director and Co – Chairman, Jesus College, Cambridge, July 2009) 3, para 5 <http://www.crimesymposium.org/PDFfiles/2009%20Programme.pdf> accessed 28 February 2014.

10 Text to n 40, 11 in chapter 1.

11 Text to n 43 in chapter 1.

Had Dr Scherrer connected the argument on the strategic deficiencies of Non-Cooperative Countries or Territories[12] posing a risk to the international financial system with the control of the redistribution of wealth, he could have delivered a more convincing justification as to why anti-money laundering and terrorism financing sanctions apply to natural persons, legal persons and Non-Cooperative Countries or Territories through a centrally administered system by the Financial Action Task Force.[13]

Even if we are not yet ready to accept the argument that the current international anti-money laundering strategy aims to control the redistribution of unaccountable or untaxed[14] wealth,[15] this reservation does not necessarily have to prevent us from agreeing that there is a genuine need at the international level to promote and protect the integrity of financial institutions and to maintain a high level of investor confidence, fairness and stability in capital markets.[16] An excellent example to consider in regard to securities is that of the American regulatory system.[17]

Of course, the Madoff affair has proven, among other things, that jurists and academics are not futurologists, and are thus unable to predict the various manifestations of human greed and delinquency. Enemies such as corruption, fraud and insider dealing[18] can at times penetrate the financial system from within, even in those jurisdictions enforcing exceptionally high standards of protection.[19] As will be demonstrated in greater detail in Chapter 6, it is precisely for these reasons that money laundering countermeasures are continuously reviewed, assessed and improved.

---

12 United States Department of the Treasury Financial Crimes Enforcement Network, 'FinCEN Advisory: Guidance to Financial Institutions Based on Anti-Money Laundering and Counter-Terrorist Financing Risks Posed by Iran, Uzbekistan, Turkmenistan, Pakistan and Sao Tome and Principe 07/09' (FinCEN website, 2009) <http://www.fincen.gov/statutes_regs/guidance/html/fin-2009-a004.html> accessed 28 February 2014; United States Department of the Treasury Advisory FinCEN, 'Withdrawal of Advisory FIN-2008-A003 regarding the area of Cyprus administered by Turkish Cypriots (northern part of Cyprus) 07/09' (FinCEN website 2009) <http://www.fincen.gov/statutes_regs/guidance/pdf/fin-2009-a005.pdf> accessed 28 February 2014.

13 US Department of the Treasury Financial Crimes Enforcement Network, 'FIN-2013-A008 Advisory on the FATF-Identified Jurisdictions with AML/CFT Deficiencies' (FinCEN website, 4 December 2013) <http://www.fincen.gov/statutes_regs/guidance/pdf/FIN-2013-A008.pdf> accessed 11 December 2013.

14 Email from Swiss Federal Administration admin.ch to author 'Federal Council authorises first banks to participate in US programme' (29 November 2013).

15 Email from Swiss Federal Administration admin.ch to author 'Federal Council decides to sign administrative assistance convention and adopts draft mandate on taxation of savings income with EU' (9 October 2013).

16 Text to n 85, 340 in chapter 1.

17 Text to n 16.

18 *The Economist*, 'The Madoff Affair' (2009) 392 (8638) 68.

19 Text to n 85 in chapter 1.

In summary, corruption is not a stereotypical phenomenon of the developing countries only. Indeed, corruption is well-rooted in the developed-world coalition countries and, paradoxically, in certain exporting countries of transparency[20] such as the United States,[21] Canada,[22] Germany[23] and the United Kingdom.[24]

Internationalism should be perceived as the spine of intergovernmental collaboration in the fight against economic crime. The current trend is to enact and enforce global transparency laws as part of an overall strategy to promote economic growth and to redistribute wealth by minimising the illicit income of corruption, bribery and unfair competition; enhance mutual legal assistance on the search, seizure and confiscation of criminal proceeds; and exercise pressure on certain countries to put their houses in order.[25]

The redistribution of wealth does not necessarily entail enforcing imperialistic norms with a view to prevent developing economies from competing as equals in world trade and international business transactions. It may well entail the enforcement of measures aiming to promote the lawful and taxable means of creating wealth, increase the income of the international tax regime, and deprive offenders of their ill-gotten gains.

The OECD

Over two decades ago the Organisation for Economic Cooperation and Development (OECD) represented a totally different multilateral initiative.[26] It was primarily concerned with consumer demand, output, employment, prices and costs, inflation, and OPEC oil pricing.[27] Presently, next to the International Monetary Fund and the World Bank, the OECD constitutes one of the main bodies of international

---

20 Simon Young, 'Why Civil Actions against Corruption?' (2009) 16 JFC 2, 146.

21 Text to n 6, 68 in chapter 1.

22 *The Economist*, 'Municipal Corruption in Canada' (2009) 391 (8637), 64.

23 *Kathimerini*, 'Former Siemens Executive Arrested' *Kathimerini English Edition* (Athens, 11 June 2009) <http//www.ekathimerini.com/4dcgi/_w_articles_politics_2_11/06/2009107991> accessed 28 February 2014.

24 *The Economist*, 'Extending Freedom of Information – Uncovering the Next Scandal' (2009) 391 (8634) 34.

25 Text to n 8 in chapter 1.

26 The Organisation for European Economic Cooperation was established in 1948 to promote cooperation among Marshall Plan recipient countries to recover in the aftermath of the Second World War. Following the Treaty of Paris of 14 December 1960, it became the Organisation for Economic Cooperation and Development.

27 Jack C Plano and Roy Olton, *The International Relations Dictionary* (4th edn, Clio Press Ltd 1988) 319–320; Graham Bannock, RE Baxter and Evan Davis, *The Penguin Dictionary of Economics* (4th edn, Penguin Group 1987) 303.

administration,[28] which interacts with transnational regulatory networks such as the Basel Committee on Banking Supervision, the International Organisation for Securities Commissions, the International Association of Insurance Supervisors and the International Organisation of Pension Supervisors.

On the reversal of the standard-setting phenomenon by transnational regulatory bodies, Armin Schafer of the Max Planck Institute has argued this phenomenon is due to the reliance of international organisations on soft law to avoid an institutional crisis and to prevent a breakdown of negotiations.[29] In academic commentary on the evolution of transnational regulatory bodies, Giulia Bertezzolo has underlined that these significant standard-setting bodies have been filling the normative gap that domestic regulators were unable to fill in an increasingly globalised world.[30]

If we are prepared to set aside the different yet important opinions of academic commentators on the justification for the rise of transnational regulation, we could confidently argue that the most probable factor for the rise of this phenomenon is that domestic regulation is no longer in a position to lay down and enforce extraterritorial and uniform measures for the prevention and control of economic crime.[31]

From the point of view of the Organisation for Economic Cooperation and Development, national legislators should adopt a multidisciplinary approach[32] based on the anti-corruption principles of anti-bribery and integrity instruments.[33] Injecting integrity in the public and private sectors is the main aim. The legal panoply comprises of the OECD Convention in Combating Bribery of Foreign Public Officials in International Business Transactions (1997)[34] and the following international instruments adopted by its Council: the 1996 Recommendation on the Tax Deductibility of Bribes; the 1997 Revised Recommendation of the Council on Combating Bribery in International Business Transactions; the 1998 Recommendation on Improving Ethical Conduct in the Public Service; the 2000

---

28 Giulia Bertezzolo, 'The European Union Facing the Global Arena: Standard Setting Bodies and Financial Regulation' (2009) 34 ELR 2, 257–280.

29 Armin Schafer, 'Resolving Deadlock: Why International Organisations Introduce Soft Law' (2006) 12 ELJ 2, 194–208.

30 Bertezzolo (n 28) 260.

31 Shehu (n 42) 237 in chapter 1.

32 Sol Picciotto, 'Constitutionalising Multilevel Governance?' (2008) 6 IJCL (3/4), 468–469.

33 Peter Johnstone and George Brown, 'International Controls of Corruption: Recent Responses from the USA and the UK' (2004) 11 JFC 3, 217–249.

34 OECD Directorate for Financial, Fiscal and Enterprise Affairs Committee on International Investment and Multinational Enterprises, 'Working Group on Bribery in International Business Transactions (CIME) Convention on Combating Bribery of Foreign Public Officials in International Business Transactions and Related Documents' (OECD website 2009) <http://www.oecd.org/dataoecd/4/18/38028044.pdf> accessed 28 February 2014.

OECD Guidelines for Multinational Enterprises; the 2003 Recommendation for Managing Conflict of Interest in the Public Service; the 2006 Recommendation on Bribery and Export Credits; and the 2008 Recommendation on Enhancing Integrity in Public Procurement.[35]

OECD Member Countries are therefore required to implement measures to disrupt, prosecute and sanction those persons offering and accepting bribes; confiscate the proceeds of corruption; cooperate in the gathering and exchange of evidence; extradition; promote integrity in the private sector; and ensure that prosecutorial interest focuses on foreign bribery issues.[36]

The 1996 Recommendation of the OECD Council on the Tax Deductibility of Bribes to Foreign Public Officials has changed the culture of bribery in that it is no longer treated as an international business usage. Of course, the initiative has extended from the social condemnation of claiming bribes to foreign public officials and political parties as tax-deductible expenditure,[37] to the criminalisation of the act. Furthermore, the issuance of the Bribery Awareness Handbook for Tax Examiners of 2003, which is available in 13 languages, aims to facilitate the tracing of suspicious payments by internal and external auditors, promote the reporting of incidents to law enforcement authorities, strengthen the network of tax partnerships with non-OECD economies, and raise awareness of the proper course of action.

The promotion of good governance through the enhancement of transparency and accountability in the public sector is of cardinal significance in combating the demand side of corruption. It is linked to the OECD's long-term strategy of equating transparency and accountability with administrative simplification; closing the loopholes of bureaucracy; encouraging legislative reform; promoting electronic government; and creating a new culture for the control of public finance.[38] Plainly the enhancement of the base of ethics is meant to be gradually accomplished through the synergy of regulation, institutions and management best practices.[39]

Fostering responsible and ethical transactional conduct is envisaged by the OECD as part of a broader notion[40] of promoting and protecting international

---

35 OECD, 'Key OECD Anti-Corruption Documents' (OECD website 2009) <http://www.oecd.org/document/42/0,3343,en_2649_37447_41799402_1_1_1_1,00.html> accessed 28 February 2014.

36 OECD, 'The OECD Fights Corruption' (OECD website 2006) <http://www.oecd.org/dataoecd/36/51/37418910.pdf> accessed 28 February 2014.

37 Text to n 33.

38 Text to n 36.

39 PwC Academy by PricewaterhouseCoopers, 'Principles of Corporate Governance: Practical Issues of Internal Audit Seminar 03/09' (PwC website 2009) <http://www.pwc.com/gr/eng/ins-sol/spec-int/09dkse_EsoterikosEleghos.pdf> accessed 28 February 2014.

40 Text to n 1.

investment. Adherence to the OECD Guidelines for Multinational Enterprises[41] aims not only to promote and protect trade and investment, but also to facilitate the establishment of a forum for the discussion of problems arising from the deficit of transparency and engagement in bribery as a means to contract with the public sector.

Against that background, it is important to appreciate the OECD's initiatives to strengthen civil society in aid recipient countries. However, capacity building for reforms and transparency[42] must be accompanied by necessary legislative changes such as the repealing of bank secrecy laws, implementing the UN Convention against Corruption (UNCAC); and joining intergovernmental partnerships – Joint Project Groups – with the Financial Action Task Force for exploring criminal links between money laundering and corruption.[43]

From a prosecutorial point of view, the International Association of Prosecutors (IAP) has submitted that it is imperative for prosecutorial discretion to be exercised independently,[44] free from political influence,[45] and uninfluenced by the media or other centres of pressure.[46] And although the IAP welcomed the progress made thus far in the implementation and review of anti-corruption measures at the international level, it did not miss the opportunity to call upon its Members to concentrate their efforts in cross-border recovery and seizure of criminal proceeds.[47]

The commentary of the Commission of the International Chamber of Commerce (ICC) on Anti-Corruption convincingly emphasised more on the need to equate the anti-corruption mechanism with the anti-money laundering mechanism. Although it recognised that the OECD's monitoring role was vital in pushing further State Parties to fulfil their obligations and responsibilities under the instruments, it stressed that the effectiveness of implementation ought to be qualitatively evaluated in line with the number of enquiries, investigations and successful convictions of cases involving corruption at the national level.[48]

The blend of new ideas that the ICC Commission contributed to the Consultation Paper Review, called upon 30 OECD Member Countries and the

41 OECD Directorate for Financial and Enterprise Affairs, 'Guidelines for Multinational Enterprises' (OECD website 2009) http://www.oecd.org/department/0,3355, en_2649_34889_1_1_1_1_1,00.html> accessed 28 February 2014.

42 OECD (n 36) 11.

43 OECD (n 36) 13.

44 *The Economist* (n 3) 85.

45 International Association of Prosecutors, 'Responses to the Consultation Paper on the Review of the OECD Anti-Bribery Instruments' (OECD website 2009) 1, para 2.1 <http://www.oecd.org/dataoecd/8/8/40498974.pdf> accessed 28 February 2014.

46 IAP (n 45) 1.

47 IAP (n 45) 2.

48 International Chamber of Commerce (ICC Commission on Anti-Corruption), 'Responses to the Consultation Paper on the Review of the OECD Anti-Bribery Instruments' (OECD website 2009) <http://www.oecd.org/dataoecd/7/27/40498870.pdf> accessed 28 February 2014.

eight Non-Member Countries (Argentina, Brazil, Bulgaria, Chile, Estonia, Israel, Slovenia and South Africa)[49] to combat the demand side of corruption by applying the multilateral anti-corruption toolkit to less explored areas that can best be summarised as follows.

Application of due diligence measures by multinational enterprises (both parent companies and controlled subsidiaries)[50] to intermediaries and, especially, in regard to the integrity criteria upon which intermediaries are hired (education, ethical conduct and financial background). Periodic assessment of service providers during the process of the provision of services.[51] Application of the same anti-corruption tools used to fight bribery, extortion and corrupt practices to combat petty corruption, which entails small payments to low-level officials to expedite routine procedures and approvals.[52] Combating bribery of foreign political parties.[53] Equate private–private corruption with the fight against public corruption since the former can disrupt competition equally to the latter.[54] And promote whistleblower protection in the corporate environment as it can substantially contribute to the detection and disruption of fraud in enterprises.[55]

In summary, it is evident that the initiatives of the OECD aim to promote and enhance the fundamental principles of anti-money laundering and anti-corruption laws.[56] Both OECD Member and Non-Member Countries are continuously called upon to cooperate and to demonstrate the efficacious implementation of all the aforementioned important instruments, which aim to create a uniform platform for the prevention and control of criminals and kleptocrats from transferring their ill-gotten gains from the illicit to the licit economies.

There are pressing needs for governments to create public records and comparable statistical data[57] of money laundering,[58] corruption,[59] bribery and fraud incidents;[60] the actions taken to prosecute and sanction the offenders; and the measures taken through international cooperation to seize, recover[61] and

49 OECD Directorate for Financial and Enterprise Affairs, 'Steps Taken by State Parties to Implement and Enforce the OECD Convention on Combating Bribery of Foreign Public Officials in International Business Transactions' (OECD website 2009) <http://www.oecd.org/document/44/0,3343,en_2649_34859_36433004_1_1_1_1,00.html> accessed 28 February 2014.

50 Article 7(d) ICC Rules of Conduct and Recommendations.

51 ICC Commission on Anti-Corruption (n 48) 3.

52 ICC Commission on Anti-Corruption (n 48) 4.

53 ICC Commission on Anti-Corruption (n 48) 5.

54 ICC Commission on Anti-Corruption (n 48) 5.

55 ICC Commission on Anti-Corruption (n 48) 7.

56 European Commission Directorate-General (n 136) in chapter 1.

57 COM (2012) 85 final (n 135) in chapter 1.

58 COM (2013) 45 final (n 147) in chapter 1.

59 COM (2011) 3673 final (n 143) in chapter 1.

60 COM (2011) 376 final (n 142) in chapter 1.

61 Council Decision 2007/845/JHA (n 142) in chapter 1.

manage[62] criminal assets. This last statement summarises the necessary actions that governments are required to take with a view to protect financial systems and anti-money laundering systems from the serious and immediate threats of corruption and penetration.[63]

The Council of Europe

An entire law textbook would not suffice to present a comprehensive analysis of the internationally recognised initiatives[64] of the Council of Europe (COE) to combat the laundering of criminal proceeds. These include the COE Committee in Crime Problems of 1977; the COE 1980 Recommendation on measures against the transfer and safekeeping of funds of criminal origin;[65] the drafting and negotiation of European Conventions and Agreements[66] in combination with the promotion and enhancement of human rights and fundamental freedoms, the rule of law, democracy and good governance, intercultural dialogue and respect for cultural diversity, education and social cohesion;[67] and the promotion of international cooperation in the areas of Laundering, Search, Seizure and Confiscation of the Proceeds from Crime[68] and combating the Financing of Terrorism[69] to name but a few.

As it is continuously demonstrated throughout the first two chapters of this book, there exists a pan-European web for the disruption of the criminal enterprise, and it must be equally underlined that the Council of Europe has made

---

62 COM (2012) 85 final, Article 10(1) (n 154) in chapter 1.

63 Commission, 'An area of Freedom, security and justice serving the citizen' (Communication) COM (2009) 0262 final, 6.

64 Denis Huber, *A Decade Which Made History: The Council of Europe 1989–1999* (Council of Europe Publishing 1999).

65 COE, 'Background Information' (COE website 2009) <http://www.coe.int/t/dghl/monitoring/moneyval/about/background_m> accessed 28 February 2014.

66 COE, 'Complete List of the Council of Europe's Treaties' (COE website 2009) <http://www.conventions.coe.int/Treaty/Commun/ListeTreaties.asp?CM)=8&CL=ENG> accessed 28 February 2014.

67 Neill Nugent, *Politics and Governance in the European Union* (5th edn, Savalas Publishers 2003).

68 COE, 'Special File: Financial Investigations and Confiscation of Proceeds from Crime' (COE website 2009) <http://www.coe.int/t/dghl/cooperation/economiccrime/SpeciaFiles/FI_en.asp> accessed 28 February 2014.

69 Economic Crime Division Directorate General of Human Rights and Legal Affairs of the COE, 'The Role of Technical Assistance in Development of Anti-Money Laundering and Counter-Terrorist Financing Systems. Lessons Learned from TA Projects Implemented by the Council of Europe, 2003–2007' (COE website 2009) <http://coe.int/dghl/cooperation/economiccrime/MoneyLaundering/Report/%20lessons%20learnt%20fin.pdf> accessed 28 February 2014.

a substantive contribution to its architecture. However, it is crucial to appreciate that the disruptive mechanism of this web, which is based on the principle of international cooperation,[70] depends to a large extent[71] on the volition of Union Member States and COE Signatory States to make effective use[72] of the wealth of instruments that can best be summarised as follows in the present context:

1. Anti-corruption instruments such as the Civil Law Convention on Corruption (ETS 174);[73] the Criminal Law Convention on Corruption (ETS 173);[74] Rec (2000) 10E of 11 May 2000 on Codes of Conduct for Public Officials;[75] Rec (2001) 11 E of 19 September 2001 Concerning Twenty Guiding Principles on the fight against Organised Crime;[76] and Rec (2003) 4 of the Committee of Ministers to Member States on common rules against corruption in the funding of political parties and electoral campaigns.[77]
2. Anti-money laundering instruments such as COE Convention on Laundering, Search, Seizure and Confiscation of the Proceeds from Crime of 8 November 1990[78] (CETS 141);[79] and COE Convention on the Financing of Terrorism of 16 May 2005 – the Warsaw Convention

---

70 Text to n 45.

71 Article 67 of the Treaty on the Functioning of the European Union (n 149) in chapter 1.

72 European Union Committee (n 8) in chapter 1.

73 Articles 3–7.

74 Articles 2–10, 12–13, 18–19 and 23.

75 COE Committee of Ministers, 'Rec (2000) 10E of 11 May 2000 on Codes of Conduct for Public Officials' (COE website 2009) <http://wcd.coe.int/ViewDoc.jsp?id=353945&Site=CM?BackColorInternet=9999CC&BackColorIntranet=FFBB55&BackColorLogged=FFAC75> accessed 28 February 2014.

76 COE Committee of Ministers, '(Rec 2001) 11E of 19 September 2001 Concerning Twenty Guiding Principles on the Fight against Organised Crime' (COE website 2009) <http://wcd.coe.int/com.intranetServlet?command=com.instranet.CmdBlobGet&InstranetImage=62085&SecMode=1&DocId=212804&Usage=4> accessed 28 February 2014.

77 COE Committee of Ministers, 'Rec (2003) 4 of the Committee of Ministers to Member States on Common Rules against Corruption in the Funding of Political Parties and Electoral Campaigns' (COE website 2009) <http://wcd.coe.int/ViewDoc.jsp?id=2183&Site=CM&BackColorInternet=9999CC&BackColorIntranet=FFBB&BackColorLogged=FFAC75> accessed 28 February 2014.

78 This instrument's scope is broader than that of the 1988 UN Convention against illicit traffic in narcotic and psychotropic substances in regard to criminal offences, confiscation measures, and sanctions (Articles 1–22).

79 COE, 'Explanatory Report to the Convention on Laundering, Search, Seizure and Confiscation of the Proceeds from Crime (CETS 141)' (COE website 2009) <http://conventions.coe.int/Treaty/en/Reports/Html/141.htm> accessed 28 February 2014.

(CETS 198)[80] in combination with the international standards set by other competent international organisations.[81]

3. Judicial cooperation[82] in criminal matters, especially against organised crime.[83]

Against this rich background, one cannot but readily identify the special properties and the dynamism of the pan-European web for the disruption of the criminal enterprise. Notwithstanding, it is underlined that the initiatives of the Council of Europe constitute a substantial part[84] of the toolkit[85] against money laundering and the financing of terrorism.[86]

In line with the above reasoning, the Explanatory Report[87] of the COE 2005 Convention has pointed out that the scope of the instrument's Third Chapter is international cooperation ranging from the stage of preliminary investigations to the final stage of enforcement of confiscation orders with a view to deprive criminals of their ill-gotten gains.

Additionally, the same Explanatory Report has underlined that the 1990 Convention had to be amended in order to properly address the evolution of money laundering techniques and anti-money laundering strategies of other international fora, such as the Financial Action Task Force, the European Union, the Egmont Group and the United Nations, over a period of 10 years.[88]

It is therefore essential to appreciate that the COE 2005 Convention has extended its scope to the fight against the financing of terrorism through existing international instruments; the promotion of adherence to international standards set by other international fora; the enhancement of measures to rapidly trace and

---

80 COE, 'Explanatory Report to the Convention on Laundering, Search, Seizure and Confiscation of the Proceeds from Crime and on the Financing of Terrorism (CETS 198)' (COE website 2009) <http://conventions.coe.int/Treaty/EN/Reports?Html/198.htm> accessed 28 February 2014.

81 COE Action against Economic Crime, 'Standards and Initiatives of other International Organisations and Mechanisms' (COE website 2009) <http://www.coe.int/t/dghl/cooperation/economiccrime/Money/Laundering/default_en.asp> accessed 28 February 2014.

82 COE Action against Economic Crime, 'Judicial Cooperation' (COE website 2009) <http://www.coe.int/t/dghl/cooperation/economiccrime/JudicialCooperation/default_en.asp> accessed 28 February 2014.

83 COE Action against Economic Crime, 'Organised Crime' (COE website 2009) <http://www.coe.int/t/dhl/cooperation/economiccrime/organisedcrime/default_en.asp> accessed 28 February 2014.

84 Kern Alexander (n 42) 182–183 in chapter 1.

85 Angela Veng Mei Leong, 'Chasing Dirty Money: Domestic and International Measures against Money Laundering' (2007) 10 JMLC 2, 146–148.

86 Text to n 80.

87 Text to n 80, 1–5, para 5.

88 Text to n 80, 3, para 15.

seize criminal property and suspicious bank accounts; and facilitate the domestic legislative systems of Member States to effectively respond to requests by other countries and to provide evidence upon request within the framework of international cooperation.[89]

From a macroscopic point of view, the Council of Europe's strategy to promote and enhance international cooperation against corruption, money laundering, the financing of terrorism, organised crime, and trafficking in human beings and sexual exploitation, is based on the following triptych: standard setting;[90] monitoring compliance with evolving standards;[91] technical cooperation for capacity building.[92]

In summary, building trust in the anti-money laundering system can be conceptually equated with creating a culture for the detection and reporting of economic crime incidents to prosecutorial, law enforcement and tax authorities for the benefit of the state and the public interest. The disruption of the criminal enterprise cannot effectively take place without the strict implementation of existing anti-money laundering standards at the national level.[93]

On the other hand, the engagement of financial institutions in the reporting system is strongly connected to the qualitative aspect of Suspicious Activity Reports.[94] As regards the important role that internal and external monitoring and evaluation practices play in assessing performance in the disruption of the criminal enterprise, the Council of Europe has suggested that anti-money laundering strategy implementation ought to be treated as project management at the national level.[95] On this particular issue, we should perhaps expect the minimum contribution from

89 Text to n 80, 19–38, paras 123–278.

90 COE, 'Council of Europe Treaties' (COE website 2009) http://www.conventions.coe.int/> accessed 28 February 2014.

91 COE, 'GRECO's 43rd Plenary Meeting (GRECO 43), Strasbourg, 29 June – 2 July 2009' (COE website 2009) <http://www.coe.int/t/dghl/monitoring/greco/default_en.asp> accessed 28 February 2014; COE, 'Committee of Experts on the Evaluation of Anti-Money Laundering Measures and the Financing of Terrorism – MONEYVAL' (COE website 2009) <http://coe.int/t/dghl/monitoring/moneyval/> accessed 28 February 2014; COE, PC – OC – Committee of Experts on the operation of European Conventions on cooperation in criminal matters, 'Human Rights and Legal Affairs' (COE website 2009) <http://www.coe.int/t/e/legal_affairs/legal_co-operation/Transnational-criminal_justice/> accessed 28 February 2014; COE, T – CY – Convention Committee on Cybercrime (T – CY), 'Convention Committee on Cybercrime (T – CY)' (COE website 2009) <http://www.coe.int/t/dghl/cooperation/economiccrime/cybercrime/T-CY/default_en.asp> accessed 28 February 2014.

92 Text to n 69.

93 Economic Crime Division Directorate General of Human Rights and Legal Affairs of the COE (n 69) 23.

94 Economic Crime Division Directorate General of Human Rights and Legal Affairs of the COE (n 69) 24.

95 Economic Crime Division Directorate General of Human Rights and Legal Affairs of the COE (n 69) 25.

the law, as it is plainly a matter of strict implementation by national authorities. The improvement of existing practices is far beyond the normative reach. In the result, meaningful technocratic solutions should be sought at the governance level on a risk-sensitive basis.

The Objectives for the Prosecutorial Toll

As any prosecutor will confirm, the objectives for the prosecutorial toll have evolved in parallel to the mental models[96] postulated by the international community to understand the threats posed by transnational organised crime and terrorism financing to the economic, social and political systems, and to develop robust, structured and meaningful regulatory responses to the various forms of serious crime targeted for prevention and control.[97]

Bringing to justice those who engage in the mingling of disguised criminal proceeds with the legitimate funds of the formal economy, is one of the main objectives for the prosecutorial toll. As Dr R.E. Bell of the Department of the Director of Public Prosecutions, Royal Courts of Justice, Belfast, has observed, the more criminal funds are invested in legitimate businesses, the more organised crime can influence the economic, social and political aspects of organised societies.[98]

In the past, prosecutors encountered enormous difficulties in obtaining substantive and incontestable inculpatory evidence from cross-border financial investigations. For this reason, the international community worked in partnership and delivered instruments that boosted national legislations through simple, clear and express provisions concerning:

1. The simplification of wrongful conduct (*actus reus*),[99] which criminalised the substantive[100] offence of money laundering without calumniating it to the predicate offence that generated the criminal proceeds.[101]
2. Guilty knowledge and wilfulness of the laundering offence, which requires prosecutors to prove the defendant's state of mind in knowing,

---

96 RE Bell, 'Prosecuting the Money Launderers Who Act for Organised Crime' (1999) 3 JMLC 2, 104.

97 International Association of Prosecutors, 'Third World Summit of Prosecutors General, Attorneys General and Chief Prosecutors (Bucharest, Romania, 24–25 March 2009) Report' (IAP website 2009) 5, para 24 <http://www.iap-association.org/resources/Bucharest_Summit_final_report_09.pdf> accessed 28 February 2014.

98 Bell (n 96) 104–106.

99 Bell (n 96) 107.

100 Stessens (n 44) 5 in chapter 1.

101 Freis Jr (n 107) 10 in chapter 1.

suspecting or having had reasonable grounds of suspecting the provenance of criminal property.[102]

3. The reversal of the burden of proof to the extent that it neither violates Article 6[103] of the ECHR[104] nor Article 6(2) of the ECHR, through which any defendant can establish defence under the necessary precondition that the overall burden of proving guilt rests with the prosecution.[105]
4. The laws and regulation for the confiscation, condemnation and forfeiture of the proceeds of crime.[106]
5. The legal infrastructure for judicial cooperation in criminal matters.[107]

In the result, the objectives for the prosecutorial toll have become synonymous with the enforcement of financial regulation and the maintenance of orderly, credible and transparent markets. Today's global anti-money laundering system comprises a uniform regulatory framework with common objectives for the prosecution and sanctioning of the different forms of economic crime.

Thus, the totality of the objectives for the current prosecutorial toll is characterised by an 'all crimes' approach, including money laundering, the financing of terrorism, corruption, market manipulation, insider dealing, fraud, tax evasion, health, safety and environmental violations, the proliferation of weapons of mass destruction, and human trafficking.

Distinct issues such as managing criminal investigations, cross-border investigations, disclosure of offences, reversal of the burden of proof, financial information gathering powers and competencies, exchange of personal data for law enforcement purposes, actions against persons and firms operating in two or more jurisdictions, and compliance, are of particular and coequal significance to the framework of application of prosecutorial powers as the suppressive environment has become all the more multifarious.[108]

Turning back to the postulation of mental models by the international community to understand transnational organised crime and terrorism financing

---

102 Trevor Millington and Mark Sutherland Williams, *The Proceeds of Crime: Law and Practice of Restraint, Confiscation, Condemnation and Forfeiture* (2nd edn, OUP 2007) 574–586.

103 Bell (n 96) 108.

104 Text to n 8 in chapter 1.

105 Sub-Committee F – Home Affairs on Money Laundering and the Financing of Terrorism (n 128) 34–35 in chapter 1.

106 Text to n 102, 363–569.

107 Council Decision 2007/845/JHA (n 142) in chapter 1.

108 EUROPOL (n 86) 1 in chapter 1; Commission, 'Proposal for a Regulation of the European Parliament and of the Council on the European Union Agency for Law Enforcement Cooperation and Training (Europol) and Repealing Decisions 2009/371/JHA and 2005/681/JHA' COM (2013) 173 final; Commission, 'Proposal for a Regulation of the European Parliament and of the Council on the European Union Agency for Criminal Justice Cooperation (Eurojust)' COM (2013) 535 final.

trends with a view to shape effective strategies against new and innovative ways to move dirty money into the licit economies, it is argued that the four justifications for the extension of the global anti-money laundering regime analysed in Chapter 1 (the war on drugs, the war on organised crime, the war on the financing of terrorism, and the war on illicit enrichment in its broadest sense), represent not only evolving mental models, but also the main forces behind the transformation of the prosecutorial toll from a narrower[109] to a broader one. Indeed, the prosecutorial toll is internationalised and all the more drastic[110] due to its all crimes approach.

It is therefore submitted with confidence that the all crimes approach of the prosecutorial toll signifies that we are dealing with an evolving trend in favour of transparency laws and against the various forms of corruption. This transformation can be accelerated if, on the one hand, the existing international anti-money laundering benchmarks used to assess and improve national anti-money laundering legislation are further enriched with transparency standards[111] and, on the other hand, a vertical diffusion of global transparency standards takes place within the internal architecture[112] of the global anti-money laundering and counter-terrorist financing system for the protection of the financial system and public wealth.

Nonetheless, it is also necessary to raise awareness of the constitutional impediments (the fundamental right to property and right to a fair trial) that a global transparency regime could potentially face in the future, mainly by civil law jurisdictions, in regard to the preclusion of non-conviction forfeiture.[113] Of course, these constitutional impediments exist even at present, and it is for this reason that international cooperation in civil recovery actions must be promoted and further enhanced.[114]

In summary, it is evident that there were pressing needs to make the prosecutorial toll wider and easier. As such, the challenge that lies ahead is about strict implementation.[115] In this regard, it is underlined that the prosecutorial toll has been made as wide and as easy as it can possibly become.

---

109 Bell (n 96) 105.

110 Sub-Committee F (Home Affairs) of the House of Lords Select Committee on the European Union, *E/08 – 09/F70 ML, Written evidence by the Crown Prosecution Society (CPS) Submission by the Director of Public Prosecutions to the Sub-Committee F (Home Affairs) of the House of Lords Select Committee on the European Union in Response to the Call for Evidence for the Inquiry into Money Laundering and the Financing of Terrorism* (HL 2008–09, 132–II) 4, para 14, Mr Jeremy Rawlins, Head of Proceeds of Crime Delivery Unit, Mr Mike Kennedy, Chief Operating Officer, <http://www.parliament.uk/documents/upload/F070DirectorPublicProsecutionsCPS120209.pdf> accessed 28 February 2014.

111 IAP (n 97) 5, para 25.

112 Text to n 110, 1–2, para 4.

113 COM (2012) 85 final (n 24) 6 in chapter 1.

114 Text to n 110, 6, para 24.

115 Professor Gilles de Kerchove (n 8) in response to Question 255 of Baroness Henig in chapter 1.

To further broaden the objectives for the prosecutorial toll without risk-sensitive reasoning, could potentially render money laundering countermeasures inoperable in the financial system. Let us recall that the cornerstone of national lawmaking is to implement and enforce measures that do not exclude legitimate businesses and consumers from the financial system.

Indeed, we have all become aware of the fact that transnational organised crime is a polymorphic nucleus, which continuously generates criminal finance. We have also become equally aware of the fact that money laundering, as a separate, substantive and acquisitive[116] offence, establishes bogus mechanisms for the making of criminal proceeds indistinguishable from lawful funds through a nexus that facilitates illicit financial activities. We should not therefore exclude the possibility of refining the objectives for the prosecutorial toll through the enforcement of transparency laws, such as anti-corruption and tax justice measures.

To promote tax justice essentially entails combating tax avoidance and tax evasion. According to the Tax Justice Network,[117] developing countries lose approximately USD $500,000,000,000 of tax revenues annually as a consequence of tax avoidance and evasion. Around USD $124,000,000,000 is lost due to the use of tax havens. Furthermore, it is estimated that the United Kingdom loses around £100,000,000,000 annually, out of which £18,500,000,000 is owed to the use of tax havens; whereas the United States[118] loses approximately USD $345,000,000,000, out of which USD $100,000,000,000 is owed to the use of tax havens.[119] Let us also recall that this was a central topic in the agenda of the G20 Summit in London in April 2009. At the same time, the OECD published a list of countries that either failed or refused to sign and adopt an international standard for the exchange of tax information.[120]

After all, improving tax justice by promoting and enhancing standards for the exchange of information on tax avoidance and tax evasion[121] and controlling unfair

116 Stessens (n 44) 5–10 in chapter 1.

117 Neil Hodge, 'A Taxing Issue: With Huge Amounts of Money being Lost by Developing Countries through Tax Avoidance and Evasion, a New G20 Communiqué Aims to Reverse the Trend – but Many Feel it Does Not Go Far Enough' (2009) 63 International Bar News 4, 21 – 23.

118 Email from Swiss Federal Administration admin.ch to author 'Switzerland and United States sign Memorandum of Understanding on FATCA agreement' (7 June 2013).

119 Text to n 117.

120 Text to n 15.

121 Europa Press Releases Reference: IP/04/1164 Date: 25/06/2009, 'European Commission Launches Strategy to Prevent Financial and Corporate Malpractice' (Europa website 2009) <http://europa.eu/rapid/pressReleasesAction.do?reference=IP/04/11...> accessed 28 February 2014.

tax competition[122] practices,[123] could be an alternative mental model for reshaping the strategy of reaching flows[124] of legitimised yet untaxed funds with a view to strengthen sustainable economic and social development.[125]

The Disruption of the Criminal Enterprise by the Union's Third Anti-Money Laundering Directive

This section focuses mainly on the interactive provisions of Directive 2005/60/EC,[126] Council Regulation 1889/2005 of 26 October 2005 on control of cash entering or leaving the Community,[127] and Council Regulation 1781/2006 of 15 November 2006 on information on the payer accompanying transfer of funds.[128] Finally, the discussion ends with a meaningful commentary on the Union's forthcoming Fourth Anti-Money Laundering Directive in the light of COM (2013) 45 final.[129] It is thus clarified that the present analysis will not compare Directive 2005/60/EC with the two aforementioned Regulations. On the contrary, the critical analysis will focus on the interrelation and interaction of the aforementioned three instruments.

The disruption of the criminal enterprise is of the utmost importance to governmental and intergovernmental organisations,[130] whose duty is to prevent and control the threats posed to the stability and integrity of the Union's financial system.[131] The concept of disruption should be perceived as the totality of preventive measures against those who act for organised crime and misuse the financial system for the purpose of laundering criminal proceeds and financing terrorism.

---

122 Nikolaos Barbas, 'Tax Competition as a Consequence of the Economic Globalisation' (2009) Business and Company Law 155, 12–22.

123 Commission, 'Communication from the Commission to the Council and the European Parliament on Preventing and Combating Corporate and Financial Malpractice' COM (2004) 611 final.

124 Email from Swiss Federal Administration admin.ch to author 'Report on taxation of cross – border commuters in Switzerland' (13 December 2013).

125 IAP (n 45) 3, para 14.

126 Text to n 2 in chapter 1.

127 Council Regulation (EC) 1889/2005 of the European Parliament and of the Council of 26 October 2005 on control of cash entering or leaving the Community [2005] OJ L209/9.

128 Council Regulation (EC) 1781/2006 of the European Parliament and of the Council of 15 November 2006 on information on the payer accompanying transfer of funds [2006] OJ L345/1.

129 Text to n 147 in chapter 1.

130 Angela Veng Mei Leong, *The Disruption of International Organised Crime: An Analysis of Legal and Non-Legal Strategies* (Ashgate 2008) 55–65.

131 Text to n 9, 3, para 5 (reference made to corruption, penetration and fraud).

In 2004, Frits Bolkestein, former Internal Market Commissioner, pointed out that the Union's First Anti-Money Laundering Directive (1991) showed that the Community was at the forefront of the international initiatives taken against the laundering of criminal proceeds.[132] However, in 2006, the Commission Staff Working Document of 19 December 2006[133] pointed out that Directive 91/309/EEC obliged the financial sector to identify their customers, report suspicious activities and establish internal control procedures, but its scope of application was limited to combat criminal proceeds emanating mainly from illicit drug trafficking.

With respect to the Second Anti-Money Laundering Directive 2001/97/EC,[134] the European Commission stressed that it had enhanced the preventive aspect of the regulatory framework established back in 1991, and that its primary goal was to make the necessary adaptations to the money laundering methods and techniques that had evolved in the previous years.[135] However, Internal Market Commissioner Bolkestein clarified that the amendment of Directive 91/309/EEC extended its scope to cover the proceeds of a broader range of crimes and to regulate a wider range of professions, such as lawyers, notaries, estate agents, accountants, art dealers, auctioneers, jewellers and casinos.[136]

The above findings strengthen the argument in Chapter 1 that the anti-money laundering regime was extended further to not only combat the proceeds of illicit drug trafficking, but also to combat a wider range of serious criminal offences. Of course, the disruption of the criminal enterprise depends to a large extent on the good performance of financial institutions in identifying their customers, reporting suspicious transactions, and establishing internal procedures and sophisticated systems internally to trace and report unusual transactions.

Whilst this might appear to be commonsensical, the principal aim is to underline that, when we refer to the legal initiatives of the European Union to disrupt the criminal enterprise through a wealth of proactive measures proposed, we should be prepared to appreciate that the overall strategy is not entirely based

---

132 Europa, Press Releases Reference: IP/04/832 Date: 30/06/2004, 'Money Laundering: Commission Proposes to Update and Improve Directive' (Europa website 2009) 1, para 1, <http://europa.eu/rapid/pressReleasesAction.do?reference=IP/04/832...> accessed 28 February 2014.

133 Commission of the European Communities, SEC (2006) 1792 of 19 December 2006 Commission Staff Working Document, 'The Application of Directive 91/309/EEC on the Prevention of the Use of the Financial System for the Purpose of Money Laundering in Relation to the Identification of Clients in Non–Face Transactions and Possible Implications for Electronic Commerce' (Europa website 2009) 3, para 1, <http://ec.europa.eu/internal_market/company/docs/financial-crime/non_face_to_face_en.pdf> accessed 28 February 2014.

134 Directive 2001/97/EC of the European Parliament and of the Council of 4 December 2001 amending Council Directive 91/308/EEC on the prevention of the use of the financial system for the purpose of money laundering [2001] OJ L344/76.

135 Text to n 133, 3, para 2.

136 Text to n 132, 1, para 2.

on what sanctions are foreseen under Directive 2005/60/EC against those who intend to misuse the financial system.

The overall repressive strategy is founded on the notion of what European Union law and national regulators oblige financial institutions and certain non-financial professionals to proactively do, in order to ensure that the criminal enterprise is disrupted and the perpetrators are brought to justice. In fact, it is through the obligation under Directive 2005/60/EC to report suspicious financial activities, to report transactions exceeding €15,000 in cash, and to establish sophisticated preventive systems within financial institutions, that the European Union is determined to strike a blow against organised crime[137] and the financing of terrorism.[138]

The aforementioned tools for the reporting of suspicions, which is the human perception of a conditional intention to engage or having engaged in a transaction that could potentially facilitate prohibited serious criminal acts, has been subjected to austere criticism. With regard to counter-terrorism financing measures taken by Western countries and particularly the United Kingdom, Dr Nikos Kotzias, Senior Associated Member of St Anthony's College of the University of Oxford and Senior Fellow in Weatherhead Centre for International Affairs of Harvard University, has supported the view that supranational terrorism facilitates the dominating groups in the West to undermine issues relating to the welfare state with a view to exercise excessive powers through the rise of the security state.[139]

On the other hand, in the light of the introduction of the euro currency and its €500 bank notes that can be misused for the purpose of cash smuggling, there are those who justify the regulatory framework of Directive 2005/60/EC and, without reservations, underline the significance of the reporting system and the special role that Financial Intelligence Units play in the facilitation of financial investigations and the prosecution and sanctioning of organised crime. Of course, as J.J. Freis Jr, Director of FinCEN, observed, the adoption and enforcement of anti-money laundering measures does not concern the millions of lawful remittances, but those transactions aiming to repatriate proceeds of crime or to finance terrorism.[140]

Against that background, it should not surprise us that today's technological advancements can be used to facilitate the uncovering of secret networks of professionals within financial institutions and enterprises taking advantage of their positions of trust and engaging in highly profitable crimes. They, too, should be considered as forming part of the criminal enterprise that falls well within the

---

137 Directive 2005/60/EC, Articles 3(4), 4(5) (a)–(f).

138 Europa, Press Releases Reference: IP/05/682 Date: 07/06/2005, 'Adoption of Anti-Money Laundering Directive will Strike a Blow against Crime and Terrorism' (Europa website 2009) <http://europa.eu/rapid/pressReleasesAction.do?reference=IP/05/682> accessed 28 February 2014.

139 Nikos Kotzias, *Political System and Identity: Globalisation and the Case of the United Kingdom* (1st edn, Kastanioti Publishers 2008) 331.

140 Freis Jr (n 107) 1–2 in chapter 1.

scope of Article 3(5)(d)–(e) of the Third Anti-Money Laundering Directive. Prior to entering into the discussion of the relevant instruments, it is important to note that software firms such as Cataphora and RenewData specialising in e-discovery, have launched new smart products that can trace unexplainable patterns of electronic communication within corporate environments and between individuals who are in different departments and have no reason to be in contact.[141]

The main mechanism for the disruption of the criminal enterprise under Directive 2005/60/EC is based on the reporting of suspicious transactions by the employees of credit and financial institutions[142] and by certain non-financial professionals to Financial Intelligence Units. The latter are the national centres for receiving, analysing and disseminating Suspicious Activity Reports and other information to competent authorities relating to potential money laundering and terrorism financing activities. The same applies for the reporting of business relationships with persons either holding or having held public positions (politically exposed persons – PEPs) and, in particular, those from countries where corruption is high.[143]

Ultimately, the preventive aspect of this strategy is based on the concept of bank employees and certain regulated professionals reporting to Financial Intelligence Units their clients'[144] suspicious transactions. But the concept of reporting suspicion clearly entails the reporting of the suspicious conduct of natural persons or the natural persons being beneficiaries of legal persons that are actually mimicking[145] the conduct of commercial people with a view to disguise criminal activity.[146] In this regard, it should also be acknowledged that the protection of reporters against threats and hostile acts is guaranteed under the said Directive.[147]

Credit and financial institutions with branches and subsidiaries located in other Member States and in third countries, especially in third countries where financial regulation may be deficient, are obliged to notify the competent authorities of the Member State in which they operate or are based for proper action to be taken[148] against global risk.[149] This obligation can have an extraterritorial legal impact on a third country as it will essentially trigger the mechanism for the exercise of peer

---

141 *The Economist*, 'Software that Spots Hidden Networks' (2009) 391 (8637) 74.

142 Preamble to Directive 2005/60/EC, para 36.

143 Preamble to Directive 2005/60/EC, paras 20, 25 and 29.

144 Articles 7–9(6) and 13 of Directive 2005/60/EC.

145 Articles 26–27 of Directive 2005/60/EC.

146 Article 20 of Directive 2005/60/EC.

147 Preamble to Directive 2005/60/EC, para 30.

148 Preamble to Directive 2005/60/EC, para 35.

149 Commission of the European Communities, SEC (2009) 939 final of 20 June 2009 Commission Staff Working Paper, 'Compliance with the Anti-Money Laundering Directive by Cross-Border Banking Groups at Group Level' (Europa website 2009) 6, para 2.9 <http://ec.europa.eu/internal_market/company/docs/financial-crime/compli_cbb_en.pdf> accessed 28 February 2014.

pressure, which can ultimately lead to the blacklisting of the country having a deficient anti-money laundering and counter-terrorist financing regime.[150]

But there is more to be said about the way in which Directive 2005/60/EC makes effective use of financial and non-financial professionals to disrupt the criminal enterprise. Financial institutions, enterprises and professionals are obliged to apply ongoing monitoring controls and enhanced due diligence measures to those persons or legal entities controlled by other persons seeking to hide their identity or politically exposed persons and their immediate family members and their close associates. In regard to politically exposed persons, the Directive's central objective is to control two different circles. On the one hand, the circle of politicians and public officials as a special category of regulated professionals. On the other hand, the social circle of these regulated professionals, which is essentially a narrower social circle within a broader social circle.[151]

As Article 3 of Directive 2006/70/EC provides, simplified due diligence is applicable only when the following criteria are met. The identity of the customer is publicly available, transparent and certain. The customer's financial activities and accounting practices are transparent if he or she is accountable to a competent institution of the Community. The customer is licensed under the national law of a Member State and is thus under a continuous obligation to adhere to mandatory rules for the maintenance of that license. The customer's financial activities, including books and records, are regularly reviewed, randomly sample-tested and continuously supervised by a competent authority.

Similarly, the financial product in question must meet the following criteria. It must have a contractual basis. It must not be linked to anonymous or complicated transactions. It must have a predetermined threshold of maximum €1,000. The benefits of the product must not extend to third parties. The realisation of the product's benefits must take place in the long term.

To reverse the reasoning of Article 3 of Directive 2006/70/EC, it is impossible for any person, group of persons or legal person to bypass the existing money laundering control mechanism, unless there is collaboration and facilitation from within the financial institution or the intermediary enterprise. In any other event, the anti-money laundering mechanism does not allow for wealth to remain unaccountable.

---

150 DG Internal Market and Services, Unit F2 'Company Law, Corporate Governance, Financial Crime', 'EU AML Info-letter: Countries with Deficient AML/CFT Regimes' (Europa website 2009) <http://ec.europa.eu/internal_market/company/docs/financial-crime/aml/news-200709_en.pdf> accessed 28 February 2014.

151 Directive 2006/70/EC of the European Commission of 1 August 2006 laying down implementing measures for Directive 2005/60/EC of the European Parliament and of the Council as regards the definition of 'politically exposed person' and the technical criteria for simplified customer due diligence procedures and for exemption on grounds of financial activity conducted on an occasional or very limited basis [2006] OJ L214/29, Article 2.

Whilst under Directive 2005/60/EC all natural and legal persons trading in goods by way of professional activity automatically fall under the risk-based supervision and monitoring when accepting payments exceeding the maximum threshold of €15,000[152] in cash, under Council Regulation 1889/2005, any person entering or leaving the Community with more than €10,000 in cash is obliged to declare the money to the competent authorities of Member States.[153]

The competent authorities (Customs) of Member States are empowered to carry out controls on natural persons travelling through airports, sea ports and train stations, their baggage, and the means of their transport. If cash, bank cheques and bills of exchange are found to exceed the maximum threshold declared or suspicions arise as to the possessors of the cash moved even though the sum in question is below the established threshold, the self-regulatory authorities of Member States can seize the funds.[154]

The information obtained by self-regulatory authorities by virtue of Articles 3–4 of Council Regulation (EC) 1889/2005, is recorded, processed and reported to the competent Financial Intelligence Unit.[155] This information may be transmitted to the competent authorities in other Member States or to the Commission when there are indications that the cash seized represent the proceeds of fraud[156] or other illegal activity that can seriously affect the financial[157] interests of the European Union.[158]

Furthermore, the information gathered can be exchanged[159] with third countries subject to the consent of the competent authorities having initially obtained the information pursuant to Articles 3–4 of the aforementioned Regulation. It is therefore apparent that the pattern for the disruption of the criminal enterprise under Council Regulation (EC) 1889/2005 is similar to that of Directive 2005/60/EC in that the public sector's self-regulatory authorities are used to deliver effective money laundering controls and to report their findings[160] to Financial Intelligence Units, which fall under the regulatory framework of Directive 2005/60/EC.

When considering the scope of application of Council Regulation (EC) 1781/2006 on the payer accompanying transfer of funds, it becomes all the more

---

152 Preamble to Directive 2005/60/EC, para 18.

153 Article 3 of Council Regulation (EC) 1889/2005.

154 Article 4 of Council Regulation (EC) 1889/2005.

155 Article 5 of Council Regulation (EC) 1889/2005.

156 Commission, 'Proposal for a Directive of the European Parliament and of the Council on the fight against fraud to the Union's financial interests by means of criminal law' COM (2012) 363 final.

157 COM (2011) 293 final (n 146) in chapter 1.

158 Article 6 of Council Regulation (EC) 1889/2005.

159 Article 7 of Council Regulation (EC) 1889/2005.

160 Europa, Press Releases Reference: IP/07/832 Date: 14/06/2007, 'Customs' New Rules to Combat Money Laundering and Terrorist Financing: Persons Entering or Leaving the EU have to Declare Cash Movements' (Europa website 2009) <http://www.europa.eu/rapid/pressReleasesAction.do?Reference=IP/07/8332> accessed 28 February 2014.

apparent that Directive 2005/60/EC is the supreme anti-money laundering and counter-terrorist financing instrument of the European Union. The reasoning behind Council Regulation (EC) 1781/2006 is to disrupt money launderers and financiers of terrorism[161] by tightening controls on the traceability of transfer of funds[162] in line with Special Recommendation VII of the Financial Action Task Force.[163]

Essentially, the payment service provider of the payee is obliged to have effective procedures in place to trace whether information on the payer is missing,[164] to transmit rapidly the relevant transaction data to the competent authorities upon request, and to store the data adequately and safely.[165] When the payment service provider of the payer is not based in the European Union, enhanced customer diligence measures must be applied pursuant to Directive 2005/60/EC, especially concerning cross-border correspondent banking relationships.[166]

When the payment service provider of the payee becomes aware that information on the payer is missing or is incomplete, then the payment service provider is obliged to automatically submit a Suspicious Activity Report to the competent authorities in accordance with Directive 2005/60/EC and national regulation.[167] Lastly, Council Regulation (EC) 1781/2006[168] also aims to facilitate the prosecution of criminals at the stage that information on the payer must be rapidly passed to the competent authorities carrying out criminal investigations.[169]

As already suggested throughout the discussion in the last two sections, the disruption of the criminal enterprise by the European Union's anti-money laundering[170] and counter-terrorist financing[171] web is based on the principle of entrusting mainly private sector stakeholders with preliminary financial

161 Cameron (n 74), paras 4–5 in chapter 1.

162 Preamble to Council Regulation (EC) 1781/2006, para 3.5.

163 Preamble to Council Regulation (EC) 1781/2006, para 5.

164 Preamble to Council Regulation (EC) 1781/2006, para 15.

165 Articles 7–14 of Council Regulation (EC) 1781/2006.

166 Preamble to Council Regulation (EC) 1781/2006, para 16.

167 Preamble to Council Regulation (EC) 1781/2006, para 18.

168 In combination with Directive 2005/60/EC implementing Financial Action Task Force Special Recommendation IX on cash couriers.

169 Preamble to Council Regulation (EC) 1781/2006, para 21.

170 Directive 2005/60/EC, Council Regulation (EC) 1781/2006, Council Regulation (EC) 1889/2005, Directive 2007/64/EC, Council Regulation (EC) 2580/2001, and Council Regulation (EC) 881/2002.

171 Council Regulation (EC) 2580/2001 of 27 December 2001 on specific restrictive measures directed against certain persons and entities with a view to combating terrorism [2001] OJ L344/70; Council Regulation (EC) 881/2002 of 27 May 2002 imposing certain specific restrictive measures directed against certain persons and entities associated with Usama bin Laden, the Al-Qaida network and the Taliban, and repealing Council Regulation (EC) 467/2001 prohibiting the export of certain goods and services to Afghanistan, strengthening the fight ban and extending the freeze of funds and other financial resources

investigation duties.[172] The key to understanding the central issue of this section is what Directive 2005/60/EC actually obliges credit institutions[173] to proactively engage in and how to synchronise their compliance and reporting obligations with supervisory authorities for the effective disruption of the criminal enterprise.

Overall, the findings have to show that the shell of Directive 2005/60/EC is a legal one, but the core of countermeasures and guiding principles are mainly technocratic, just as commercial people perform and pursue their activities. It is all about disrupting those who intend to misuse the financial system by mimicking ordinary commercial people and corporate entities. In this regard, the Union and the Financial Action Task Force have grasped the deceitful and evolving techniques of the criminal enterprise and have shaped the repressive strategy accordingly.

Commentary on the Forthcoming Fourth Anti-Money Laundering Directive in the Light of COM (2013) 45 Final

With COM (2013) 45 final, the European Union aims to deliver an improved, more comprehensive, and accessible anti-money laundering regulatory framework that is consistent with the new set of Recommendations adopted by the Financial Action Task Force in 2012.

The proposal's objectives are to guarantee efficiency in business environments, reduce cross-border complexities, and enable Member States to deliver consistent national rules through flexible implementation. Of course, it remains to be seen whether Member States will strengthen existing national rules through meaningful amendments or will opt to overload their national regulatory framework with new risk-focused measures.

The measures[174] proposed aim to secure financial stability and protect the soundness of the Internal Market by strengthening the Union's repressive strategy

---

in respect of the Taliban of Afghanistan [2002] OJ L139/9. The latter Council Regulation implements part of Financial Action Task Force Special Recommendation III.

172 Valsamis Mitsilegas and Bill Gilmore, 'The EU Legislative Framework against Money Laundering and Terrorist Finance: A Critical Analysis in the Light of Evolving Global Standards' (2007) 56 ICLQ 1, 136–140.

173 Directive 2007/64/EC of the European Parliament and of the Council of 13 November 2007 on payment services in the internal market amending Directives 97/7/EC, 2002/65/EC, 2005/60/EC and 2006/48/EC and repealing Directive 97/5/EC [2007] OJ L319/1.

174 COM (2013) 45 final (n 147) in chapter 1, 3. Setting a high level of common standards by strengthening the elements of the revised Recommendations of the Financial Action Task Force; the threshold for providers of gambling services and dealers in goods is set to €7,500 instead of €15,000; beneficial ownership information must be made available to obliged entities and to competent authorities; and obliging Member States, Supervisory Authorities, and obliged entities must assess risks and enforce measures that are proportionate to the risks involved.

in the light of the changing nature of money laundering and terrorism financing threats. The criminal enterprise is continuously seeking to exploit gaps in the regulatory system with a view to take advantage of technological advances[175] and create new and more innovative techniques[176] to transform criminal proceeds into legitimate and thus investable funds.[177]

In regard to the consistency of the proposed measures with the new set of Recommendations adopted by the Financial Action Task Force in February 2012, a number of key observations should be taken into consideration in order to properly understand the Union's determination to make Europe open and secure for its citizens.[178]

The Stockholm Programme[179] requires Member States and the Commission to further expand the exchange of information[180] between Financial Intelligence Units[181] in order to effectively combat money laundering and terrorism financing. Yet the restrictive measures already taken under Council Regulation (EC) 881/2002[182] against persons and legal entities to prevent money laundering and the financing of terrorism, fall within the scope of the five strategic objectives of the European Union's Internal Security Strategy for 2011–2014.[183] Plainly the enhancement of the transparency of legal persons and legal arrangements (beneficial ownership information) is one of the strategic objectives of the Union's revised strategy.[184]

It is important to promote electronic commerce, electronic transactions, the use of electronic signatures and the purchase of cross-border trust services for electronic transactions for the purpose of economic development. However, it is

175 Financial Crimes Enforcement Network, 'Statement of Jennifer Shasky Calvery, Director Financial Crimes Enforcement Network United States Department of Treasury Before the United States Senate Committee on Homeland Security and Government Affairs' (FinCEN website, 18 November 2013) 1 <http://www.fincen.gov/news_room/testimony/pdf/20131118.pdf> accessed 19 November 2013.

176 Text to n 175, 1–2 on the misuse of virtual currency.

177 COM (2013) 45 final (n 147) in chapter 1, 2. The Union's repressive strategy will be enhanced in order to effectively combat newly emerging threats and the criminal law will be harmonised for the offence of money laundering on the basis of Article 83(1) of the Treaty on the Functioning of the European Union.

178 Text to n 84 in chapter 1, 1–6.

179 Commission, 'Communication from the Commission to the European Parliament, the Council, the European Economic and Social Committee and the Committee of the Regions Delivering an area of freedom, security and justice for Europe's citizens Action Pan Implementing the Stockholm Programme' COM (2010) 171 final, 70.

180 Text to n 109 in chapter 1.

181 Text to n 110 in chapter 1.

182 Council Regulation (EC) 881/2002 (n 171).

183 Commission, 'Communication from the Commission to the European Parliament and the Council, the EU Internal Security Strategy in Action: Five Steps towards a More Secure Europe' (COM) 2010 673 final.

184 COM (2013) 45 final (n 147) in chapter 1, Articles 12, 29–30.

equally important that Member States have in place an efficient system for the control and simulation of the use of electronic identification, electronic signature and trust services for electronic transactions, in order to prevent criminals from taking advantage of new technological advancements[185] to conceal their transactions and identities. Under COM (2012) 238/2[186] specific measures have been proposed for the protection of digital citizenship and the prevention of cybercrime, but the aforementioned measures are further strengthened by COM (2013) 45 final.[187]

By COM (2012) 85 final,[188] the European Commission called upon Member States to take appropriate measures for the establishment of an efficient system to freeze, manage and confiscate criminal proceeds and to provide for sufficient institutional setup, financial and human resources. But in order for national authorities to be successful in the implementation of the measures proposed under COM (2013) 45 final, they must also be institutionally fit to prevent financial institutions from violating the Union's rules by sanctioning violations within their jurisdictions in cooperation with the new European Supervisory Authorities (ESAs).[189]

The Union's supervisory authorities are responsible for the coordination of the enforcement activities of national authorities by COM (2010) 716 final.[190] In the result, those Member States lacking a centralised system for the reinforcement of sanctions in the financial sector will be rapidly identified and will be obliged to put their houses in order through meaningful reforms at the national level.

Furthermore, under COM (2013) 45 final, the Union has shifted the obligation to national authorities to implement strengthened yet meaningful measures, which are not meant to financially exclude[191] legitimate businesses and consumers from the financial system. Thus the Union expects Member States to efficaciously enforce strengthened measures against money laundering and the financing of terrorism, but proportional to the national goal of financial inclusion.[192]

---

185 Text to n 175.

186 Commission, 'Proposal for a Regulation of the European Parliament and of the Council on electronic identification and trust services for electronic transactions in the internal market' COM (2012) 238/2, 2–8.

187 COM (2013) 45 final (n 147) in chapter 1, Articles 2–3, 19, 30, 44.

188 Text to n 24 in chapter 1.

189 The European Securities and Markets Authority (ESMA), the European Banking Authority (EBA), and the Occupational Pensions Authority (EIOPA).

190 Commission, 'Communication from the Commission to the European Parliament, the Council, the European Economic and Social Committee and the Committee of the Regions' COM (2010) 716 final.

191 After a fruitful public–private sector dialogue on anti-money laundering and countering the financing of terrorism that is compatible with financial inclusion as set out by the Financial Action Task Force in June 2011.

192 Vladimir Nechaev, FATF President 2013–2014, 'G8 Public–Private Sector Dialogue on Anti-Money Laundering and Countering the Financing of Terrorism (AML/

In regard to the Commission's recent data protection proposals,[193] the proposed amendments are compatible with Article 21 of COM (2012) 11 final (General Data Protection Regulation), which empowers European Union or national legislation to either maintain or introduce restrictions of the principles laid down in Article 5 and the data subject's rights (Articles 11–20 and 32) for the investigation and prosecution of criminal offences.[194]

As already suggested in the second and fifth sections of this chapter, there are pressing needs to combat tax fraud and tax evasion by making efficacious use of the anti-money laundering web. Whilst the control and prevention of tax crimes already falls under the scope of application of COM (2012) 722 final,[195] COM (2013) 45 final defines criminal activity as any form of criminal involvement in the commission of tax crimes (Articles 3(4)(f) and 31 for direct and indirect taxes) in accordance with the revised Recommendations of the Financial Action Task Force. It shouldn't therefore surprise us if we see in the immediate future national rules considering tax crimes as predicate offences to money laundering.

By way of comparison, the Third Anti-Money Laundering Directive and the forthcoming Fourth Anti-Money Laundering Directive constitute the cornerstone of the Union's strategy to combat money laundering and the financing of terrorism in line with the standards set and revised by the Financial Action Task Force.

The main difference between the Third Directive and the forthcoming Directive is that the Fourth will be an improved supreme instrument based on the principles of enhancement and clarification of the measures presently in force. With respect to the proposed enhancement and clarification of existing measures under COM (2013) 45 final, we can only hope that the responsibility of qualitative lawmaking that is shifted to Member States will not lead to disproportionate national rules that can impede economic growth.

Indeed, under COM (2013) 45 final, the measures proposed are strengthened and meaningful. Gambling is covered as opposed to casinos only. Thresholds for traders in goods in cash are reduced by 50 per cent. The sanctions regime must

CFT)' (FATF website 2013, 6 September 2013) <http://www.fatf-gafi.org/topics/financial inclusion/documents/ppsdsept13.html> accessed 28 October 2013.

193 Commission, 'Proposal for a Regulation of the European Parliament and of the Council on the protection of individuals with regard to the processing of personal data and on the free movement of such data (General Protection Regulation)' COM (2012) 11 final; Commission, 'Proposal for a Directive of the European Parliament and of the Council on the protection of individuals with regard to the processing of personal data by competent authorities for the purposes of prevention, investigation, detection or prosecution of criminal offences or the execution of criminal penalties, and the free movement of such data' COM (2012) 10 final.

194 On 21 October 2013, the Civil Liberties Committee voted new amendments for the provision of stronger safeguards for data transfer to non-European Union countries.

195 Commission, 'Communication from the Commission to the European Parliament and the Council; An Action Plan to strengthen the fight against tax fraud and tax evasion' COM (2012) 722 final.

efficaciously employ the administrative law. Statistical data must be collected and reported to central supervisory authorities. The processing, movement and storage of personal data is protected. Tax crimes are treated as predicate offences to money laundering under specific conditions. In the interests of transparency and accountability beneficial ownership falling under the 25 per cent threshold cannot remain secret. Branches and subsidiaries of financial institutions in other Member States are obliged to perform their home and host supervisory responsibilities for anti-money laundering purposes. Financial Intelligence Units will have increased powers in order to facilitate cross-border cooperation. Member States are obliged to carry out national risk assessments and then take appropriate measures to mitigate the risks. Enhanced due diligence measures must be conducted for high risk prevention only, while simplified due diligence measures must be promoted for low risk cases. The white list no longer exists in the equivalence of third country anti-money laundering regimes. European Supervisory Authorities must perform their duties on a risk-sensitive basis. Domestic politically exposed persons working in international organisations are finally regulated.

In summary, Directive 2006/70/EC, Directive 2005/60/EC and COM (2013) 45 final reflect the European Union's genuine need to prevent negative economic impacts as a consequence of uncontrolled money laundering and terrorism financing evolving trends. Indeed, money laundering, corruption and terrorism financing can destabilize financial systems, create financial instability, and ruin the integrity and reputation of financial markets. In short, under the forthcoming Fourth Directive, the enemy within financial systems continues to exist and to evolve.

The challenge that lies ahead is not only about delivering strengthened and risk-sensitive measures to Member States; it is also about implementing the Union's measures with pragmatism at the national level. And it is all the more necessary for the Union to continuously supervise and evaluate both the implementation and enforcement performance of national authorities without any compromise because the shifting of the obligation by the Union to Member States with a view to implement strengthened yet meaningful measures can potentially constitute the Achilles' heel of the forthcoming Fourth Anti-Money Laundering Directive.

Chapter 3

Transnational Organised Crime and Corruption

The Critical Function of Anti-Money Laundering Laws in Combating Transnational Organised Crime: A Critical Analysis from the UN Perspective

As any jurist will confirm, the prevention and control of transnational organised crime is an objective that ought to be pursued through the approximation of substantive criminal law, the mutual recognition of judicial decisions, and the enhancement of law enforcement and judicial cooperation in criminal matters.[1] In accordance with EUROPOL's Organised Crime Threat Assessment (OCTA) 2008, there are pressing needs for Europe to combat the threats posed by transnational organised crime in four hot spots: the North-West (Atlantic) region,[2] the North-East (Baltic Sea) region,[3] the South-East region,[4] and the South-West (the Iberian Peninsula) region.[5]

Consequently, neither the transnational dimension of organised crime nor the development of criminal alliances should be perceived as an exaggeration on the part of international standard-setting fora to concentrate efforts on the protection of universal legal goods, such as the financial system, fair competition, public policy and the administration of justice.[6]

This section sets out the role of anti-money laundering laws in the fight against transnational organised crime[7] from the perspective of the United Nations.[8]

---

1 Council Framework Decision 2008/841/JHA of 24 October 2008 on the fight against organised crime [2008] OJ L300/42, Preamble, para 3.

2 EUROPOL (n 53) 33–35 in chapter 1.

3 EUROPOL (n 53) 36–37 in chapter 1.

4 EUROPOL (n 53) 38–39 in chapter 1.

5 EUROPOL (n 53) 38–39 in chapter 1.

6 PP Tsirides, *The New Law for Money Laundering: Law 3691/2008* (Nomiki Bibliothiki SA 2009) 47–52.

7 Articles 2–3, 5–6, 8 and 23 of UNTOC.

8 The UN's Global Programme against Money Laundering (GPLM) was established in 1997 in response to the mandate given to UNODC by the 1988 UN Convention against Illicit Traffic in Narcotic Drugs and Psychotropic Substances. GPML was further strengthened in 1988 by the UNGASS Political Declaration and Action Plan against Money Laundering that extended to all serious crime. The three additional Conventions adopted

It addresses the critical function of anti-money laundering laws in combating transnational organised crime and identifies key findings to support the position in the fifth section of this chapter, that the UN Convention against Transnational Organised Crime (UNTOC), besides promoting international cooperation for the effective prevention and control of transnational organised crime,[9] contributes to the approximation of legislation with regard to international standards on transparency, integrity, accountability and good governance.

Prior to entering upon a detailed discussion of the critical function of anti-money laundering laws in combating transnational organised crime, it would be appropriate to set the scene in regard to what UNTOC[10] constitutes. It is argued with confidence that UNTOC is the main international instrument[11] requiring its State Parties[12] to criminalise the laundering of criminal proceeds, lay down and enforce measures against money laundering,[13] and establish frameworks for mutual legal assistance, extradition, law enforcement cooperation, sharing of expertise, and international cooperation.[14]

In political terms, UNTOC is not only a product of internationalism, but has also pooled intergovernmental volition, responsibility and obligation for the adoption of international standards in national legislation to uphold the rule of law,[15] prevent and control transnational crime effectively,[16] and ensure[17] that organised crime neither pays nor finances further crime and terror. Yet anti-money

are: the 1999 International Convention for the Suppression of the Financing of Terrorism, the 2000 UN Convention against Transnational Organised Crime, and the 2003 UN Convention against Corruption, This section focuses in particular on UNTOC.

9 Article 1 of UNTOC.

10 Adopted by General Assembly Resolution 55/25 of 15 November 2000 and entered into force on 29 September 2003.

11 Including the Protocol to Prevent, Suppress, and Punish Trafficking in Persons, Especially Women and Children; the Protocol against the Smuggling of Migrants by Land, Air and Sea; and the Protocol against the Illicit Manufacturing of and Trafficking in Firearms, Their Parts and Components and Ammunition.

12 Council Decision (EC) 579/2004 of 29 April 2004 on the conclusion, on behalf of the European Community, of the United Nations Convention Against Transnational Organised Crime [2004] OJ L261/69.

13 European Union Committee, *Money Laundering and the Financing of Terrorism* (HL 2008–09, 132 I) 20, para 49 <http://www.publications.parliament.uk/pa/ld200809/ldselect/ldeucom/132/132i.pdf> accessed 28 February 2014.

14 UNODC treaties, 'Crime-related Treaties' (UNODC website 2009) <http://www.unodc.org/uncode.org/unodc/en/treaties/index.html> accessed 28 February 2014.

15 Emmanuel Roukounas, *International Law I* (3rd edn, Ant N Sakkoulas Publishers 2004) 181–194.

16 Article 1 of UNTOC.

17 Council Framework Decision 2008/841/JHA (n 1), Preamble, para 6, the Union aims to build further on the UNTOC.

laundering measures operate at the interface[18] of the criminal law and the civil law. We should therefore inquire into the abstract notions of the administration of justice in the criminal law context and restitution in the civil law context to set out properly the basic parameters of these measures.

More specifically, the commission of one or more cross-border predicate[19] offences violates public policy in at least two jurisdictions. Until the predicate offences committed are prosecuted,[20] the obstruction of justice in the jurisdictions concerned is perpetuated.

Money laundering countermeasures are more likely to have the maximum repressive impact on the inflow of criminal proceeds into the financial system.[21] More specifically, at the zero point that criminal funds are unusable until they are cleaned.

It is thus through the application of effective money laundering controls, including the filtering of qualitative Suspicious Activity Reports, that national authorities are enabled to trace and seize the alleged proceeds of transnational organised crime,[22] prosecute money laundering offences, and where possible, prosecute and sanction predicate offences.[23]

The confiscation of the proceeds of criminal organisations, which unfortunately usually takes place after the sentencing of the members of a structured association and their facilitators, does not restitute the violation of public policy and the misuse of the financial system. Plainly put, what is intentionally and wantonly done cannot be undone. The reasoning behind the seizure and confiscation of the proceeds of the predicate offences committed is to restrain criminal finance and render it useless to finance further the same or new forms of cross-border criminal activity.[24]

In legal terms, UNTOC does not exclude the possibility of prosecuting money launderers for participation in a criminal organisation, provided that the offenders intentionally and wantonly pursued a criminal plan and acted in concert with those having committed the predicate offence with a view to facilitate the criminal organisation by disguising the true origin of the proceeds. The same principle is applicable to the offenders of the underlying crime who can be prosecuted for money laundering as well, provided that the offenders' actions aimed to facilitate the financial and material objectives of the criminal organisation.

---

18 Barry Rider, 'A Murkey World' (2003) 24 Comp Law 7, 193.

19 Articles 2, 6 and 6(2)(f) of UNTOC.

20 Article 1(5) of Directive 2005/60/EC.

21 Barry Rider, 'Taking Money Launderers to the Cleaners: Part 1' (1996) PCB 2, 144–145.

22 Articles 2(b), 5, 23 and 26(3) of UNTOC.

23 Articles 2–3, 5–6, 8 and 23 of UNTOC.

24 Articles 13–14 of UNTOC.

To recapitulate, the critical function of anti-money laundering laws has four repressive dimensions. First, to create the conditions within financial systems for the rapid tracing and seizure of criminal assets on the basis of the principle of the origin and lawfulness of the funds. Second, to facilitate the prosecution of money laundering offences on the basis of the principle of preventing the cloaking of predicate offences. Third, to disrupt the facilitation of the financial and material objectives of criminal organisations on the basis of the principle of combating the facilitation of criminal organisations. Fourth, since criminal organisations do not have the right to possess wealth, let alone wealth in disposable form, to subject money laundering offences to the same prosecutorial and judicial treatment as predicate offences.

The critical function of anti-money laundering laws is reflected in a number of key provisions of UNTOC. Under Article 7 of UNTOC, State Parties are expected to: establish a comprehensive anti-money laundering regime for the regulation and supervision of credit and financial institutions, non-financial institutions, and other enterprises exposed to money laundering risks; enforce measures for customer identification, record keeping, the submission of Suspicious Activity Reports; ensure that the competent regulatory, administrative and law enforcement authorities cooperate and exchange information at the national and international levels through Financial Intelligence Units; lay down measures for monitoring cross-border movement of cash and negotiable instruments; and deliver money laundering controls on cross-border transfer of funds through the reporting system and the gathering of financial intelligence.

Of significant substance is also the provision of Article 2(f) of UNTOC on the temporary freezing of property by court order in that it facilitates the rapid seizure of criminal property, particularly in civil law jurisdictions, where considerable delays can take place between the stage of the criminal prosecution of the offender and the offender's actual sentencing in court. Similarly, the confiscation and seizure procedures[25] are carefully drafted to effectively and equitably deal with the problem of criminal proceeds having been intermingled with legitimately acquired property by limiting the confiscation up to the assessed value of the allegedly intermingled proceeds.[26]

Furthermore, offences committed outside the jurisdiction of a State Party will constitute predicate offences on condition that the conduct is a criminal offence in the State where the offence was committed, and would be a criminal offence under the substantive criminal law of the State Party applying the provision of Article 6(2)(c) had it been committed there (the principle of dual criminality).

25 Article 12(6)–(7) of UNTOC.

26 Article 12(4) of UNTOC.

Pursuant to Article 18[27] of UNTOC, State Parties are expected to be fully cooperative particularly when the requesting State Party has reasonable grounds to suspect that the offence referred to in Article 3(1)(a)–(b) is transnational and involves an organised criminal group.[28] However, Article 27(1)(a) of UNTOC on law enforcement cooperation is of particular significance because it expressly refers to the establishment of channels of communication amongst the agencies and repressive authorities of State Parties for the rapid exchange of information concerning all aspects of the offences covered by the Convention.

State Parties are also required to collect, analyse and exchange information on the evolving trends of organised crime in parallel to technological advances misused for criminal purposes,[29] and to share analytical experience under the auspices of regional and international organisations.[30] Under Article 31 of UNTOC, State Parties are required to continuously assess repressive initiatives and promote best practices and policies for the prevention and control of transnational organised crime.[31] Last but not least, State Parties are also required to adopt a series of comprehensive transparency, integrity and accountability measures to enhance the financial system and to ensure that the corruptive powers of transnational organised crime do not penetrate the public and private sectors from within.[32]

By way of summary, it is evident that the anti-money laundering system has become notionally inseparable from the universal principle of promoting and enhancing the stability of the financial system. Indeed, anti-money laundering standards constitute UNTOC's spinal column. Without the seamless web established by anti-money laundering laws, it would be impossible to trace, disrupt, prosecute and sanction predicate offences and the offences of laundering the proceeds of criminal organisations into the formal economy.

It is also underlined that UNTOC's arsenal of money laundering countermeasures, which are pooled under the framework of international cooperation, reflects the mental model postulated by the international community to understand and assess the threats posed by transnational organised crime and to respond effectively to the various forms of serious crime. Nevertheless, the important point to note is that, underneath UNTOC's canonistic surface, anti-money laundering principles, which interconnect with the international standards set by the Financial Action Task Force, play the role of the centrifugal regulatory force. In this regard it is also

27 Article 18(8) of UNTOC, bank secrecy cannot be an impediment to transnational mutual legal assistance.

28 Article 18(3)(a)–(i) of UNTOC, mutual legal assistance is to be offered in the widest possible extent.

29 Article 28(1) of UNTOC.

30 Article 28(2) of UNTOC.

31 Article 31(1) of UNTOC.

32 Article 31(2)–(7) of UNTOC.

suggested that, besides using the criminal law as a weapon against transnational organised crime, it is of the utmost importance to make efficacious use of the civil law and the tax law.

The findings in UNTOC's specific provisions[33] enable us to confidently suggest that this invaluable instrument, among other things, contributes to the approximation of international legislation on transparency, accountability and good governance in the public and private sectors.[34] This view is all the more reinforced by the key findings of Chapter 2 on the strengthened repressive anti-money laundering strategy[35] of the Union in the light of the recently published draft of the forthcoming Fourth Anti-Money Laundering Directive.[36]

Money Laundering in the Context of Organised Crime and Corruption

This section focuses mainly on the United Nations Convention against Corruption (UNCAC).[37] It also goes deeper into the notion that evolving international standards aim to strengthen criminal law and civil law measures in national regulatory frameworks[38] with a view to combat corruption, promote transparency, integrity and accountability in the public and private sectors, and enhance international cooperation in the recovery of illicitly acquired assets.[39]

All together, this section underlines the significant contribution of the UNCAC to the promotion of the civil law and the tax law[40] as effective weapons for the recovery of the proceeds of corruption.[41] The Convention's devotion to asset recovery has to show, amongst other things, that the illicit acquisition of wealth is an anti-social phenomenon against good morals, which can seriously impede sustainable economic development.

33 Articles 8–9 of UNTOC.

34 Articles 9 and 31 of UNTOC.

35 Text to nn 137–142 in chapter 1 on the Union's existing regulatory framework.

36 COM (2013) 45 final (n 147) in chapter 1, 3, paras 2 – 3.

37 The Convention was adopted by GA Resolution 58/4 of 31 October 2003. By GA Resolution 57/169 of 18 December 2002, the UN General Assembly accepted the Mexican government's offer to host the high-level Conference in Merida for the signing of the UNCAC. Pursuant to Article 68(1) of GA Resolution 58/4, UNCAC entered into force on 14 December 2005.

38 Preamble and Articles 1, 43 and 51–59 of UNCAC.

39 UNODC, 'United Nations Convention against Corruption: Convention Highlights' (UNODC website 2009) 2–3 <http://www.unodc.org/unodc/en/treaties/CAC/convention-highlights.html> accessed 28 February 2014.

40 Barry Rider (ed.), *Corruption: The Enemy Within* (Kluwer 1997).

41 Barry Rider, 'In Pursuit of Fees' (2007) 10 JMLC 4, 389.

The transmogrification of secret[42] and unaccountable wealth through the financial system is the stereotypical objective pursued by the offenders of serious crimes including that of corruption. Serious crime offenders, including corrupted persons, are mainly motivated by the illicit acquisition and possession of wealth in disposable form. Thus after having committed the predicated offences, the offenders are primarily concerned with securing the safety and immediate accessibility of their ill-gotten gains to finance criminal operations and normal commercial activities.

But the problem lies in that it is not often fully appreciated that the central role of international anti-money laundering and anti-corruption instruments is to oblige and guide national authorities to implement money laundering countermeasures within their jurisdictions with a view to effectively deal with serious threats.

Of course, we should not fail to also recognise that by the time anti-money laundering standards are transposed from the international to the national level, let alone from one legal system to another, they can be unintentionally altered due to the constitutional, legal and institutional peculiarities of different legal traditions called upon to implement them.

Nonetheless, national authorities are expected to create the proper conditions within their national legal systems to effectively trace and attack the assets of organised crime and corruption during the laundering process, that is, prior to be being placed in the financial system.[43] It is precisely for this reason that, under Article 14 of the UNCAC,[44] State Parties are obliged not only to criminalise[45] money laundering and corruption offences,[46] but also to institute a comprehensive, accessible and consistent regime to effectively regulate and supervise credit and financial institutions, non-financial institutions, professionals and obliged legal entities.

There are two crucial points that should be kept in mind with regard to the aforementioned observation. First, neither the UNTOC nor the UNCAC provide detailed provisions as to how money laundering operations should be intercepted during the cleaning process. As it has been underlined by HM Treasury,[47] it is the duty of the national legislator to continuously feed the financial system

42 Garry W Potter, '1980s USA: Money Laundering for Contras, the Mob and the CIA' <http://coat.ncf.ca/our_magazine/links.issue43/articles/more_launderi> accessed 28 February 2014.

43 Text to n 21.

44 Article 7 of UNTOC is equivalent.

45 Article 23 complementing Article 14 of the UNCAC.

46 Indira Carr and Miriam Goldby, 'The UN Anti-Corruption Convention and Money Laundering' 5–8 <http://idec.gr/iier/new/CORRUPTION%20CONFERENCE/The%20UN%20Anti-corruption%20convention%20and%20money%laundering-INDIRA%CARR.pdf> accessed 28 February 2014.

47 Text to n 5, para 1.8 in chapter 1.

with improved, smarter and more cost-effective tools for the disruption of the criminal enterprise.

But these tools, which must also be risk-sensitive to reflect the Union's revised repressive strategy, must be based on the fundamental principles of effectiveness, proportionality, mitigation of risks, financial inclusion, and continuous engagement of stakeholders and gatekeepers from all sectors. Second, what makes the UNCAC drastically different from the UNTOC is its devotion[48] to the fundamental principle of asset recovery[49] under Article 51.

Moreover, the provisions of Chapter V of the UNCAC (Articles 52–59) not only promote the civil law as an effective weapon for tracing and attacking the assets of corruption, but in their totality, they also remind us that those jurisdictions applying the most effective money laundering controls will always be at the top of the list of serious crime offenders because the more reputable the jurisdiction is, the safer and less suspicious will be the placement of the laundered criminal proceeds.[50]

Undoubtedly, the Convention contains other equally important provisions aiming to strengthen transparency, integrity and accountability in the public[51] and private[52] sectors; the prudential management of national wealth,[53] and the criminalisation of the illicit enrichment of those public officials[54] who cannot explain the acquisition of assets beyond their declared income. It is important to note that the UNCAC calls upon its State Parties to adopt uniform measures to prosecute corruption along with other forms of economically motivated serious crime.[55]

Making use of the civil law as an effective weapon for the seizure of the assets of economic crime is commendable, but it does not constitute the final solution to the problem of dealing with those who possess huge amounts of unaccountable wealth and are obliged to justify the origins of that wealth to the judicial authorities, let alone to declare it to the tax authorities.

Yet it is of the utmost importance not to miss the essential point that, like under the UNTOC, under the UNCAC it is still necessary to establish the nexus between wealth and serious crime. Anti-money laundering laws provide national authorities

48 Text to n 41, 389.

49 Chapter V (Asset Recovery), Articles 52–59 of the UNCAC.

50 Barry Rider, 'Organised Crime and Terrorism: Tracking and Attacking the Assets of Economic Crime and Terrorism 06/02' (ICC Commercial Crime Services Annual Lecture, Director of the Institute for Advanced Legal Studies, Skinners' Hall, London, 2002) 1, para 10 <http://www.iccwbo.org/iccbjfh/index.html> accessed 28 February 2014.

51 Articles 5–11, 14–20 and 23–30 of the UNCAC.

52 Articles 5, 12–14, 18–21 and 23–30 of the UNCAC.

53 Chapters III–IV (Articles 15–50) of the UNCAC.

54 Article 20 of the UNCAC.

55 Text to n 41, 389.

with an effective booster to trace and attack the assets of economic crime on the condition that prosecutorial authorities will prove to judicial authorities and to juries that the wealth seized represents the proceeds of crime.

Alternatively, it could also be argued that if the anti-money laundering system is capable of tracing the fruits of economic crime with a view to seize them and to facilitate the prosecutorial work in bringing the perpetrators and, potentially, the predicate offenders to justice, then it must also be capable of establishing the nexus between money laundering activity and those individuals who intentionally collaborated with organised crime or wantonly acted incompetent[56] because they were corrupted insiders.

It is no secret that those in possession of criminal funds, including organised crime groups, will always be in a position to threaten financial stability[57] by laundering criminal proceeds[58] and corrupting those who hold positions of trust and mind other people's wealth.[59] In this regard, those who shape the European Union's anti-money laundering strategy must not fail to recognise that the criminal enterprise will be attracted by jurisdictions delivering the most effective money laundering controls[60] because such reputable jurisdictions unintentionally offer to criminals the maximum degree of safety and immediate access to their laundered criminal assets.

By way of summary, it is evident that both the criminal law and the civil law are effective weapons for the seizure of criminal assets and the prevention and control of corruption, which generates criminal profits.[61] The supranational method[62] of proposing measures for the implementation of strengthened[63] national

56 Barry Rider, 'Here We Go Again' (2008) 15 JFC 3, 241.

57 Peter J Quirk, 'Money Laundering: Muddying the Macroeconomy' <http://www.worldbank.org/fandd/english/0397/articles/0110397.htm> accessed 28 February 2014.

58 Albert F Tellechea, 'Economic Crimes in Capital Markets' (2008) 15 JFC 2, 218.

59 Michael Levi, 'Money Laundering: Private Banking becomes Less Private' 204–205 <http://transparency.org/content/download/4267/26206/file/gi_money_laundering.pdf> accessed 20 December 2008.

60 The World Bank, World Bank Committee on Payment and Settlement Systems, 'General Principles for International Remittance Services 02/07' (World Bank website 2007) <http://www.bis.org/publ/cpss/76.pdf> accessed 28 February 2014.

61 Lois M Mousikali, 'Why Criminal Sanctions still Matter in Corporate Governance' (2009) 20 ICCLR 4, 133–141.

62 Estella Baker, '"From Past Imperfect to Future Imperfect?" A Longitudinal Study of the Third Pillar' (2009) 20 ICCLR 4, 133–141.

63 Email from Swiss Federal Administration admin.ch to author 'Federal Council adopts dispatch on implementation of revised FATF recommendations' (13 December 2013).

rules on the criminalisation[64] of corruption[65] and the seizure and recovery of criminal assets, is commendable and in line with upholding the rule of law. However, as it has already been pointed out in Chapter 2, delivering effective money laundering controls constitutes only part of the solution because prosecutorial authorities must prove to courts and juries that the wealth seized represents the proceeds of crime.

Perhaps, the remaining half of the solution can be given by dealing more radically with the problem, that is, by mobilising the civil law and the tax law to trace unaccountable wealth on the basis of the presumption of corruption.[66] Let us also recall that tracing and seizing the criminal profits of insider fraud[67] and market abuse is extremely difficult if not almost impossible, unless the anti-money laundering mechanism is triggered by the Suspicious Activity Report. The latter must clearly specify the particulars of the alleged fraudulent act that will then become the subject of the prosecutorial investigation. After all, the combination of taxing unaccountable wealth and injecting transparency, accountability and good governance standards in the financial system cannot but contribute to the solution of the problem.

Lastly, setting aside that under the UNCAC it is necessary to establish the nexus between criminal property and a specific form of serious crime, it must be acknowledged that this excellent Convention binds its State Parties to lay down national rules that not only contribute to the prevention and control of corruption and economic crime[68] as a whole, but also promote the concept of the redistribution of wealth.

---

64 Indira Carr, 'Corruption in Africa: Is the African Union Convention on Combating Corruption the Answer?' [2007] JBL March, 11–36.

65 Email from Swiss Federal Administration admin.ch to author 'The Federal Council extends the freezing of assets of several individuals from Tunisia and Egypt' (18 December 2013) referring to Presidents Ben Ali of Tunisia (CHF 60,000,000) and Mubarak (CHF 700,000,000).

66 Kenneth L Bryant, 'Senior Foreign Political Figures (SFPFs) or Politically Exposed Persons (PEPs) Scandals' (Kenneth l Bryant website 2009) <http://www.amlcft.com/cases.html> accessed 28 February 2014.

67 RCH Alexander, 'Insider Dealing and Money Laundering in the EU: Law and Regulation' (2009) 34 ELR 2, 341–343; *The Economist*, 'The Galleon Affair | All at Sea' (2009) 393 (8654) 77.

68 CIA, 'Speeches & Testimony > Appendix A: Chronology of Nuclear Smuggling Incidents > The Continuing Threat from Weapons of Mass Destruction' (CIA website 2009) <http://www.cia.gov/news-information?speeches-testimony/1996/go_appendixa_032796.html> accessed 28 February 2014.

Corruption as an Internal Enemy of the Anti-Money Laundering System

Benjamin Franklin, in his memoirs,[69] highlighted that our dealings should always be based on the principles of truth, sincerity and integrity. In legal terms, the application of these principles can suffice to preclude corruption from our political and financial dealings. Contrastingly, the question may be asked, what do mega scandals, such as the BCCI,[70] Enron,[71] HealthSouth,[72] Worldcom,[73] Madoff,[74] Siemens,[75] and Papandreou,[76] to name just a few, have to show about the crime[77] of corruption[78] in the context of the anti-money laundering system?

INTERPOL Secretary General, Ronald K. Noble, points out that corruption[79] undermines the work of the law enforcement community, impoverishes communities, threatens national security for the benefit of the few, and generates more than USD $1,000,000,000,000 in bribes annually. At the same time, the World Bank Institute[80] estimates the size of the world economy to be approximately USD $30,000,000,000,000.

---

69 JA Leo Lemay and PM Zall (eds), *Benjamin Franklin's Autobiography: An Authoritative Text* (1st edn, WW Norton & Co 1986) 46.

70 United States Senate, Report to the Committee on Foreign Relations by Senator John Kerry and Senator Hank Brown 12/92, 'The BCCI Affair' US 102nd Congress, 2nd Session Senate Print, 102–140, Executive Summary, 1 paras 1–16 (Federation of American Scientists website 2009) <http://www.fas.org/irp/congress/1992_rpt/bcci/01exec.html> accessed 28 February 2014.

71 Adam Lashinsky, 'The Enron Scandal' *What Really Happened* (New York, 30 November 2001) <http://whatreallyhappened.com/WRHARTICLES/ENRON.html> accessed 28 February 2014.

72 Washingtonpost.com Staff, 'Timeline of Accounting Scandal at HealthSouth' *The Washington Post with Bloomberg* (Washington, 30 September 2004) <http://www.washingtonpost.com/wp/dyn/articles/A24671-2003Oct14.html> accessed 28 February 2014.

73 BBC News, 'WorldCom: Wall Street Scandal' *BBC News Business* (London, 1 July 2002) http://news.bbc.co.uk/2/hi/business/2077838.stm> accessed 28 February 2014.

74 *The Economist* (n 18) 68 in chapter 2.

75 DW.DE staff (jc), 'Report: Siemens Scandal May Involve Top Executives' *De Deutsche Welle Top Stories/Business* (27 November 2006) <http://www.w.de/report-siemens/scandal/may/involve/top-executives/a-2249977-1> accessed 28 February 2014.

76 John Ward, 'Papandreou Accused of Greek Debt "Lifebelt" Fraud' *The Slog* (London, 1 June 2011) <http://hat4uk.wordpress.com/2011/06/01/papandreou/accused-of-greek-debt-lifebelt-fraud/> accessed 24 December 2013.

77 Graham Rodmell, 'Corruption – Economic Crime or Economic Reality?' (2007) 28 Comp Law 9, 259.

78 Henry H Rossbacher, 'The Business of Corruption, or is the Business of Business Corruption?' (2006) 13 JFC 2, 204.

79 JT Noonan Jr, *Bribes* (Macmillan 1984).

80 Interpol, 'Corruption: About Corruption' (Interpol website 2009) 1–2 <http://www.interpol.int/Public/Corruption/about.asp> accessed 28 February 2014.

Indeed, there exists a mountain of international anti-corruption instruments.[81] Yet it is impossible to totally eradicate this multifaceted phenomenon.[82] But this harsh reality should not prevent us from pursuing further research, sharing our knowledge with a view to contribute to the strengthening of the repressive strategy against corruption, and discovering new ways of improving the existing mechanism to trace, attack and recover the internationally distributed proceeds of corruption.

As we already had the opportunity to review in Chapter 1, the repressive nucleus of the anti-money laundering system comprises two fundamental components: the reporting system and the gathering and exchange of financial intelligence. The important point to note, however, is that the dynamic of the anti-money laundering system is not only the statutory transformation of financial institutions and financial intermediaries into reporting entities at the stage of having traced suspicious or unusual transactions, but also the submission of Suspicious Activity Reports by reporters to their national Financial Intelligence Unit in conformity with national regulation. It logically follows, therefore, that whenever Suspicious Activity Reports are not submitted, the anti-money laundering system is not triggered to trace, attack and seize criminal assets.

The particular stage is equated with the zero point discussed in this chapter, at which reporters are expected to trace and then to specify in their Suspicious Activity Reports the alleged criminal assets targeted for attack by the anti-money laundering system. Although criminal profits are unusable in the laundering process, they have the prospect of becoming usable when they re-enter the legitimate financial system. Therefore, the higher the level of integrity of private sector reporters, the higher will be the level of integrity of the anti-money laundering system as a whole. Yet as we already had the opportunity to analyse earlier in this chapter, those jurisdictions applying the most effective money laundering controls will always be at the top of the list of the criminal enterprise because the more reputable the jurisdiction is, the safer and less suspicious will be the placement of the criminal proceeds.

The reader is thus encouraged to bear in mind that the enemy of the anti-money laundering system has two dimensions, an external and an internal. On the one hand, reporters are obliged to trace the proceeds of crime, the external enemy of the financial system, at the stage that they are unusable. On the other, the employees of reporting entities may become the internal enemy of the financial system when they both intentionally and wantonly refrain from submitting Suspicious Activity Reports to their Financial Intelligence Unit or when they tip off their clients in regard to financial investigations in progress.

81 Interpol, 'About Corruption: Conventions regarding Anti-Corruption' (Interpol website 2009) 1–2 <http://www.interpol.int/Public/Corruption/Conventions/default.asp> accessed 28 February 2014.

82 Text to n 80, 1.

The main purpose of this section is to analyse the threat posed to the integrity of the anti-money laundering system by commercial[83] corruption at the zero point of the money laundering cycle. This threat is particularly insidious because it stems from the nefarious alliance between money launderers acting for organised crime as bribe givers and the employees of reporting entities acting as bribe recipients and facilitators of the laundering of criminal proceeds.[84] The epicentre of the present discussion therefore concerns those persons holding positions of trust within financial institutions having a price to commit the crime of facilitating the distribution of the proceeds of serious crimes and corruption from within the financial system.

It should also be pointed out that the role of corruption as the internal enemy of the anti-money laundering system[85] has constituted the subject of serious debate since the 14th Cambridge International Symposium on Economic Crime in 1996. In 2006, Henry H Rossbacher, Fellow of the Institute for Advanced Legal Studies, confirmed that the issues elucidated at the 1996 Symposium contributed to the adoption of the Convention on combating bribery of foreign public officials in 1997 by the OECD.[86] In 2008, David Chaikin, a barrister and former Expert Consultant to the Financial Action Task Force and Asia/Pacific Group on Money Laundering (2006–2007), highlighted that the policies adopted to combat corruption and money laundering may have an almost identical repressive impact.[87]

Taken together, these submissions suggest that organised crime and corruption can penetrate financial institutions by bribing the employees of private sector reporting entities who are then transformed into the internal[88] enemies of the anti-money laundering system. In this regard, Chaikin's observation is not only convincing, but it also raises awareness of how money launderers and organised criminals can persuade insiders to abuse their positions of trust by refraining from submitting Suspicious Activity Reports in circumstances that they are obliged to (passive facilitation) or by revealing inside information concerning financial investigations in progress.

Active facilitation can be described as wantonly structuring or facilitating bogus transactions from within financial institutions. This form of facilitation cannot constitute the work of one or two corrupted employees only. It requires the collaboration of a number of insiders acting secretly for money laundering networks and criminal organisations. This view is reinforced by taking into consideration that financial institutions have in place multiple levels of internal

83 David Chaikin, 'Commercial Corruption and Money Laundering: A Preliminary Analysis' (2008) 15 JFC 3, 269–272.

84 Text to n 83, 272.

85 Barry Rider, 'Corruption: The Enemy Within' (1998) 13 JIBL 9, 321–322.

86 Text to n 78, 203.

87 Text to n 83, 269.

88 Barry Rider, 'An Insider Paradox' [2008] 29 Comp Law 1, 1.

controls and compliance procedures,[89] during which a number of employees from different departments must review and approve the documentation required for the realisation of domestic[90] and cross-border[91] transactions.[92]

Passive facilitation can be described as wantonly acting incompetent[93] or unsuspicious to facilitate criminal money to bypass the internal controls of financial institutions. The act of turning a blind eye to a suspicious transaction and refraining from submitting a Suspicious Activity Report to the national Financial Intelligence Unit may be owed to already having knowledge that criminal funds are transferred from another corrupt[94] financial institution used[95] for the initial stage of the laundering cycle.[96] This conspiratory act entails a certain aura of legality and it is based on the notion of 'hear no evil, see no evil'[97] on the part of insiders acting as undercover white-collar criminals.[98]

Compendiously, the preceding analysis articulates and defends four central views. The first is that money laundering and corruption often occur together, but the former mainly owes its existence to the latter. There would not exist a laundering mechanism for the proceeds of corruption, if corrupt conduct did not generate illicit profits in the first place.

The second is that the employees of private sector reporting entities will always be exposed to the threat posed by organised crime, which is its ability to corrupt professionals and penetrate institutions. Due to the lack of comparable statistical data, it would be appropriate to temperately speculate that organised crime groups, in collaboration with insiders, can access confidential information as to how financial institutions manage their compliance risks.

---

89 Basel Committee on Banking Supervision, 'Revisions to the Basel II Market Risk Framework' (Bank for International Settlements website 2009) <http://bis.org/publ/bcbs148.pdf?noframes=1> accessed 28 February 2014.

90 Council Regulation (EC) 1889/2005 (n 127) in chapter 2.

91 COM (2013) 45 final (n 147) in chapter 1.

92 Text to n 60, 11–55.

93 Text to n 56, 241.

94 Martin Mann, 'Corrupt Banks Identified' (Liberty Lobby website 2009) <http://www.libertylobby.org/articles/2000/20000402banks.html> accessed 28 February 2014.

95 David Crawford and Like Esterl, 'Inside Bribery Probe Siemens' (Liechtenstein – Athens, 3 January 2008) <http://www.adslgr.com/forum/archive/index.php/t-161266.html> accessed 28 February 2014.

96 US Department of the Treasury, 'US Customs Service Takes Down Major Drug Traffickers, Corrupt Banks and Bankers in Largest Drug Money Laundering Case Ever' (Office of Public Affairs: RR-2452, 18 May 1998) <http://www.treasury.gov/press/releases/rr2452.htm> accessed 28 February 2014.

97 Peter Alldridge, 'Reforming Bribery: Law Commission Consultation Paper 185: (1) Bribery Reform and the Law – Again' [2008] Crim. LR 9, 671–686.

98 Margaret E Beare, 'The Devil Made Me Do It: Business Partners in Crime' (2007) 14 JFC 1, 36.

The third is that active facilitation, passive facilitation and tipping off[99] clients by insiders are manifestations of the inherent vice of those who cannot control their greed and are willing to prostitute their personal and professional ethics.[100] The good news is that not all professionals are susceptible to corruption, consequently, the integrity of the anti-money laundering system cannot be simultaneously attacked from all possible angles. Private sector stakeholders should be more engaged in social dialogues and anti-money laundering assessments. They should be encouraged by national authorities to share their experiences and field expertise, and should be invited more frequently to exchange their views on the improvement of internal control and compliance compatibility with anti-money laundering regulation. Only this way we will be able to safeguard the integrity of the anti-money laundering system, prevent the creation of criminal institutions,[101] and enhance fair competition[102] within the financial system.

The fourth is that legislators should appreciate that anti-corruption laws should not be applied only to those public officials who cannot explain their wealth beyond their declared annual income. Similar measures should also apply to those who hold positions of trust in financial institutions if we are seriously concerned with controlling abusive dealings within financial institutions and enterprises.

After all, the central objective of Directive 2006/70/EC is to control politicians and public officials as a special category of regulated professionals and to also control the circle of persons related to politically exposed persons.[103] The question may be asked, why shouldn't we apply similar, proportionate and risk-sensitive measures to the employees of private sector reporting entities? Of course, financial institutions should equally appreciate that there are pressing needs to intervene by providing increased financial resources to improve the income of their employees with a view to make them less vulnerable to the threats posed by corruption and organised crime.

The Current Trend: Corruption

The present section epitomises that the previous trends were drugs, organised crime, terrorism financing and money laundering; but the current trend is corruption. This proposition has been diffused in the first three chapters of the book, but within the broader context that we are dealing with combating illicit enrichment with a

---

99 Text to n 83, 274.

100 Commission of the European Communities, Commission Staff Working Paper, 'Compliance with the Anti-money Laundering Directive by Cross-border Banking Groups at Group Level' SEC (2009) 939 final, 30 June 2009, Annex 4, 31.

101 Text to n 78, 202.

102 H Argyroiliopoulos, *Private and Public Corruption as a Crime of Unfair Competition* (Nomiki Bibliothiki SA 2006).

103 Article 2 of Directive 2006/70/EC.

view to control and, where the circumstances permit, to restructure unaccountable wealth. All the more so, this broader concept will be analysed in the second part of this book. What follows below is a succinct recapitulation of the key findings justifying the submission that the fifth and current trend is corruption.

Chapter 1 presented the reader with the three justifications for the extension of the anti-money laundering regime, which, among other things, aims to trace, seize and recover criminal assets emanating from drug trafficking, money laundering, organised crime, corruption and the financing of terrorism. But the first chapter went one step deeper into the notion that the current trend is corruption by setting out that the Union proposed measures that will: tighten money laundering controls to repress tax evasion, private corruption, fraud, insider dealing, market manipulation and the misappropriation of public funds; establish the European network of offices for the recovery of criminal proceeds; set strategic objectives on transparency, accountability and the fight against corruption in public procurement; and combat counterfeiting and piracy.

Chapter 2 presented the reader with the seamless anti-corruption web and referred to a mountain of laws created as a result of international cooperation, which is plainly what internationalism has made of it. The proposition that the current trend is corruption has unfolded in those sections focusing in particular on the initiatives of the OECD, the Council of Europe and the European Commission. Yet the aforementioned proposition was put to the test on two separate occasions. First, in Chapter 2, on the occasion of analysing the objectives for the prosecutorial toll. And, second, in Chapter 2, on the occasion of analysing how the European Union's Third Anti-Money Laundering Directive in combination with other European secondary anti-money laundering instruments aims to disrupt the criminal enterprise.

But Chapter 2 also underlined the centrality of the pooling of: policies for crime prevention and criminal justice; the strengthening of national rules on the exchange of information to effectively combat tax avoidance and tax evasion; and the prevention and control of unfair tax practices, which above all, confirms that the fight against corruption ranks at the top of the list of priorities of the Union's agenda in the area of freedom, justice and security.

Chapter 3 explained that anti-money laundering laws create the proper systemic conditions to trace and seize the proceeds of organised crime and corruption. It raised awareness of the fact that both the UNTOC and the UNCAC call upon national authorities to make use of the civil law as an effective weapon for the tracing, seizure and confiscation of criminal proceeds.[104] The findings have to show that corruption is a multifaceted and transnational phenomenon, which can seriously threaten the integrity of the anti-money laundering system.[105]

104 Emmanuel Ioannides, 'Country Spotlight: Greece – Anti-Corruption Developments in Greece' [2009] IBA Anti-Corruption Committee Newsletter 1, 10.

105 Text to n 78, 205.

It is for this reason that, in the present chapter, this author suggested the application of more radical anti-corruption measures, such as the taxation of unaccountable[106] wealth and the implementation of strengthened transparency, integrity, accountability and good governance[107] measures in conformity with the set of Recommendations adopted by the Financial Action Task Force in February 2012.

The invaluable international instruments frequently referred to in all the three chapters reflect the mental model postulated by the international community to understand and assess: the threats posed by corruption to the economic, social and political systems of our societies, and the genuine need to work in collective partnership to develop uniform, robust, cost–benefit,[108] and risk-sensitive responses to effectively trace, seize and recover[109] the proceeds of the different forms of corruption.

Indeed, money laundering and corruption often occur together. However, it is important to appreciate that corruption[110] generates criminal finance, but money laundering reinforces corruption. Member States are thus obliged to implement the Union's risk-focused repressive strategy by ensuring consistency between the national and the international approach to combat economic crime, organised crime, corruption and the financing of terrorism.

It is therefore imperative to draw a distinction between the UN, which is a supranational organ setting out fundamental principles that interconnect with the international anti-money laundering standards of the Financial Action Task Force for vertical implementation, and the Union's proposed measures requiring Member States to ensure strict horizontal consistency with the aforementioned standards through the application of risk-sensitive measures at the national level. Nevertheless, we should acknowledge not only the supremacy, but also the efficacy of UN instruments. In the future, we should not be surprised if supranational standard-setting will absorb regional and national lawmaking in the interests of achieving more effective implementation of anti-money laundering standards in an increasingly globalised world.

But as we had the opportunity to review in the first three chapters of this book, not all State Parties to UN instruments have the same legal traditions and the

106 David Gow, 'UBS Uncovers Tax Fraud Cases' guardian.co.uk (London, 27 November 2008) <http://www.guardian.co.uk/business/2008/nov/27/ubs-europe-fraud> accessed 28 February 2014; Anna Rembelou, 'For the First Time Bank Accounts Open In Switzerland: In the Nails of Ex … wives 4,450 Clients of UBS in USA', *Kosmos Tou Ependiti* (Athens, 29–30 August 2009) 15.

107 Text to n 76.

108 Text to n 100.

109 Simon NM Young, 'Why Civil Actions against Corruption?' (2009) 16 JFC 2, 144–149.

110 U4 Anti-Corruption Resource Centre, 'Political Corruption Cases' (U4 website 2009) <http://www.u4.no/themes/political-corruption/cases.cfm> accessed 28 February 2014.

same economic systems. It is therefore absolutely necessary that European Union Member States ensure horizontal consistency with the forthcoming Fourth Anti-Money Laundering Directive on the basis of the principles of proportionality, mitigation of risks, financial inclusion and the continuous engagement of stakeholders from all sectors, as opposed to searching for solutions through the comparison of two fundamentally different normative centres at this point in time: the UN on the one side, and the European Union on the other.

Finally, the tension identified in the first three chapters of this book in regard to the diametrically opposite perspectives on anti-money laundering legislation: those of governments and European Supervisory Authorities on the one hand, with their duty to surveil financial transactions in the public interest, and those of financial institutions and their clients on the other, with their genuine need for the protection of financial privacy and trade secrecy, undoubtedly, merits the European Union's immediate attention for the following reasons.

The financial privacy of financial institutions and their clients when engaging in legitimate financial transactions involving funds, which do not interconnect with the financing of terrorism or with the financing of any other illegal activity, ought to be strengthened in the light of the forthcoming Fourth Anti-Money Laundering Directive. The current deficit of risk-sensitive measures in the Union's existing regulatory framework, conflicts with the Charter of Fundamental Rights (Articles 16–17 and 21).

Let us recall that all persons and all corporations controlled by natural persons have the right to financial privacy because they create wealth and contribute to economic growth. To safeguard and to strengthen further the fundamental right to financial privacy should be equated with the promotion and enhancement of fair competition in an efficient European business environment.

The financial stability and soundness of the Internal Market is based on the principle of fair and healthy competition for the economic wellbeing of those persons and enterprises that create wealth and for the Member States in which they operate. In this regard, the Union, European Supervisory Authorities and governments must realise that the right to financial privacy is synonymous with safeguarding corporate strategic assets and trade secrets from rivals.

Indeed, the gathering and exchange of financial intelligence is an invaluable anti-money laundering tool. Financial institutions and other obliged entities are obliged to filter financial transactions with a view to assess whether they are legitimate or suspicious. Inevitably, private sector reporters are obliged to gather and to store the data of the financial transactions of their clients, such as sales contracts, strategic alliance agreements, marketing plans, trade plans and commercial contracts, which have a commercial value and could be unlawfully acquired by insiders engaged in industrial and corporate espionage, bribery and theft.[111]

111 Dirk Kaufmann, 'Corporate Espionage: The Spy in Your Cubicle' *DW.DE* (DW

It is important to appreciate that trade secrets are neither trademarks nor patents. Unfortunately, those who hold trade secrets have no exclusive rights under the Union's regulatory framework. The European Union's Single Market Commissioner, Michel Barnier, has recently pointed out that cybercrime and industrial espionage have increased the risk of misappropriation of commercially valuable information that is secret but not covered by a patent. It has also been estimated that 20 per cent of European companies were the victims of those who have attempted to unlawfully obtain trade secrets in the past 10 years.[112] Furthermore, Member States such as Germany, Denmark and Spain do not expressly define trade secrets in their civil law, whereas the United Kingdom, Belgium, the Netherlands and France have no specific provisions for trade secrets under their civil law statutes.[113]

Last but not least, as already analysed in Chapter 2, in the light of COM (2013) 45 final, this is the opportune moment for the Union to delegate the proper powers to European Supervisory Authorities[114] to work in collective partnership with governments, financial institutions and obliged entities to put in place proportionate and risk-sensitive measures that will harmonise and strengthen national rules on the right to financial privacy of financial institutions and their clients through concrete safeguards against unlawful disclosures of financial information.

With respect to the effective protection of strategic company assets and trade secrets against the risks posed by the misuse of the financial information gathered and stored by private sector reporters, Member States' central banks can play an active role by supervising the application of due diligence measures in the control of the origin of funds of legitimate financial transactions. And, if the base of these controls is risk-sensitive and proportionate, the right to financial privacy of financial institutions and their clients will not be unnecessarily compromised. This way the Commission can succeed in aligning the Union's policy with the effective protection provided under the civil law statutes of other jurisdictions and competitors such as the United States and Japan.

---

website 2013, 9 November 2013) <http://www.dw.de/corporate-espionage-the-spy-in-your-cubicle/a-17215294> accessed 20 December 2013.

112 Alex Barker, 'Brussels Takes Aim at Industrial Espionage' *Financial Times* (Brussels, 28 November 2013) <http://www.ft.com/cms/s/0/b7fb43ae-57af-11e3-86d1-00144feabdc0.html#axzz2od3CtdCK> accessed 24 December 2013.

113 Text to n 112.

114 Text to nn 189–192 in chapter 2.

PART II
Advanced Principles

Chapter 4
Restructuring Unaccountable Wealth and the Tax Issue

Setting the Scene of Unaccountable Wealth

One of the main arguments developed in Part I of this book was that the reporting system is used as a vehicle[1] for the collection of intelligence on persons, legal persons and legal arrangements, business relationships, and financial transactions by law enforcement and prosecutorial authorities.[2] One of the main arguments developed in this part is that one of the underlying rationales of money laundering control should be to trace, seize and tax unaccountable wealth by making more effective use of the tax law.

Admittedly, this is a radical approach to unaccountable wealth. Yet it is a dynamic one in that it switches the limited view that the role of anti-money laundering laws is to merely enable national authorities to trace and seize criminal assets before they enter the formal economy. The question may be asked, what is wrong with tolerating the idea that unaccountable wealth has wittingly or unwittingly escaped money laundering controls and should therefore be taxed in the public interest?

The general presumption is that consumers and companies tend to increase spending when their incomes and balance sheets are increased. Stated differently, a good year for consumers and taxable plutocrats, in general, means a good year for the taxman. As Harold James, Professor of History and International Affairs at Princeton University, rightly observed, during financial crises our uncertainty in monetary value transforms us into a more altruistic kind of species with a profound interest in the reconsideration of values in the deepest possible fundamental sense.[3] On this occasion, an additional question may be asked, what is wrong with reconsidering our values in a more radical way that imposes the tax burden on unaccountable wealth as opposed to favouring policies and practices that continue to impose the tax burden on lawful yet static wealth?

---

1 David Chaikin, 'How Effective are Suspicious Transaction Reporting Systems?' (2009) 12 JMLC 3, 238–245.

2 Text to n 1, 246.

3 Harold James, *The Creation and Destruction of Value: The Globalization Cycle* (HUP 2009) 231.

In 2009, *The Economist* published an article[4] on the developments at Buttonwood. Among other things, the article reminded us that the Beatles may have joked when they wrote their famous lyrics of 'Taxman', but the authorities were tempted to raise taxes again. In the light of the current financial crisis, it is anticipated that tax revenues to be collected from capital market transactions will not cover budgetary needs. Consequently, governments need to find new ways to raise consumption taxes, which will inevitably affect the poor more than the rich.[5]

Taxing lawful wealth through consumption and property taxes reflects any government's fiscal policy. One the one hand, there are those who find ways to veil unaccountable mobile[6] wealth and escape taxation. On the other, all those who create and preserve lawful wealth cannot escape taxation, let alone increased taxation. Yet the offshore economy, which shelters the proceeds of economically motivated serious crimes, such as international bribery, tax fraud, tax evasion, tax avoidance, corruption and commercial transfer mispricing abuse, should be targeted by tax authorities for the purpose of widening the tax base.[7]

Money is indeed amoral[8] and mobile. However, unaccountable mobile wealth is equally amoral but traceable by the anti-money laundering system.[9] It is therefore up to governments to decide to trace and seize it with a view to tax it and close revenue gaps, as opposed to focusing on taxing static wealth. The first suitable example was indirectly offered in Chapter 1, where reference was made to the North African underground economy absorbing financial resources that would otherwise have been available for reinvestment in the formal economy of the European Union.[10] The second proper example was directly offered in Chapter 3, where it was demonstrated that the application of more radical measures by the American government to trace and uncover unaccountable wealth parked in Switzerland was successful.

Against the background of fiscal crime and the stereotypical tendency of those in possession of unaccountable wealth to move their bank accounts to more popular tax havens,[11] it is important to also take into consideration that, in 2007, the estimated value of criminal assets for seizure and taxation in the United

---

4 *The Economist*, 'Buttonwood: Be Thankful They Don't Take it All' (2009) 392 (8647) 79.

5 Text to n 4.

6 Text to n 4, 79, commentary of Britain's 'Red Adair' Turner, Head of the FSA.

7 Tax Justice Network, 'Magnitudes: Dirty Money, Lost Taxes and Offshore' <http://www.taxjustice.net/cms/front_content.php?idcat=103> accessed 28 February 2014.

8 Hinterseer (n 3) 69 in chapter 1.

9 Megan Harris, 'Dirty Money Cleanup Gains Speed' *UPI.com* (29 January 2009) <http://www.upi.com/Emerging_Threats/2008/01/29/Analysis-Dirty> accessed 28 February 2014.

10 Text to n 21 in chapter 1.

11 Diane Francis, 'Opinion: Unearth the Dirty Money' *Financial Post* (22 August 2009) <http://www.financialpost.com/opinion/story.html?id=7b0e55b9–61d9> accessed 28 February 2014.

Kingdom amounted to £2,000,000,000, whereas in the same fiscal year, some £3,300,000,000 were sent to offshore accounts.[12]

Of course, there are those who have taken the opposite view on the issue of uncovering criminal money merely because, since 2001, the number of FSA enforcement actions against violations of anti-money laundering compliance are too low in comparison with the actual size of the United Kingdom's financial sector.[13] However, it is also important to appreciate that one of the underlying rationales behind the idea of taxing unaccountable wealth is to put pressure on other countries to cooperate in the Global Forum,[14] to adopt and implement transparent practices, and to effectively exchange information in the interests of promoting tax justice and the soundness and proper functioning of the financial system.

Compendiously, the concept of the taxation of unaccountable wealth is all about restructuring wealth in the hands of non-taxpayers and widening the tax base in an equitable way. But the problem lies in that it is not often fully appreciated by legislators and fiscal policy-makers that developing countries lost approximately USD $858,600,000,000–1,060,000,000,000 in illicit capital outflows in 2006, whereas cross-border flows[15] of dirty money in the same year ranged from USD $1,100,000,000,000 to $1,600,000,000,000, half of which originated from transitional economies.[16]

Moreover, in accordance with the Tax Justice Network publication on *The Price of Offshore* (March 2005), which was based on data from Boston Consulting Group, McKinsey, Merrill Lynch, Cap Gemini and the Bank for International Settlements, the world's High Net Worth Individuals (HNWI) held USD $11,500,000,000,000 offshore, which resulted in tax losses of USD $255,000,000,000. The latter figure represents three times the assistance offered to OECD countries for development.[17] Ultimately, if the OECD estimates the total size of wealth held offshore by High Net Worth Individuals between USD $5,000,000,000,000 and $7,000,000,000,000, then it is only reasonable for prudent governments to widen the taxation toll with a view to combat tax evasion, restructure unaccountable wealth, and promote economic growth during the financial crisis.[18]

---

12 Jeffrey Simser, 'Tax Evasion and Avoidance Typologies' (2008) 11 JMLC 2, 123.

13 Jackie Harvey, 'The Search for Crime Money – Debunking the Myth: Facts versus Imagery' (2009) 12 JMLC 2, 98.

14 Richard Murphy, 'Where is the OECD Going?' *Taxresearch.org.uk* (London, 14 August 2009) <http://www.taxresearch.org.uk/Blog/2009/08/14/where-is-the-oecd-g> accessed 28 February 2014.

15 Text to n 50 in chapter 3.

16 Text to n 7, 2.

17 Text to n 7, 2.

18 OECD Centre for Tax Policy and Administration, 'OECD Global Forum Consolidates Tax Evasion Revolution in Advance of Pittsburgh' (OECD website 2009) <http://www.oecd.org/document/43/0,3343,en_2649_33767_436015> accessed 28 February 2014.

The Tax Issue and its Dynamic

In October 2008, the Director of Public Prosecutions, Sir Ken MacDonald QC, warned us of the dangers involved in the expansion of state surveillance in the light of the decisions on the nature of State power that had to be taken in the next few years. Moreover, he underlined that the use of these powers and their extent will be irreversible as they will shape the world that we decide to build for the future. He therefore called upon the country's policy-makers to enquire deeper into the notion of whether society will bear the use of the surveillance powers of the State in the future.[19]

Indeed, the issue of the expansion of State surveillance[20] in Great Britain cannot but equally appeal to Parliamentarians and Constitutionalists, especially in the context of the tax issue. In the area of tax law, taxes can be levied only with the consent of Parliament,[21] in the public interest, subject to national law, and in accordance with the general principles of international law.[22] But the levying of taxes ought to satisfy the political criterion of proportionality and must not violate the constitutionally guaranteed right of persons, legal persons and legal arrangements to peacefully enjoy their possessions.[23] On the other hand, it is equally important to recognise that the State has the right to enforce laws for the control of the use of property and to secure the payment of taxes and contributions in the public interest.[24]

At the State level, these constitutional safeguards provide for the proper balance between those empowered to levy proportionate taxes in the general interest of the public and the taxpayers who can peacefully enjoy their possessions as long as they fulfil their tax obligations. But the issue in question here does not have to do only with the effect of taxes in general. We are all aware of the fact that taxes take way a certain percentage of our earnings as opposed to the entire amount of income earned.[25] It is therefore important to appreciate that the tax issue has a certain dynamic[26] to explore, which is notionally inseparable from the

---

19 Jonathan Schwartz, 'Rights and Powers: Protecting the Legitimate Interests of Taxpayers' [2009] BTR 3, 308–309.

20 Text to n 139 in chapter 2.

21 *R v Customs and Excise Commissioners, ex p Kay & Co Ltd* [1996] STC 1500 (QB).

22 Text to n 19, 311, the Bill of Rights of 1688.

23 *R (on the application of Federation of Tour Operators & Ors) v HM Treasury & Ors* [2008] EWCA Civ 752.

24 Text to n 19, 312, reference made to the ECHR.

25 M Michelle Gallant, 'Tax and Terrorism: A New Partnership?' (2009) 14 JFC 4, 454.

26 Text to n 25.

international community's volition[27] to tax unaccountable wealth and to prevent and control tax evasion[28] and tax avoidance.[29]

In October 2005, Raymond Baker and Jennifer Nordin, in their excellent article in the *Financial Times*, identified the following four forces of dirty money that can prevent the true course of legitimate business transactions: the cross-border smuggling of profits through abusive transfer pricing, the outflow of tax-evading money from one country, the inflow of tax-evading money in another country, and money laundering.[30] Of equal note is Raymond Baker's description of the 40-year-old parasitical mechanism for the laundering of criminal proceeds,[31] which has been channelling criminal and tax-evading funds to Western countries, and must be destroyed if capitalism is to achieve its maximum potential.[32]

In September 2009, 178 delegates from 84 jurisdictions and international organisations met in Mexico to discuss the progress made in regard to the implementation of international standards of transparency and exchange of information for tax purposes as reflected in the Model Tax Information Exchange Agreement, Article 16 of the OECD Model Tax Convention, and UN Model Tax Conventions. According to the Summary of the Meeting of the Global Forum on Transparency and Exchange of Information for Tax Purposes Held in Mexico on 1–2 September 2009, the Global Forum will be continuously monitoring legal instruments for the exchange of information, double taxation treaties, and tax information exchange agreements both for Global Forum members and non-member countries as of 2010.[33]

In accordance with the Overview of the OECD's Work on Countering International Tax Evasion, the standards of transparency and exchange of tax information (reliable, unrestricted and confidential) constitute the model for the good majority of the 3,600 bilateral tax conventions entered into by OECD and non-OECD countries, and are thus recognised as the international norm for cooperation in tax matters.[34] Moreover, pursuant to the progress report of 11 September 2009

27 Text to n 18.

28 Text to nn 121 and 195 in chapter 2.

29 Articles 3(4)(f) and 31 of COM (2013) 45 final.

30 Raymond W Baker and Jennifer Nordin, 'How Dirty Money Thwarts Capitalism's True Course' (*Financial Times*, 11 October 2005) <http://www.gfip.org/index.php?option=com_content& task=view?id> accessed 28 February 2014.

31 Raymond W Baker, *Capitalism's Achilles Heel: Dirty Money and How to Renew the Free-Market System* (John Wiley & Sons 2005) 337–351.

32 Text to n 31, 1.

33 OECD Centre for Tax Policy and Administration, 'Summary of the Meeting of the Global Forum on Transparency and Exchange of Information for Tax Purposes Held in Mexico on 1–2 September 2009' (OECD website 2009) <http://www.oecd.org/dataoecd/44/39/43610626.pdf> accessed 28 February 2014.

34 OECD Centre for Tax Policy and Administration, 'Overview of the OECD's Work on Countering International Tax Evasion: A Background Information Brief 11 September

(Original Progress Report, 2 April 2009),[35] all the jurisdictions surveyed by the Global Forum are currently committed to the internationally agreed tax standards. For example, Austria and Switzerland[36] withdrew their reservations to Article 26 of the OECD Model Tax Convention and have informed their Treaty Partners that they are willing to revise their treaties to include the aforementioned new article.

By way of synopsis, it is evident that tax evasion interconnects with uncooperative and non-transparent jurisdictions offering offshore[37] harbours mainly to those in possession of unaccountable wealth. Besides promoting and strengthening international standards to tax unaccountable wealth in the hands of non-taxpayers with a view to restructure and to widen the tax base in an equitable way, it must be pointed out that the main toolbox to be used is the anti-money laundering regime. This is the pragmatic view of the tax issue's dynamic and the international tax revolution progressing in our times.

The initiatives referred to in this section reflect our genuine need to reform the financial system by taking away investible capital from jurisdictions that have played for too long the parasitical role of harbours of unaccountable wealth. In practical and political terms, fanciful cases of corruption or grand corruption apart, unaccountable wealth can and should be taxed and legitimised with the ultimate goal of being reinvested in the financial system. In view of the current financial crisis, there are pressing needs for governments to reassure the general public that they are in a position to make fiscal policy credible again. It is for these good reasons that the aforementioned standards of transparency and exchange of tax information should be welcomed and strengthened further.[38]

The Future: Transparency Laws

Transparency and accountability are appraised as the antidotes to the threats posed by corruption to good governance and the prudent management of public assets.[39]

2009' (OECD website 2009) 4, para 5 <http://www.oecd.org/dataoecd/32/45/42356522.pdf> accessed 28 February 2014.

35 Text to n 34.

36 Email from Swiss Federal Administration admin.ch to author 'Double taxation: revised agreement with Ireland and new agreement with Turkmenistan in force' (23 December 2013).

37 OECD Centre for Tax Policy and Administration, 'Countering Offshore Tax Evasion: Some Questions and Answers in the Project 11 September 2009' (OECD website 2009) 19 <http://www.oecd.org.dataoecd/32/45/42356522.pdf> accessed 28 February 2014.

38 OECD Centre for Tax Policy and Administration, 'Tax Co-operation 2009: Towards a Level Playing Field – 2009 Assessment by the Global Forum on Transparency and Exchange of Information' (OECD website 2009) <http://www.oecd/org/document.23/0,3343,en_2649_33767_435556> accessed 28 February 2014.

39 Denis Osborne, 'Transparency and Accountability Reconsidered' (2004) 11 JFC 3, 292–293.

Truly, these broad notions of ethical, responsible and accountable conduct have been embraced by the supranational fora to such an extent that they have become an integral part of the broader yet abstract concept of the rule of law.[40]

This section delivers a critical analysis of the reasons why transparency laws are currently evolving. In this regard, the following meaningful question may be asked, if the lack of an effective transparency regulatory regime is one of the main reasons why wrongdoers succeed in laundering criminal assets and channelling unaccountable wealth into offshore jurisdictions, then doesn't the restructuring of unaccountable wealth through taxation facilitate the reformation of the financial system?

The international volition to achieve serious international tax transparency for the prevention and control of offshore tax avoidance and evasion[41] is manifested in the Code of Good Practices on Fiscal Transparency (2007),[42] the Manual on Fiscal Transparency[43] and the Guide on Resource Revenue Transparency[44] of the International Monetary Fund (IMF). Of particular note is the IMF's first pillar, the Code of Good Practices on Fiscal Transparency of 2007, which established a set of principles and practices (Reports on the Observance of Standards and Codes for fiscal transparency – ROSCs) to assist governments in providing their citizens with a comprehensive view of public finances.[45]

As this is not the proper place to enter into a detailed discussion of the particulars of transparency in the public sector, two crucial points should be kept in mind. First, that the aforementioned developments reflect the international consensus on the application of uniform standards for fiscal transparency. Second, that the purpose of the standards for fiscal transparency is to make more straightforward the management of public wealth by governments – the agents, and thus more accountable these entrusted agents to their principals – the citizens.

Yet fiscal policy is far more complex because it involves tax rates and structured spending schemes, which are ultimately political choices of how public funds are spent and how citizens are taxed.[46] Notwithstanding, transparency and

40 Philip R Wood, 'Predictions for the Future of Financial Law and Lawyers' (2008) 9 BLI 3, 248.

41 HM Revenue & Customs and HM Treasury, 'Policy: Reducing Tax Evasion and Avoidance' (GOV.UK website 2013, 8 October 2013) <http://www.gov.uk/government/policies/reducing-tax-evasion-and-avoidance> accessed 20 November 2013.

42 IMF, 'Code of Good Practices on Fiscal Transparency (2007)' (IMF website 2009) 1–4 <http://www.imf.org/external/np/fad/trans/code.htm> accessed 28 February 2014.

43 IMF, 'Manual on Fiscal Transparency: 2007 Revised Edition' (IMF website 2009) 1–106 <http://www.imf.org/external/np/fad/trans/manual.htm> accessed 28 February 2014.

44 IMF, 'Guide on Resource Revenue Transparency: 2007 Revised Edition' (IMF website 2009) 1–57 <http://www.imf.org/external/np/fad/trans/guide.htm> accessed 28 February 2014.

45 Text to n 42, 1.

46 *The Economist*, 'Making Fiscal Policy Credible: Bind Games' (2009) 392 (8648) 77.

accountability can facilitate citizens to determine with clarity how well governments spend the tax revenues collected. According to George Kopits, Senior Scholar at the Woodrow Wilson International Centre for Scholars and a former member of the National Bank of Hungary's monetary council, a good fiscal policy must have the following basic features: a clearly defined target for the debt ratio, spending schemes funded by taxes, supervision by an independent but authoritative body, and complete, clear and accessible public accounts that include all the costs.[47]

Admittedly, the first two features suggested by Kopits are not directly related to the present context, and perhaps economists would be in a better position to properly assess them. However, the last two features reconfirm that transparency laws are needed to keep governments honest and to ensure that sound public finances are achieved on the basis of prudence, transparency and accountability. One could therefore hardly imagine a symbiotic relationship of transparent and accountable public sectors with corrupted and unaccountable private sectors.[48]

Another aspect of the critical function of transparency laws is that they provide the guiding principles upon which the activities of financial institutions can become socially useful.[49] If we recall the numerous times that reference has been made in this book to those professionals (the agents) entrusted with the duty of minding other people's (the principals') wealth, particularly in the context of the credit crunch and the huge amount of money that international investors lost because their funds were invested in toxic (American) mortgage-backed securities, the picture can become all the more clear. Ultimately, the issue in question has to do with applying transparency standards with a view to prevent and control abusive dealings in the context of the problematic relationship between the agent and the principal.

In accordance with Paul Woolley of the London School of Economics and Political Science, Centre for the Study of Capital Market Dysfunctionality, the agents have always access to more information than their clients – the principals. And, due to the complex and long-term nature of financial products, the principals – the investors – are not always in a position to mitigate the risks involved, but the agents – the financial intermediaries – have the opportunity to gain huge profits at the expense of their clients.[50]

This is precisely what we are actually dealing with, the critical function of transparency laws. They aim to prevent and control dysfunctionalities arising from the abuse of vital information[51] that should be comprehensive and accessible

47 Text to n 46.

48 Text to n 46.

49 *The Economist*, 'Buttonwood | Too Big for its Gucci Boots: The Causes of the Overexpansion of the Finance Industry' (2009) 392 (8648) 79.

50 Text to n 49.

51 Neil Fagan and Lucy Thompson, 'Corporate Responsibility and Group Redress Mechanisms' (2009) 10 BLI 1, 53.

to all parties involved in fiscal and financial relations.[52] On the one hand, there are those governments that do not spend well but choose to tax cleverly their citizens in order to disguise the defects of public finances. Yet there are those who create wealth and pay their taxes, while others engage in offshore tax avoidance and evasion. On the other, there are those private sector professionals who earn a high level of rent[53] by wittingly selling to investors high-risk financial products. Yet there are those who lack the expertise to recognise that they will be facing financial loss in the immediate future.

By way of summary, all of what has been discussed thus far aimed to sketch the corpus of transparency laws. Anti-money laundering, anti-corruption, and anti-tax evasion measures are integral parts of the supreme principle of transparency and tax justice. It is not symptomatic that transparency laws are enforced to prevent and control the accumulation of unaccountable wealth held offshore through the evolving international tax revolution.[54] In the light of the global financial crisis, one of the lessons we have learned is that a non-transparent financial sector will always be in a position to earn a high level of rent[55] at the expense of those investors lacking financial expertise and direct access to vital information on corporate liquidity, performance and capital market ratings.[56]

On the other hand, the enforcement of enhanced transparency and accountability measures may slow down innovation and reduce the rate of returns,[57] but it can secure financial stability and the protection of the financial interests of private and public sector investors[58] in the process of overhauling financial regulation. It would therefore be only fair to suggest that those who will have to shoulder the cost of filling the gaps of liquidity for the overhauling of the financial system, will be those few in possession of unaccountable wealth. As already suggested, there is a niche for the international and the national tax authorities.[59]

52 Nicole Stolowy, 'Transparency and Prevention of Corporate Bankruptcy: A US–France Comparison' [2009] JBL 6, 531.

53 Text to n 49.

54 Text to n 18, 1.

55 Dimitri Vayanos and Jiang Wang, 'Liquidity and Asset Prices: A Unified Framework' (The Paul Woolley Centre for the Study of Capital Market Dysfunctionality website 2009) 1–41 <http://www.lse.ac.uk/collections/paulWoolleyCentre/publications/PWC5.pdf> accessed 28 February 2014.

56 Text to n 52.

57 *The Economist*, 'Overhauling Financial Regulation: The Regulatory Rumble Beings' (2009) 391 (8633) 75.

58 Text to n 49.

59 Alicia Fraerman, 'SPAIN: Dirty Money Used for Construction and Pollution' *IPS News Net* (Madrid, 7 November 2006) <http://ispnews.net/news.asp?idnews=35401> accessed 28 February 2014.

Lastly, we should not fail to take into consideration the prediction of Philip R. Wood,[60] which constitutes a mirror reflection of the observation of the Director of Public Prosecutions,[61] and reveals with pragmatism the two models that may dominate legal regimes in the future. The first is a group of jurisdictions with a restrictive and punitive regime, which has turned its citizens into informers. The second is a group of jurisdictions with a prudential regime, which has efficaciously used the law to serve its citizens as opposed to restricting and oppressing them. This author genuinely believes that transparency laws cannot but meaningfully contribute to the placement of the European Union in the second group of jurisdictions.

Power and Reinvestment

There has always been scepticism in regard to monitoring and controlling financial transactions[62] through the reporting system and the exchange of financial intelligence. We should therefore enquire deeper into the tension between power and reinvestment, rather than confining the critical analysis on the evolution of measures for the criminalisation of the different forms of economic crime.

The present section extends the analysis by suggesting that there is another reason for the progressive developments taking place in the criminal,[63] civil[64] and tax[65] laws of Member States already demonstrated in Chapter 2. More specifically, it suggests that political power is the main force behind the reform of the Union's

60 Philip R Wood, 'Predictions for the Future of Financial Law and Lawyers' (2008) 9 BLI 3, 244.

61 Text to n 19.

62 M Kaifa Gbandi, 'The Penal Confrontation of Laundering Dirty Money: Between International, European and National Legislation' [2007] Penal Chronicles NZ, 3–4.

63 Council Framework Decision 2002/584/JHA on the European arrest warrant and the surrender procedures between Member States of 13 June 2002 [2002] OJ L190/1; Council Framework Decision 2008/978/JHA of 18 December 2008 on the European evidence warrant for the purpose of obtaining objects, documents and data for use in proceedings in criminal matters [2008] OJ L350/72; Council of the European Union, (COD) 2010/0817 Initiative of the Kingdom of Belgium, the Republic of Bulgaria, the Republic of Estonia, the Kingdom of Spain, the Republic of Austria, the Republic of Slovenia, and the Kingdom of Sweden for a Directive of the European Parliament and of the Council of regarding the European Investigation Order in criminal matters [2010] 9288/10, 21 May 2010.

64 Europa, 'Judicial Cooperation in Civil Matters' (Europa website 2009) <http://www.eur-lex.europa.eu/Repview.do?rep=19> accessed 28 February 2014. There are more than 250 instruments related to judicial cooperation in civil matters.

65 Text to nn 123–124 and 195 in chapter 2.

financial and fiscal[66] regulatory framework. This political power aims to keep under control reinvestment as a means of safeguarding the economic prosperity of the European Union and strengthening the stability and integrity of the financial system within the context of the new global economic order.[67]

According to Colin Bradford and Johannes Linn of the Brookings Institution, the passage from the old economic order (sovereignty; national interest; unilateralism; competing blocks; fixed alliances; predominance; hard power; and singular economic models) to the new global economic order is owed to the following cognitive factors: poor macroeconomic management; insufficient financial regulation; long-term financial imbalances amongst key economies; insufficient management of an interdependent globalised financial system in the absence of internationally agreed-upon standards of financial surveillance and supervision; domestic and cross-border conflicts and terrorism; and the loss of traditional industries and jobs by the leading industrialised countries.[68]

The aforementioned cognitive factors, in combination with new emerging threats, should be conceptually approached as constituting the main reasons for the international community's volition to exercise power over reinvestment. After all, when it comes to appreciating the social usefulness of effective money laundering controls through financial surveillance, supervision and regulation, we should be equally open-minded to also appreciate that the morality of this legal discussion is all about amoral wealth and how it should be restructured with a view to generate more economic growth, which can in turn minimise the existing financial imbalances amongst key economies.

Moreover, what Colin Bradford and Johannes Linn suggested does not exclude the following four main challenges to international financial governance, which Britain's former prime minister, Gordon Brown, pointed out during the one-hour session with the Prime Minister in view of the preparation for the London G20 Summit in 2009: global financial supervision, the environment, energy and inequality.[69] Of particular relevance is that in the 1990s, William Nicoll of the Council of the European Communities and Trevor Salmon of the University of

66 Europa, 'Prevention of Tax Evasion and Avoidance' (Europa website 2009) <http://eur-lex.europa.eu/Result.do?RechType=Reach_repertoire&rep=0950*&repihm=Prevention%20of%20tax%20evasion%20and%20avoidance> accessed 28 February 2014; Commission, 'Protection of the Communities' Financial Interests – Fight against Fraud – Annual Report 2008' (Commission Report to the European Parliament and to the Council Communication) COM (09) 372 final, 7–30.

67 Colin I Bradford and Johannes F Linn, 'Is the G-20 Summit a Step Toward a New Global Economic Order?' (Brookings Institution website 2009) 1–2 <http://www.brookings.edu/papers/2009/09_g20_bradford_linn.aspx> accessed 28 February 2014.

68 Text to n 67, 75.

69 Brookings Institution, 'International Financial Governance: Toward the London G-20 Summit' (Brookings Institution website 2009) <http://www.brokings.edu/events/2009/~/media/Files/2009/0209_g20/20090209_g20_Summary.pdf> accessed 28 February 2014.

St Andrews had already pointed out that since there were areas of prosperity and areas of deprivation, necessary steps had to be taken to redistribute wealth and to allocate the use of resources in the European Union in order to encourage integration and prevent opposition.[70]

The American government's exercise of power for the repatriation of tax-sheltered profits at an unusually low tax rate for the purposes of promoting employment and domestic reinvestment is a relevant example to consider.[71] Although there may be diametrically opposite views on the disadvantages of this fiscal measure, mainly the reduction of tax revenues in the long term, it is important to briefly underline that, in 2005, more than USD $300,000,000,000 held in offshore accounts, repatriated to the United States in the light of a 5.25 per cent tax rate (instead of the standard 35 per cent) deal offered by the American government.[72]

This example demonstrates the interaction between the exercise of governmental power and the restructuring of wealth[73] in the interests of promoting employment and encouraging the reinvestment of repatriated capital into the national economy.[74] Furthermore, the example demonstrates the macroeconomic dimension of restructuring wealth by the American government as the transatlantic central tank of receiving the flows of international: anti-corruption,[75] transparency, exchange of information, and cooperation standards to effectively combat the new emerging threats posed by corporate fraud, money laundering and tax evasion.[76]

---

70 William Nicoll and Trevor Salmon, *Understanding the European Communities* (1st edn, Philip Allan 1990) 225–226.

71 Citizens for Tax Justice (CTJ), 'Will Congress Make Itself a Doormat for Corporations that avoid US Taxes? Senate Should Reject Proposal to Allow "Repatriation" of Offshore Profits as Super-Low Tax Rate' (CTJ website 2009) 2 <http://www.ctz.org/pdatiation.pd> accessed 28 February 2014.

72 Tax Justice Network, 'Levin, Dorgan Question Repatriation Lobbying Effort' (Tax Justice Network website 2009) <http://www.levin/senate.gov/newsroom/release.cfm?id=307617> accessed 28 February 2014.

73 Urika Lomas, 'Italy Launches Tax Amnesty' Tax – News.com (Brussels, 17 September 2009) <http://www.lawandtax-news.com/asp/story.asp?storyname=3910> accessed 28 February 2014.

74 US Congressional Research Service, 'Tax Cuts on Repatriation Earnings as Economic Stimulus: An Economic Analysis' <http://www.levin.senate.gov/newsroom.supporting/2009/CRS.RapatriationAnalysis.013009.pdf> accessed 28 February 2014.

75 Kenney McCafferty Qui Tam Lawyers, 'US Treasury Moves to Thwart Offshore Tax Evasion with Further Implementation of New Law' Kenney McCafferty Blog (31 October 2013) <http://blog.tax-fraud.net/2p=533> accessed 26 December 2013.

76 The White House President George W Bush, 'The United States and the European Union Initiative to Enhance Transatlantic Economic Integration and Growth ANNEX' 1–2 <http://www.iasplus.com/usa/0506useupressrelease.pdf> accessed 28 February 2014.

In synopsis, two central ideas lie behind the power versus reinvestment issue. The first is that money laundering, corruption, tax evasion, abusive dealings and market manipulation not only facilitate the long-term imbalances amongst key economies,[77] disrupt a highly interdependent global financial system,[78] and encourage tax injustice,[79] but also make law-abiding citizens and enterprises lose their confidence in good corporate citizenship,[80] the integrity[81] of markets and the rule of law.[82]

The second is that money laundering control is a multipurpose tool, which empowers prudent governments not only to enforce financial surveillance and supervision measures to ensure the sound operation of the financial system, but also legitimises the exercise of power by governments to trace and seize wealth that must be restructured in the interests of protecting traditional industries, jobs and wages. Undoubtedly, this second idea can also serve as the main vehicle for those governments that may wittingly choose to legitimise the repatriation of grey capital from the offshore economy to stimulate the formal economy, especially in the aftermath of a financial crisis.[83]

Shifting Legal Obligations to Public Servants and Officials to Explain the Source of their Wealth

The argument developed in this section aims to raise awareness of the significance of the tracing remedy of anti-corruption measures for the protection of public wealth and the disruption of public corruption, bribery, transnational corruption and grand corruption. Setting aside the shifting of responsibility to financial institutions and their employees to disclose offences on the basis of the presumption of suspicious or unusual financial activities, which is well-founded on the sound notion of not failing to prevent what is foreseeable, it is equally important to appreciate that there are pressing needs for governments to devise a mechanism that disrupts those public officials and politicians who possess unexplained property or mobile wealth in excess of their official emoluments.

It is for the above reason that this section suggests that the strategy of governments to prevent and control the peculation of public wealth must be based on the pragmatism of the common law and its unique susceptibility to the exercise of judicial discretion in regard to: the presumption of corruption in the absence of satisfactory and innocent explanations for the possession of unaccountable

77 Text to nn 67, 69 and 70.
78 Text to n 67.
79 Text to nn 33–34 and 37–38.
80 Text to n 175 in chapter 2, 10.
81 COM (2013) 45 final (n 147) in chapter 1, 3.
82 Text to n 67.
83 Text to n 74.

wealth by public officials; the maintenance of the balance of procedural fairness in the judicial process of subjecting unaccountable wealth to the presumption of corruption; and the endorsement of credible judicial opinions in regard to what Parliament intended[84] the law to be in those compelling circumstances that statutory words must be properly interpreted so as to not constitute the main obstacle to the imposition of the legal obligation on those in possession of unaccountable wealth to explain, to the satisfaction of the court, its true sources.

It is thus necessary for governments to implement national rules that facilitate the maintenance of criminal assets within the reach of the law by enabling prosecutors to prove that unaccountable wealth represents the proceeds of crime or a broader form of criminal activity as opposed to establishing the nexus between the wealth traced and a specific crime committed.[85]

On the one hand, national courts will inevitably have to lower the threshold for the prosecution to prove that the property traced and seized represents the proceeds of corruption without necessarily having to establish the link between the wealth acquired and the specific pattern of criminal conduct pursued for the acquisition of unaccountable property. On the other, this lighter burden of prosecutorial proof will be balanced with the heavier burden that the defence should shoulder in order to prove that the presumed fruits of corruption represent lawful wealth that can be satisfactorily explained by revealing its legitimate sources.[86]

For example, under Chapter 201, Section 10, Prevention of Bribery Ordinance[87] of Hong Kong, a Chief Executive or a prescribed officer is not only legally obliged to satisfactorily explain: how he maintains a standards of living above that which is commensurate with his present or past emoluments declared – Section 10(1)(a)–(c) and how the property came under his possession – Section 10(1)(b); but also where the court is satisfied that an offence under Subsection (1)(b) is consummated, any person possessing pecuniary resources of property as a gift from the accused person, will be presumed to have been in control of the accused – Section 10(2).[88]

Stated differently, the possession of unexplained property is presumptive of corruption. Consequently, the accused is under an obligation to explain, to the satisfaction of the court, that the property he possesses is lawful by revealing its

84 *The Economist*, 'The New Supreme Court: Separation of Powers' (2009) 393 (8651) 46.

85 Text to n 85 in chapter 1, 353.

86 Text to n 85 in chapter 1, 353.

87 Hong Kong Ordinances, 'Prevention of Bribery Ordinance – Section 10: Possession of Unexplained Wealth' (Hong Kong Legal Information Institute website 2009) <http://www.hklii.org/hk/legis/ord/201/s10.html> accessed 28 February 2014.

88 Text to n 18 in chapter 3, 193 with reference to the tracing remedy in *Attorney General for Hong Kong v Reid* [1994] 1 AC 324.

true sources, and that the standard of living that he maintains in excess of his present or past emoluments, is owed to lawful resources.[89]

But there is more to be said in regard to countries' conventional obligation to implement measures that disrupt the illicit enrichment of public servants and officials. As a matter of fact, the UNCAC imposes the legal obligation on its State Parties to lay down national rules that effectively disrupt and sanction: corrupted national and foreign public officials,[90] corrupted officials of public organisations,[91] and those who accept bribes in the private sector[92] or become concerned in arrangements to embezzle private wealth[93] or to launder criminal proceeds.[94]

However, it is not often fully appreciated that, under Article 20 of the UNCAC, State Parties are legally obliged to implement measures that criminalise the acquisition of property by a public official that is not in a position to reasonably explain. Of course, the provision of Article 20 of the UNCAC covers transparency, whereas the complementary provisions of Articles 30(2) and 31(2) and (8) of this invaluable instrument[95] cover the confiscature of the alleged criminal proceeds by shifting the burden of proof in those circumstances that the convicted person cannot justify their origin.[96]

By way of summary, the above findings demonstrate that there is a conventional obligation on State Parties to the UNCAC to lay down national rules that enable the judiciary to effectively address the highly complex nature of corruption and the illicit enrichment of public servants and officials. This conventional obligation for strict implementation is confirmed by the UNODC's Legislative Guide for the implementation of the UNCAC (2006), which not only aims to facilitate national authorities to place unaccountable wealth well within the reach of the law, but it also clarifies that there is no presumption of guilt and that the burden of proof remains on the prosecution to prove that the alleged enrichment is beyond one's lawful income.[97]

Truly, there are pressing needs for civil law jurisdictions to adopt the pragmatism of the common law, that is, if the prevention and control of public and

89 Attorney General for Hong Kong v Hui Kin Hong [1005] HKCA Crim 351 (CA).

90 Articles 15–19 of the UNCAC.

91 Article 16 of the UNCAC.

92 Article 17 of the UNCAC.

93 Article 22 of the UNCAC.

94 Article 23 of the UNCAC.

95 UNODC, Division for Treaty Affairs of UNDOC and the Justice, Protection and Ethics Unit of UNICRI, 'Technical Guide to the United Nations Convention Against Corruption' (UNODC website 2009) 82 <http://www.unicri.it/wwk/publications/books/docs/Technical_Guide_UNCAC.pdf> accessed 28 February 2014.

96 Text to nn 95, 91–92 and 98.

97 UNODC, 'Legislative Guide for the Implementation of the United Nations Convention against Corruption' (UN Office on Drugs and Crime Division for Treaty Affairs website 2006) 103–104 <http://www.unodc.org/pdf/corruption/CoC_LegislativeGuide.pdf> accessed 3 January 2010.

grand corruption is not a cosmetic[98] element in the agenda of the international anti-corruption strategy. Indeed, as we had the opportunity to ascertain on numerous occasions, international cooperation aims to combat the laundering of peculated public wealth. What has been submitted thus far should not be perceived as this author's predisposition to contravene Article 6(2) of the ECHR, but rather as an appropriate means to strengthen the protection of public wealth and to contribute to the administration of justice in those trials that it is absolutely necessary to ascertain beyond any reasonable doubt whether corruption[99] and the possession of unexplained property by public servants, officials[100] and politicians[101] are worthy of confiscature and conviction.

The present distillation of ideas neither aims to conflict with the fundamental right to be presumed innocent until proven guilty nor reflects an inclination on the part of this author to square the circle of the well-founded criminal standard of proof. It should rather be interpreted as a means of raising awareness of the significance of making uniform and proportionate use of the tool of the tracing remedy within the different legal systems of Member States.

98 Barry Rider, 'A Bold Step?' (2009) 30 Comp Law 1, 2.

99 *The Economist*, 'French Corruption Scandals: Peering into the Murk' (2009) 393 (8655) 36.

100 *The Economist*, 'Spain's Political Scandals: The Problem with Don Vito's Friends' (2009) 393 (8655) 38.

101 Text to n 76 in chapter 3.

Chapter 5

Disclosure of Offences, the Anatomy of the Conspiracy Charge and the Burden of Proof

Shifting Statutory Responsibility to Professionals

Shifting statutory[1] responsibility to credit and financial institutions, financial intermediaries[2] and professional legal advisors[3] handling money on behalf of their clients is one of the hottest topics, if not the hottest of all, in the context of the prevention and control of economic crime. Trevor Millington and Mark Sutherland Williams[4] have underlined the necessity to align obligatory disclosure of offences with statutory exemptions from civil liability when clients bring suits against financial institutions for breaches of confidentiality. In their view, the repressive advantages are twofold: the prosecution of money laundering offenders and the effective recovery[5] of criminal assets.[6]

The imposition of this statutory burden does not constitute an unexplored topic in anti-money laundering legislation. Yet what makes it more conceptually

1 Part 7 of POCA (ss 328(1), 333, 335(1), 335(2)–(6) and 338).

2 *Squirrell Ltd v National Westminister Bank Plc* [2005] EWHC 664 (Ch); *N2J Limited v Cater Allen* [2006] EWHC B10 (QB); *K Ltd v National Westminister Bank Plc* [2006] EWCA Civ 1039 (CA); *UMBS Online Ltd, R (on the application of) v Serious Organised Crime Agency Rev 2* [2007] EWCA Civ 406 (CA); and *Shah & Anor v HSBC Private Bank (UK) Ltd* [2009] EWHC 79 (QB).

3 Except when the information came to the legal advisor in privileged circumstances (s 330(6)(b) POCA) or when lacking knowledge or suspicion that another person in engaged in money laundering activity (s 330(7)(a) POCA). POCA's money laundering provisions were amended by the Serious Organised Crime and Police Act 2005 (SOCPA). Thus, s 330(7)(a) was amended by Part 2, c 6, s 104(6)(a)–(c) of SOCPA.

4 Text to n 102 in chapter 2, 597, para 27.01.

5 Adrienne Margolis, 'Follow the Money: Recovering Ill-gotten Gains' [2009] International Bar News, October 2009, 29–33; Han Moraal, 'Speech of Prosecutor-general Han Moraal, on the Occasion of the 9th IAP European Regional Conference' 1–3 (Speech 03/09, Openbaar Ministerie website 2009) <http://www.om.nl/actueel/toespraken@150377/speech_of> accessed 28 February 2014.

6 Part 5 of POCA (ss 240(1), 241(3)(a), 242(1)(a)–(b), 266, 272 and 304–310). The position is clearly reflected in *Serious Organised Crime Agency v Pelekanos* [2009] EWHC 2307 (QB) paras 6–18.

challenging to readdress is the noticeable concern demonstrated at the international level for the clarification of public and private sector responsibilities to strictly implement the Financial Action Task Force 40 Recommendations on money laundering and the 9 Special Recommendations on terrorist financing (the international standards set for the repressive strategy),[7] and the promotion of a protected level of sharing information generated by Suspicious Activity Reports amongst the affiliates of financial institutions and law enforcement authorities across jurisdictions.[8] According to the Director of FinCEN, J.J. Freis Jr, the best source of information is front-line bank personnel because they know their clients' normal business and are thus in the best position to trace anomalous activities by self-induced suspicion and systemic alerts.[9]

The rationale underlying this approach is a reconfirmation that the efficacy of anti-money laundering and confiscation laws, as underlined by Trevor Millington and Mark Sutherland Williams, ultimately depends on the following three necessary conditions. First, the front-line personnel of financial institutions must be sufficiently trained to trace suspicious activities. Second, the back-office personnel must be equally trained to filter the findings of automated[10] alerts and self-induced suspicions in regard to those financial transactions that do not make sense. Third, the findings of the alleged suspicious activities must be submitted to the nominated reporting officer of the compliance department, who is the last professional to decide whether the suspicion must be disclosed to the Financial Intelligence Unit in the form of a Suspicious Activity Report.

It is therefore evident that the genesis of the financial investigation by the Financial Intelligence Unit, let alone the prosecution of the alleged offenders, essentially depend on the following two contributory factors: first, the ability of the reporters to trace the suspicious transactions allegedly involving criminal property, and, second, the financial institutions' strict conformity with the statutory obligation to disclose offences.

The reactive aspect of money laundering controls can be encapsulated in the following five interconnected repressive phases. First, the rising of automated or self-induced suspicion of an unusual financial transaction. Second, the internal processing of the suspicion within the financial institution. Third, disclosure through the submission of the Suspicious Activity Report to the Financial Intelligence Unit. Fourth, the investigation of the financial affairs of a person or a

---

7 FATF Recommendations 1 and 13–16 on SARs as currently revised.

8 James H Freis Jr, 'Prepared Remarks of James H Freis Jr, Director, Financial Crimes Enforcement Network, US Department of the Treasury Delivered at the ABA/ABA Money Laundering Enforcement Network' 7 *FinCEN* (FinCEN website 2009, Washington DC, 13 October 2009) <http://www.fincen.gov/news_room/speech/pdf/20091013.pdf> accessed 28 February 2014.

9 Text to n 8, 5.

10 Massimo Nardo, 'Building Synergies Between Theory and Practice: Countering Financial Crime on a Systemic Approach' (2006) 13 JFC 3, 292–295.

legal entity by the Financial Intelligence Unit through the exchange of information between law enforcement authorities, which may also lead to the immediate freezing of criminal property. And, five, the prosecution of the offenders for money laundering, the bringing of the indictment for the offences, and trial.

Despite the importance for financial institutions to put controls in place to deal with money laundering threats, and to meet their record keeping and reporting obligations, the tension identified in the first three chapters of this book in regard to the diametrically opposite perspectives on anti-money laundering legislation – those of governments and supervisory authorities on the one hand, with their duty to monitor financial transactions in the public interest, and those of financial institutions and their clients on the other, with their genuine need for the protection of financial privacy and trade secrecy – continues to escalate.

On the one hand, professionals in the financial sector are under a strict obligation not to fail to trace, filter and disclose suspicious activities allegedly aiming to transmogrify criminal property. It is their statutory responsibility to be constantly on alert to trace suspicious transactions and to review with a critical eye their clients' transactional conduct and commercial objectives. This peculiar responsibility is statutorily shifted to them to make them not only the eyes of the prosecutorial and law enforcement authorities, but also criminally liable when they wantonly fail to disclose money laundering offences.

On the other hand, the majority of those law-abiding clients of financial institutions, engaging in financial transactions that involve funds that neither emanate from criminal activities nor intend to finance terrorism, not only experience the interference with their right to financial privacy, but they also have to deal with the state of mind of those professionals handling their money. It is therefore absolutely necessary that, in all cases, there should be more than an apparent evidential burden within financial institutions for their employees to step forward and report that their clients' accounts are allegedly criminal property or that their clients have somehow become concerned in arrangements to facilitate the acquisition, retention and use of the control of criminal property for benefit or otherwise.

Moreover, it should not be overlooked that financial institutions are in possession of their clients' sensitive commercial, financial and personal information. As such, their employees are the first of all people to come across a transaction which must not only make no commercial sense, but must also conflict with the usages of the trade in question, let alone the individual transactional profile of their clients.[11] As much as suspicion may essentially be a matter of subjective fact, we should not fail to appreciate that this statutory obligation inevitably triggers the suspension of the banking contract.

However, it must be pointed out that the rationale upon which the banking contract is suspended conflicts with the rights to the protection of fiduciary

11 Dionysios S Demetis and Ian O Angell, 'The Risk-based Approach to AML: Representation, Paradox, and the 3rd Directive' (2007) 10 JMLC 4.

interests and financial privacy. Yet the reporting entity is exempted from liability for the breach of confidentiality under those compelling circumstances that the offence must be disclosed for the commencement of the anti-money laundering investigation.[12]

So much is clear on the mental ingredient of suspicion of private sector reporting entities and their employees. The reporters either suspect or they do not. And, if they suspect, the legal obligation is automatically imposed on them to inform the authorities[13] and to seek the appropriate consent in breach of the banking contract, but in the interests of facilitating the administration of justice.

In the *Shah*[14] case, Mr Justice Hamblem did not miss the opportunity to stress that financial institutions have in place procedures for reporting suspicion, which involves a number of stages during which different professionals apply enhanced due diligence standards and review each other's suspicion prior to reaching the final decision to disclose offences to authorities.

Practically, this process may be referred to as the safety valve of filtering self-induced suspicion. It is therefore of the utmost importance to appreciate that financial institutions have in place a control and verification process of suspicion prior to submitting their Suspicious Activity Reports to the Financial Intelligence Unit, which safeguards not only their clients' interests and their reputation up to the stage of the mandatory suspension of the banking contract, but also ensures, to the maximum possible degree, that their conduct remains unimpeachable in those compelling situations that they must make the disclosure and block their clients' account.[15]

Against that background, it is appropriate to stress the importance of two additional issues. The first concerns the principle of fairness that a Suspicious Activity Report is expected to be based upon. The second concerns the sound observation of those who support the view that anti-money laundering legislation is draconian. In an endeavour to avoid unnecessary complexity, each issue is analysed separately.

First, Suspicious Activity Reports must be well founded upon the principle of elementary fairness, which is meant to safeguard in the first instance the interests of the clients of financial institutions. It is not often fully appreciated that Suspicious Activity Report filers must explain to competent authorities not only the reasons for which a particular transaction is considered to be suspicious, but are also expected to make an express reference to the totality of the circumstances surrounding the transaction reported. In other words, financial institutions are

---

12 *K Ltd v National Westminster Bank Plc* [2006] EWCA Civ 1039 (CA) para 21.

13 British Bankers' Association, 'Annual Report 2008/09' (BBA website 2009) 23 <http://www.bba.org.uk/content/1/c6/66/53/BBA%20Annual%20Review%202009.pdf> accessed 28 February 2014.

14 *Shah & Anor v HSBC Private Bank (UK) Ltd* [2009] EWHC 79 (QB) paras 42.1–42.5.

15 Text to n 14, paras 42.3–42.5.

obliged to explain in their narratives why a financial transaction was suspicious and worthy to report as unusual.[16]

Second, there are those who believe that the enforcement of this draconian legislation in the public interest may have serious consequences for financial institutions and their clients, let alone the legitimate interests of defendants. In the *UMBS*[17] case, Lord Justice Ward not only referred to the parallel drawn by the appellant to the Athenian legislator, Dracon, but also acknowledged that the operation of the anti-money laundering Act can: blow away the affected person's presumption of innocence until proven guilty; block the bank account of the person for 40 days; and potentially ruin the affected person under suspicion without a straightforward case for the recovery of the damages suffered.[18] Lastly, Lord Justice Ward emphasised the minimum price that Parliament decided to pay for the adoption and implementation of the strategy of taking profit out of crime[19] (Criminal Justice Act 1988).

But in the *K Ltd*[20] case, Lord Justice Longmore pointed out that the 2002 Act interfered with the freedom of trade for seven working days, and that this was a limited interference that could be extended for an additional period of 31 days if the competent authority decides to apply for a Restraint Order for the purpose of reviewing all the particulars of the case.

Against that background, if we take into consideration the wall of silence that affected persons face from their financial institutions concerning the concurrent investigation of their financial affairs, we will be in a better position to appreciate that the remaining part of the rationale of this statutory obligation is to prevent financial institutions and their employees from tipping off their clients that they have become the subjects of a money laundering investigation. However, the temporary freezing of bank accounts inevitably tips clients off that an overt[21] financial investigation is progressing.[22]

In summary, three central ideas lie behind the topic under consideration. The first is that Suspicious Activity Reports are multipurpose tools with an enormous potential to trigger the financial investigation and create financial intelligence. They play a central role in tracing, disrupting and restraining criminal finance. Undoubtedly, the financial cost of pursuing money launderers and financiers

16 FinCEN, 'The SAR Activity Review: Trends Tips & Issues – Issue 16' (The BSA Advisory Group, October 2009, FinCEN website 2009) 48–49 <http://www.fincen.gov/news_room/rp/files/sar_tti_16.pdf> accessed 28 February 2014.

17 *UMBS Online Ltd, R (on the application of) v Serious Organised Crime Agency Rev 2* [2007] EWCA Civ 406 (CA) para 8.

18 Text to n 17, para 8(1)–(5).

19 *Bank of Scotland v A Ltd* [2001] EWCA Civ 52 1 WLR 751 and *Amalgamated Metal Trading Ltd v City of London Police Financial Investigation Unit* [2003] EWHC 703 (Comm) [2003] 1 WLR 2711.

20 Text to n 12, para 22.

21 *Shah* case (n 14) para 79.

22 Text to n 1 in chapter 4, 241.

of terrorism is too high, if not almost unbearable, and it frequently raises serious questions in regard to proportionality and the sacrifice at times of the competitiveness of financial markets. But when it comes to considering that investigators in New York found in the laptop of a 24-year-old Afghan immigrant specifications for triacetone triperoxide (TATP), the kind of explosive used in the London Underground bombings in 2005, or that, out of the 693 terror suspects arrested in accordance with New York University's Centre on Law and Security, at least a third were charged with terrorism, one is in a better position to appreciate that the USD $300,000,000 spent in 2008 by New York City on counter-terrorism must have been spent under compelling circumstances.[23]

The second is that the wealth of information that can be extracted from financial institutions though Suspicious Activity Reports constitutes a universe of financial, commercial and personal data, which through the proper and secure processing and analysis can be exchanged to identify criminal trends and typologies,[24] which can be used by different law enforcement agencies irrespective of their geographical location, for different repressive purposes, and at multiple stages.

The third is that Suspicious Activity Reports constitute the starting point for the financial investigation because they trace and expose[25] to law enforcement and prosecutorial authorities those who cannot innocently explain the possession or control of unaccountable wealth. In legal and practical terms, Suspicious Activity Reports sketch the skeleton of the class of offence, which must be proved by prosecutors after the investigation of the financial affairs of those persons lacking a credible and reasonable explanation as to how they acquired the assets traced by the anti-money laundering system.[26] It is therefore less surprising that, across the Atlantic, the commonly held view is that there are pressing needs for the sharing of Suspicious Activity Reports amongst the affiliates of financial institutions irrespective of their geographic location.[27]

---

23 *The Economist*, 'Foiling Terrorist Attacks: Home-grown Bombers' (2009) 393 (8651) 60.

24 Text to n 16.

25 *Ahmed v Her Majesty's Advocate* [2009] ScotHC HCJAC 60 (AC) para 30.

26 Text to n 175 in chapter 2, 6 (FinCEN Director, Jennifer Shasky Calvery, referred to an alleged USD $6,000,000,000 money laundering operation through the centralised virtual currency of Liberty Reserve involving credit card fraud, identity theft, investment fraud, computer hacking, narcotics trafficking and child pornography).

27 FinCEN, 'Financial Institutions Outreach Initiative: Report on Outreach to Large Depository Institutions, October 2009' (FinCEN website 2009) 26 <http://www.fincen.gov/news_room/rp/reports/pdf/Bank_Report.pdf> accessed 28 February 2014.

The Anatomy of the Conspiracy Charge

Where the Defendant Suspected but did not Know the Money was Criminal Proceeds

To know that property, especially in disposable form, is the proceeds of crime, and to consciously decide to deal with it, is a distinct state of mind or true belief upon which the offender engages in criminality and must be sanctioned for wrongdoing. However, one's decision to deal with property suspected to be criminal proceeds is a different issue involving a lesser state of mind.

As we had the opportunity to review in the previous section, a reporting entity is obliged to submit a Suspicious Activity Report in those circumstances that something knotty is suspected to have taken place, but cannot be proved until an investigation takes place. In an effort to reverse the value of this legal reasoning, the following question may be asked, why shouldn't we accept that suspicion cannot be equated with knowledge to deal with hot property on the part of the alleged offender? In other words, it would be paradoxical if we were to give the benefit of the doubt to the reporting entities, but not to the alleged offenders.

In a hypothetical situation, if a person is walking with a view to reach a final and safe destination, but has the option to take a shortcut through a dangerous pathway where people have been stabbed in the past, and decides to walk an extra mile to avoid potential harm, the person's decision is not based on knowledge, but on mere suspicion that the odds are against him to suffer fatal harm. He only suspects so, but he does not know for certain that harm may be awaiting in the dangerous pathway.

Notwithstanding the fact that fanciful and hypothetical examples like the one offered previously may have their own practical or perceptive value, jurisprudence[28] is the main source of the standards of proof in the criminal and civil justice systems. In the *Squirrell*[29] case, Mr Justice Laddie held that, even if a bank account was not pregnant with criminal proceeds, Section 328(1) of the 2002 Act applied[30] where the financial institution suspected that the account holder had somehow dealt with criminal proceeds.[31]

The statutory offence of criminal conspiracy to facilitate the laundering of criminal proceeds should not be tried on the basis of the defendant's knowledge of his own state of suspicious mind.[32] On the contrary, this offence should be tried on the basis that the defendant got beyond the agreement to conspire with others to

28 In section 3, reference will be made to Parts 5 and 7 of POCA because the authorities examined dealt with money laundering offences committed prior to the amendments that took place by the Serious Organised Crime and Police Act 2005 (SOCPA).

29 *Squirrell Ltd v National Westminister Bank Plc* [2005] EWHC 664 (Ch).

30 *Hussein v Chong Fook Kam* [1970] AC 942.

31 *Squirrel* case (n 29) para 13.

32 *R v Sakavickas and Another* EWCA Crim 2686 (CA).

commit an offence in time future, and thus acted beyond that stage, in pursuance of the conspiracy by true engagement[33] in the laundering of the property. In other words, with knowledge or intent, and it must be proved or admitted in court[34] that the property emanated from crime[35] at the specific time the conspirators made the agreement.[36]

Contrastingly, it can be argued that the notional difference between knowledge and suspicion is marginal. This is precisely the reason for which conspiracy is a controversial criminal conduct on its own proper definition, let alone to be proved in court. It is a different thing if X knows that the property is the proceeds of crime, and the other person, Y, only suspects that the property is criminal. Indeed, X can be charged with knowledge, but can Y, the alleged co-conspirator, be charged with a thought crime or strictly on the basis of the knowledge of his own state of suspicious mind?

As any prosecutor will corroborate, if X knows but Y only suspects, isn't the intention of Y to convert the money even if it represents the proceeds of crime? At the same time, any sufficiently experienced defence attorney could seriously challenge this position by arguing that the accused may have committed the substantive offence of money laundering merely by not having agreed to do so in the absence of knowledge.

Contrastively, an experienced criminologist could argue that any defendant's doing so could be equated with a disguised plot to recklessly become concerned in arrangements to launder criminal proceeds or participation in a disguised plot of wilful blindness. In any case, this knotty issue cannot but constitute the core subject of judicial review, but in parallel to the examination of the evidence submitted concerning the state of mind of the defendant within the specific circumstantial context of the case.

There is a carefully balanced niche of equal probabilities to be explored in the triangular process of judicial review: Bench, Crown and Defence; and besides the existence of the strong probability of guilt for conspiratory conduct, there remains to be explored the other probability as to whether, on the facts known to the defendant, the act he agreed to commit was a lawful one. Inevitably, the judicial quest has to take the evidential and inferential pathway to examine the facts that were presented to the alleged conspirator by another person who might have known that the property was the proceeds of crime, but nevertheless, either did not make the disclosure to the accused or intentionally kept secret the true provenance of the property with a view to deceive the accused.[37]Admittedly, this is a conundrum, but as Lord Hope of Graighead pointed out in the *Saik* case, in the interests of fairness, the prosecutor must prove before the court that the accused

33 *R v Saik* [2006] UKHL 18 para 23.
34 *R v Ali* [2006] WLR 316 (CA) 351 para 148.
35 *R v Montilla* [2004] 1 WLR 624, 633 (CA) para 35.
36 *R v Saik* [2006] UKHL 18 paras 25–26.
37 *R v Churchill* [1967] 2 AC 224.

suspected (the subjective test) and that there were reasonable grounds to suspect (the objective test).[38]

The statutory offence of criminal conspiracy is complete at the stage of an agreement made by the parties concerned. It is complete even if the parties do not carry out what they have agreed in time past.[39] The real problem to be solved by the prosecution is when the conspiracy progresses and the conspirators act during different stages for the realisation of the money laundering plot. In such circumstances, whilst the conspiratory agreement is made once and for all, it still looks sinisterly into the future. The money laundering offence can have a sequential plan of action, and may involve different periods of time and different perpetrators. It is precisely this anomalous nexus of duplicity that leaves the prosecution with only two choices to charge. Either as a single conspiracy, which overcomes the majority of the difficulties involved or as a series of separate substantive offences, which will inevitably overload the indictment.

To elucidate further this issue, let us consider the following hypothetical example. If X agreed to deal once and for all with £10,000,000 in bank notes, which were the proceeds of Y from drug trafficking, by laundering the full amount in 20 separate stages through 20 different financial institutions, that is, £500,000 at a time, would it be correct to presume that offender X will be prosecuted and sentenced 20 different times, that is, 14 years for each of the 20 offences or 280 years for an offence he agreed to commit for personal benefit once, but practically in 20 different stages in order to avoid his arrest and the confiscation of the criminal proceeds? Perhaps the most appropriate answer to this question would be probably not, unless the particular facts of the case absolutely dictate the absurd overloading of the indictment.

It therefore arises with a considerable degree of certainty that the prosecution's work is extremely difficult when it comes to explaining to juries the use of the conspiracy counts in relation to the criminal conduct that was pursued by the different perpetrators involved. On this last point, Lord Justice Hopper rightly pointed out in the *Liaquat* case that the prosecution may decide not to charge separately each delivery of laundered money in order to avoid an overloaded indictment, but in order to prove the substantive offence, the conspiracy count may be presented to overcome the rules against duplicity.[40]

Knowing, Suspecting or Having Reasonable Grounds to Suspect the Laundering of Criminal Proceeds

As we do not live in a world of saints, a person cannot know whether property is criminal unless he participated in the predicate crime or was told that the property in question is criminal. Consequently, trial judges and juries seek to ascertain

38 *R v Saik* [2006] UKHL 18 paras 52–53.

39 *Crofter Hand – Woven Harris Tweed Co v Veitch* [1942] AC 435, 439.

40 *R v Liaquat and Others* [2005] EWCA Crim 87 (CA) paras 150–151.

whether the accused knew, suspected or had reasonable grounds to suspect the money to have been the proceeds of crime, and deliberately closed his eyes.

Those who engage in financial transactions in the regulated sector are under an obligation, which arises from the governing statutory presumptions, not to fail to obtain reasonable explanations from their clients in regard to the true sources of the wealth in their possession prior to providing their services for reward or otherwise. In the result, any person, legal person, legal arrangement and financial institution that will be found to have failed[41] to seek reasonable explanations concerning the provenance of their clients' money before deciding to handle it, will be exposed to the risk of being held criminally liable for the offence of facilitation or for the substantive offence of money laundering, depending on the force of the circumstantial evidence of the case.[42]

Indeed, the key phrase to consider in regard to the previous submission is the totality of the circumstantial evidence, which may be conceptually equated with the true force of the entirety of surrounding circumstances under which the property was handled by the defendant. Of course, the burden on the shoulders of the Crown is to prove that the property was or represented benefit from criminal conduct. In the *Ahmed* case, the Advocate Depute confirmed that all the Crown had to do was to prove that the property was or represented entirely or partly benefit from criminal conduct without necessarily having to specify the nature of the crime committed.[43] Indeed, under the Act, the Crown was not expected to prove the type of crime committed that generated the benefit, but rather to prove that the source of the proceeds was criminal.[44] Stated differently, the Crown's duty is not to solve the criminal equation by particularising the crime that generated the ill-gotten gains, but to prove that the source was criminal.[45]

Moreover, the statutory footing of Part 7 of the Act, and, more specifically, the language of Section 340(2) does not require to particularise the specific offence that the property derived from.[46] It can therefore be deduced that the current width of the prosecutorial toll should be equated with the legislator's volition that the prosecution must shoulder the lighter burden of proving that any property constitutes the fruits of criminal conduct[47] as opposed to shouldering the heavier burden of proving the specific offence from which the property derived in each and every case.[48]

41 Text to n 38.

42 Text to nn 39–40.

43 *Ahmed v Her Majesty's Advocate* [2009] ScotHC HCJAC 60 (AC) para 8.

44 Text to n 43.

45 *Ahmed v Her Majesty's Advocate* [2009] ScotHC HCJAC 60 (AC) para 9.

46 *R v NW and Others* [2008] EWCA Crim2 (CA) paras 16 and 22.

47 *Ahmed v Her Majesty's Advocate* [2009] ScotHC HCJAC 60 (AC) para 12.

48 *R v Montilla and Others* [2004] UKHL 50 para 42.

Yet there is another good reason for which the courts maintain the position that the evidential and inferential pathway meets the criminal standard of proof.[49] The evidence either proves knowledge or reasonable grounds to suspect the criminal provenance of the property under Section 340(2). Consequently, inference can sufficiently put to the test the origin of the property next to the actual state of mind of the accused.[50] This position was also accepted in the *R v Craig*[51] case, but its enhancement is mainly owed to the comparative approach to the decisions in *R v NW and Others* and in *Director of the Assets Recovery Agency v Green*[52] taken by Lord Justice Latham in *R v Anwoir and Others*.[53]

However, it is in the *R v IK* case that the scene was properly set in regard to the two ways in which the Crown can prove that the property derives from crime.[54] Either by specifying the kind of unlawful conduct the property derives from or by relying on the circumstances under which the property was handled, which must be sufficient to infer that the property could have only derived from criminal conduct.[55]

In synopsis, four central ideas lie behind this crucial topic. The first is that, suspicion is a lesser state of mind from knowledge, yet their difference is marginal. Setting aside the force of circumstantial evidence as to the way in which the alleged criminal property was handled, which may in many cases point towards the one-way direction of the defendant's guilt, it is extremely difficult for any prosecutor to prove that the conduct of the accused is worthy of sanctioning for a thought crime.

The second is that the statutory offence of conspiring to launder the proceeds of crime should be tried on the basis that the defendant actually got beyond the agreement to conspire with others to commit an offence or a series of offences, and acted in pursuance of the plan of that conspiracy agreement knowingly, suspecting or by having had reasonable grounds to suspect the laundering of criminal property at that time. Of course, at the commencement of any hearing, the innocence of all defendants is presumed and therefore ranks at the top of the barometer of innocence. However, it should be appreciated that the more the defendant fails to explain, to the satisfaction of the court, that the property in his possession or control is not unexplainable, the barometer of innocence will increasingly fall down to the bottom level where nothing but guilt will be established.

The third is that the prosecution does not necessarily have to particularise the specific offence having generated the primary source of the criminal proceeds, especially when the particulars of the case do not enable prosecutors to do so.

49 *NW* case (n 46) para 16.

50 *Montilla* case (n 35) para 43.

51 *R v Craig* [2007] EWCA Crim 2913 (CA) para 29.

52 *Director of the Assets Recovery Agency v Green* [2005] EWHC 3168 Admin (HC) paras 33–34.

53 *R v Anwoir and Others* [2008] EWCA Crim 1354 (CA) para 12.

54 *R v IK* [2007] EWCA Crim 491 (CA) para 10.

55 *R v Gabriel* [2006] EWCA Crim 229 (CA).

Nevertheless, the prosecution must prove the class of crime committed. Alternatively, the prosecution can prove that the source was criminal by demonstrating that the circumstances under which the property was handled suffice to draw conclusions that the property could have only derived from criminal conduct, and that those who became concerned in such arrangements could have only acted knowingly, with suspicion, or had reasonable grounds to suspect the laundering of criminal proceeds.

The fourth and last is that, in the absence of proof as to the origin of the property handled, possessed or acquired by the defendant, the prosecutor's force will depend on the true force of circumstantial evidence. Henceforth, the inference that the jury will be invited to draw will have to pass the criminal standard of proof on the balance of probabilities. Where the jury will be permitted to infer from circumstantial evidence the elements of guilt, truthful and credible explanations must be offered to the court by the defendant. It is this peculiar process that is sometimes fallaciously associated with the burden of proof where the force of the facts of the case completes the elements of guilt as opposed to consolidating the elements of innocence.

The Burden of Proof

The Serious Organised Crime Agency (SOCA)[56] must prove that the property was acquired by or in return for unlawful conduct. The Director does not have to prove a specific criminal offence, but must identify the kind of unlawful conduct that was pursued by the respondent in order for the court to be satisfied that the allegations have been established.[57] In the *Pelekanos* case, Mr Justice Hamblem clarified the scene by confirming that the burden of proof is on the claimant, whereas the standard of proof is the balance of probabilities.[58]

But in criminal cases, if the defendant's explanation is rejected as untruthful or unsatisfactory by the court, in the interests of preventing a serious risk of injustice, the judicial review is extended beyond the defendant's explanation offered to the court. In practical terms, the court examines the defendant's explanation next to the circumstantial evidence. In the result, the defendant's explanation becomes more or less convincing, let alone that it can be rebalanced by the evidence. In fact, the prosecution and the defence fulfil diametrically opposite roles with a view to affect the verdict. The defendant will be called upon to offer explanations to the court at various stages concerning cryptically interrelated questions that arise in relation to the evidence.

56 SOCA was established by the Serious Organised Crime and Police Act 2005. In June 2011, SOCA operations were merged into the National Crime Agency by the Crime and Court Act 2013, which commenced operations as of 7 October 2013.

57 *Serious Organised Crime Agency v Pelekanos* [2009] EWHC 2307 (QB).

58 *Pelekanos* case (n 57) para 19.

At the same time, it is important to enquire into whether the defendant's explanation offered to the court constitutes the reversal of the burden of proof, and if it is legally permissible to construe that the burden of proof is reversed repeatedly until guilt or innocence is established. On this crucial point, Lord Justice Laws rightly observed in criticism that there is no reversal of the burden of proof, and that the only legitimate mode of proof in trials is inference from circumstance.[59] We should not therefore confuse the establishment of guilt by critical inference from circumstance with the reversal of the burden of proof.

The commonly held view is that, in criminal cases, the prosecution must prove to the criminal standard that the defendant's conduct is blameworthy because he committed the prohibited act with intention or knowledge of wrongdoing as required by the criminal statute. However, the important point to keep in mind is that the prosecution does not necessarily have to particularise the criminal activity from which the criminal proceeds emanated. This should not be associated with the reversal of the burden of proof or the imposition of an unfair burden on the defence to establish that the defendant did not know that the property represented the proceeds of crime.

There are thus two live issues to be appreciated in criminal trials. First, whether the prosecution can prove that the defendant obtained or became concerned in any pattern in the concealment, disguise, conversion, transfer or removal of the property, which will be either known property in his possession or control, or that the defendant knew of the fact that the property he possessed or handled was criminal property. Second, whether the defendant can show within his knowledge that the prosecutor's allegations must not affect the verdict because his explanation proves beyond reasonable doubt a genuine lack of knowledge that the property possessed or handled was criminal and that, in the absence of blameworthy intent, he must not be found guilty of the offence.

But given the gravity of the money laundering offence and the centrality of circumstantial and documentary evidence that may interconnect with the nature of the offence, the accused's position is peculiar because he must establish strictly within the sphere of his knowledge that his explanations are sufficiently reasonable and truthful to set aside the facts that may be drawing the picture of the state of mind of a person who had knowledge or reasonable grounds to suspect that the property was criminal. Consequently, circumstantial evidence is the main source that places the defendant in the position to give explanations as to how he obtained the assets and what happened to these assets.[60]

While the prosecution shoulders the lighter burden of proving that the property in the defendant's possession represents the benefit from some criminal conduct, it must still prove what class of crime was consummated,[61] and establish the elements

59 *NW* case (n 46) para 18.

60 *R v Whittington* [2009] Crim 1641 (AC) paras 40–42.

61 *NW* case (n 46) para 16.

of the criminal offence to a criminal standard.[62] But on the other hand, the defence shoulders the heavier burden of proving that the source of the property was not criminal or that the accused did not know at the time that the property was criminal by offering truthful explanations to the court each and every time the evidential scene turns against the accused. In the result, the judicial review of the defendant's explanations concerning his presumably criminal lifestyle or the possession of presumably criminal property, and the circumstantial[63] evidence as to the way in which the property was handled, constitute the main criteria for testing whether on the balance of probabilities the property in the defendant's hands was obtained as a result of the criminal conduct alleged.[64]

Of course, what has been submitted thus far by this author is no panacea. As it was already pointed out,[65] ultimately, everything depends on the particular facts of the case, and it is a well established fact that defendants are protected in that such inference can only be drawn if it meets the criminal standard of proof.[66] As a general rule, the prosecution must prove on the balance of probabilities not only the defendant's motive[67] to become concerned in the laundering of criminal proceeds, but also his wish to conceal the truth.[68] The accused's position will always be peculiar because he must prove within his knowledge that the explanations offered to the court are reasonable and truthful in order to maintain the presumption of his innocence and to overcome the force of the circumstantial evidence that can paint the colourful picture of the realisation of his guilt.[69]

Moreover, while the overall burden of proving guilt rests with the prosecutor, the evidential burden will always be on the defendant. Indeed, the standard of proof constitutes the balance of probabilities,[70] and it is an equally well established fact that circumstantial inference can rebalance the probabilities upon which juries decide whether the property in the defendant's hands represented the proceeds of crime or was acquired as a result of criminal conduct. Henceforward, it is impossible to equate the evidential burden with the reversal of the burden of proof.[71]

In conclusion, all of what has been addressed in this section is highly representative of the state of balance of two separate standards in criminal trials.[72] On the one hand, the burden is on the prosecution to prove the defendant's guilt.

---

62 *Whittington* case (n 60) para 15.

63 *Assets Recovery Agency v Olupitan & Anor* [2007] EWHC 162 (QB) para 23.

64 *Assets Recovery Agency v Jackson & Ors* [2007] EWHC 2553 (QB) para 116.

65 *NW* case (n 46) para 16.

66 Text to n 62.

67 *R v Lucas* [1981] QB 720.

68 *Grayson & Barnham v The United Kingdom* App no 19955/05 (ECtHR, 23 September 2008) para 9.

69 *Grayson & Barnham* case (n 68) paras 11, 16 and 18.

70 *Pelekanos* case (n 57) para 19.

71 *NW* case (n 46) para 18.

72 *Hogan v The Director of Public Prosecutions* [2007] EWHC 978 Admin (QB) para 43.

On the other, the evidential burden is on the defence. Two crucial points should be kept in mind in regard to the second standard. First, that the defence must offer reasonable and truthful explanations to the court that will prove the complete absence of blameworthy knowledge and intent on the defendant's part. Second, that the foundations of the accused's explanations must not be shaken by the force of the inferential source during the judicial quest of seeking to sanction those who knowingly engage in money laundering conspiracies. Undoubtedly, they must be sufficiently fit and enduring to rebut the diametrically contrary pieces of evidence that may be pointing towards unlawful conduct.

Chapter 6
Financial Intelligence

The Basic Parameters

The imposition of the obligation on reporting entities to disclose offences in the narratives of Suspicious Activity Reports constitutes the starting[1] point for the investigation of the financial affairs of those having allegedly become concerned in the laundering of criminal proceeds or the financing of terrorism. However, as much as Suspicious Activity Reports interconnect with the receipt of raw[2] financial intelligence by FIUs before the commencement of the financial investigation, it should not be equated with the final form of financial intelligence,[3] which is delivered at a subsequent stage and as the end result of cooperation amongst FIUs, law enforcement and intelligence authorities.

Suspicious Activity Reports do not constitute evidence of crime because they are based on the reporters' subjective belief that the facts exist, and can thus provide the necessary leads to prevent crime and terror. On the one hand, it is permissible for reporting entities to suspect wrongdoing and obligatory to report alleged criminal conduct in the interests of discharging their statutory duties. On the other hand, it is imperative for FIUs to validate the proportionality of the purpose that Suspicious Activity Reports sought to achieve in their narratives before issuing a production order for evidence. This is the reason for which not all Suspicious Activity Reports[4] received[5] will be justified.[6]

It is therefore important to review with a critical eye what makes financial intelligence analysis unique and invaluable, and why, in the result, financial intelligence enables law enforcement and intelligence agencies to trace and disrupt those who engage in the transmogrification of criminal proceeds. As Mike Wells, Director of the Risk and Intelligence Service, HM Revenue and Customs,

1 Anthony Kennedy, 'Winning the Information Wars: Collecting, Sharing and Analysing Information in Asset Recovery Investigations' (2007) 14 JFC 4, 389.

2 *R v Da Silva* [2006] EWCA Crim 1654 (CA).

3 Suspicious Activity Reports are collected, processed and stored by the UKFIU on the ELMER database. Thereupon, end users in law enforcement make multiple use of them.

4 George Brown and Tania Evans, 'The Impact: The Breadth and Depth of the Anti-money Laundering Provisions Requiring Reporting of Suspicious Activities' (2008) 23 JIBLR 5, 274–277.

5 Text to n 1, 389.

6 SOCA, 'Review of the Suspicious Activity Reports Regime (The SARs Review) Sir Stephen Lander March 2006' (SOCA website 2009) 29–30, para 65 <http://www.soca.gov.uk/downloads/SOCAtheSARsReview_Final_Web.pdf> accessed 28 February 2014.

highlighted in SOCA's Annual Report 2008, the initiation of money laundering investigations is mainly owed to Suspicious Activity Reports (raw financial intelligence), whereas the 400 HM Revenue and Customs officers (human resources) are trained (financial resources) to use Suspicious Activity Reports (technological resources) to trace and disrupt organised crime networks in high level criminal intelligence operations.[7]

The Financial Transactions and Reports Analysis Centre of Canada (FINTRAC), in its Annual Report 2008, underlined that financial intelligence provides law enforcement and intelligence agencies with unique advantages to combat crime and terrorism.[8] But as Anthony Kennedy succinctly put it in commentary, in order for FIUs to effectively receive, analyse and disseminate vast volumes of information,[9] let alone to produce reports and recommendations for repressive actions, they must have operational independence and sufficient financial and human resources.[10] It therefore becomes all the more apparent that FIUs shoulder the burden of making sense of all the information submitted to them by reporters in the interests of disrupting the criminal enterprise, facilitating the prosecution of offenders, and assisting in the recovery of criminal proceeds.[11]

As we will have the opportunity to review in what follows, the gathering and exchange of financial intelligence can establish the links between persons, enterprises and bank accounts wantonly moving criminal money through the different financial institutions and sectors of the formal economy.[12] Taken together, SOCA's and FINTRAC's examples raise the following central issue. The optimum gathering, analysis and dissemination of financial intelligence depends on governments' volition to put their houses in order,[13] enact and strictly implement proportionate measures for the cooperation of their law enforcement authorities, intelligence agencies and regulatory authorities.

The crucial point to keep in mind is that financial intelligence analysis and the exchange of information are conventionally secured[14] for the purpose of establishing the necessary links between transnational organised crime,[15] corruption[16] and

7 SOCA, 'The Suspicious Activity Reports Regime Annual Report 2008' (SOCA website 2009) 29 <http://www.soca.gov.uk/assessPublications/downloads/SAR-Annual-Report-08-pn.pdf> accessed 28 February 2014.

8 Financial Transactions and Reports Analysis Centre of Canada, 'FINTRAC – 2008 Annual Report – Financial Intelligence' (FINTRAC website 2008) 1 <http://www.fintrac-canafe.gc.ca/publications/ar/2008/41-eng.asp> accessed 28 February 2014.

9 Text to n 1, 389.

10 Text to n 7, 29.

11 Text to n 7, 6.

12 Text to n 8, 1.

13 Text to n 8 in chapter 1, Question 391.

14 Articles 7(1)(b), 18(4), and 27(1)(a) of the UNTOC.

15 Recommendation 26 of the FATF; the Egmont Group definition of a national FIU; and Articles 24 and 28 of Directive 2005/60/EC.

16 Articles 36, 46(13) and 58 of the UNCAC.

money laundering offences. By way of bringing together the discussion held in Chapter 5 and the present analysis, it is suggested that the effective receipt, analysis and exchange of financial intelligence can be an invaluable asset in trials for the following two reasons. First, financial intelligence can contribute to the qualitative aspect of indictments because it provides accurate financial data. Second, it can guide trial judges to give sound directions to juries to infer from documentary evidence the intention or knowledge of accused persons to launder criminal finance.

Moreover, admissible evidence originating from financial intelligence can be used in courts to prove the defendant's or the respondent's deliberate choice not to comply with the regulations for record keeping with intent to conceal unlawful conduct or to cheat the Revenue. Alternatively, in many cases, the absence of documentary evidence corroborating compliance with the regulatory framework can equally establish unlawful conduct and tax evasion.

For example, in *R v IK*,[17] Lord Justice Dyson observed in criticism that the production of more than 2,500 false receipts; the absence of evidence of the provenance of the £5,900,000 handled in cash transactions; the forged statement summaries; and the absence of proper records, constituted the basis for the jury to properly infer that the money handled by the accused was the product of criminal conduct. Similarly, in *Ali & Anor*,[18] Lord Justice Moses underlined that the defendants had deliberately[19] failed to identify the sources of the cash handled for others, let alone that they had not kept a record of the sources of that money in accordance with the 1993 Regulations.

In an effort to make better sense of the qualities of the different arguments offered in favour of the interconnection between Suspicious Activity Reports and the gathering, storing, analysis and exchange of financial intelligence, reference is made to the Madoff errors recently admitted by JPMorgan. The bank had suspicions about Bernard Madoff since 1994. But JPMorgan allowed the transactions to reach the amount of USD $6,800,000,000 up to Madoff's arrest and failed to report suspicions (red flags) to its anti-money laundering department, which was consequently prevented from submitting a Suspicious Activity Report to FinCEN.[20]

As part of the deferred prosecution agreement, JPMorgan's criminal prosecution was waived in exchange for the payment of massive penalties amounting to USD

---

17 *R v IK* [2007] EWCA Crim 491 (CA) paras 9–10 and 34.

18 *Ali & Anor v Revenue & Customs Prosecution Office* [2008] Crim 146 (CA) para 11.

19 *R v El Kurd* [2007] EWCA Crim 1888 (CA) para 64.

20 Financial Crimes Enforcement Network, a bureau of the US Department of the Treasury, 'JPMorgan Admits Violation of BSA for Failed Madoff Oversight; Fined $461 Million by FinCEN' (*FinCEN*, 7 January 2014) <http://www.fincen.gov/news_room/nr/pdf/20140107.pdf> accessed 8 January 2014.

$2,600,000,000[21] and the bank's undertaking to reform its practices. Last but not least, these developments also demonstrate the consequences of failing to discharge statutory duties.

But there is another qualitative aspect of the analysis of financial intelligence to address. The macro analysis of Suspicious Activity Reports sets out criminal patterns and trends when the following two criteria are satisfied. First, the Suspicious Activity Reports received by the FIUs must be complete and accurate. Second, FIUs must process the Suspicious Activity Reports in parallel to the information received from other sources,[22] such as law enforcement authorities, intelligence agencies, commercial databases and foreign FIUs if necessary.[23]

Governments should therefore be primarily concerned with the achievement of the following two goals in pursuing money launderers and financiers of terrorism. First, to deliver effective money laundering controls by taking full advantage of the enormous IT potential of the Financial Intelligence Regime. Second, to make their territories hostile environments to organised crime and terror.[24]

In synopsis, on the one hand, the function of the Suspicious Activity Report Regime is critical. On the other hand, what is commonly referred to as the law of intelligence, which governs the receipt, analysis and exchange of financial intelligence, plays an equally critical role in the prevention and control of organised crime and the financing of terrorism. At the same time, the Suspicious Activity Report Regime and the Financial Intelligence Regime are conventionally secured.[25]

Prior to closing this section, it is underlined that there are pressing needs for all FIUs, not only to make efficacious use of the law of intelligence, but also to work in collective partnership with their counterparts to ensure that the performance achieved is of the same repressive level. More specifically, in the absence of a symmetry in the repressive strategies of governments to make their territories hostile environments to organised crime and terror, there is the risk of unintentionally shifting criminal trends to vulnerable jurisdictions and regions[26] lacking the financial, technological and human resources or the appropriate anti-money laundering regulatory frameworks to cope with evolving criminal patterns[27]

---

21 Tom Braithwaite and Kara Scannell, 'JPMorgan Admits Madoff Errors' *Financial Times* (London, 8 January 2014) 15.

22 Text to n 16 in chapter 5.

23 Text to n 8, 2.

24 Text to n 7 and 12.

25 Text to nn 14–16.

26 Steven Pifer, 'Global Trends and Shocks in the National Security Environment: Russia and Eurasia' (The Brookings Institution website 2009) 220–223 <http://www.brookings.edy/~/media/Files/rc/articles/2009/20_global_trends_russia_eurasia_pifer/10_Global_trends_russia-eurasia_pifer.pdf> accessed 28 February 2014.

27 FinCEN, 'Advisories/Bulletins/Fact Sheets' (FinCEN website 2009) <http://www.fincen.gov/news_room/advisory/index.html> accessed 28 February 2014.

and trends.[28] It is for this reason that the Council of Europe has cooperated in partnership with international organisations[29] to promote and enhance standard-setting, compliance supervision and technical cooperation for capacity building.[30]

The Fundamentals of the Law of Intelligence

Financial Intelligence Units (FIUs)[31] control the system for the reporting of suspicious financial activities or transactions that automatically present higher risk for money laundering and terrorism financing[32] within their jurisdiction. As independent units, their core function is to gather, analyse and exchange information, and ensure that vital pieces of information are promptly delivered to investigating authorities and prosecutors entrusted with the tasks of sanctioning criminals and restraining criminal assets.[33]

Egmont Group FIUs are firmly committed to the enhancement of cross-border[34] exchange of information on the basis of the principles of the uninhibited[35] and confidential[36] exchange of financial and personal data through the Egmont Secure Web (ESW).[37] It is therefore important not only to address the principles of the free exchange of information, the permitted use of the information received, and the confidential treatment of the information shared and exchanged at the FIU level,

28 The Egmont Group of Financial Intelligence Units, '100 Cases from the Egmont Group' (The Egmont Group website 2009) 2–172 <http://www.egmontgroup.org/library/cases> accessed 28 February 2014.

29 United States Department of the Treasury, FinCEN Advisory, 'FATF – VII Report on Money Laundering Typologies' 2–14 (FinCEN website 2009) <http://www.fincen.gov/news_room/rp/advisory/pdf/advissu4.pdf> accessed 28 February 2014.

30 Text to nn 66, 79, 76, 90, 92–95 in chapter 2.

31 Text to n 85 in chapter 1, 355.

32 FATF, 'FATF Guidance: Anti-Money Laundering and Terrorist Financing Measures and Financial Inclusion' (*FATF*, February 2013) <http://www.fatf-gafi.org/media/fatf/documents/reports/AML_CFT_Measures_and_Financial_Inclusion_2013.pdf> accessed 10 December 2013.

33 The Egmont Group, Egmont Group Library: Egmont Documents, 'Information Paper on Financial Intelligence Units and the Egmont Group' (Egmont Group website 2009) <http://www.egmontgroup.org/library/egmont-documents> accessed 28 February 2014.

34 The Egmont Group, Egmont Group Library: Egmont Documents, 'Best Practices for the Exchange of Information Between Financial Intelligence Units' (Egmont Group website 2009) 1, para 1 <http://www.egmontgroup.org/library/egmont-documents> accessed 28 February 2014.

35 By national rules and privacy laws conflicting with the principle of the cross-border sharing and exchange of information.

36 In regard to the permitted users of the information shared and exchanged.

37 Text to n 34, 1, para 2.

but also to draw the necessary distinctions between the legal[38] and best practices[39] standards involved.

The Free Exchange of Information

The free exchange of information is based on the concept of the uninhibited exchange of intelligence amongst the different types of national FIUs (administrative, law enforcement, judicial or prosecutorial, and hybrid).[40] The exchange of information is expected to take place rapidly, directly and informally, but the process must guarantee the privacy and the confidentiality of the sensitive information shared. Moreover, FIUs must be independent national centres, with proper authority and sufficient powers to promptly negotiate and sign MOUs at the FIU level.[41]

FIUs are expected to treat requests from their counterparts in the same way they would have handled a domestic disclosure. They are also expected to have instant access to: all national registries, law enforcement data, financial information stored by financial institutions and other reporting entities, and information on beneficial ownership and control of all legal persons and legal arrangements in their jurisdiction.[42]

The requested FIU providing the information to the requesting FIU, must not refuse to grant its consent for the subsequent dissemination of the information shared, unless that dissemination can result in the impairment of the criminal investigation or the infringement of the interests of the person or legal entity concerned or the violation of the fundamental legal principles of its jurisdiction. In any case, refusals to grant consent for subsequent dissemination must always be justified.[43]

Permitted Use of Information

Requests for information must be made through the submission of a Standard Egmont Group Form, which must clearly state the urgency of the issue, the contact details of the designated person sending the request, and the request for prior consent to make further use of the information requested upon the reply is sent to the counterpart FIU.[44]

The reports must be accompanied by a comprehensive summary of the relevant facts known to the requesting FIU. More specifically, these reports must clearly specify: the identities of the persons or the details of the companies involved (names

38 Text to n 34, 1–2.
39 Text to n 34, 3–5.
40 Text to n 34, 2, para 2.
41 Text to n 34, 2, paras 4–6.
42 Text to n 34, 2, para 7.
43 Text to n 34, 2, para 8.
44 Text to n 34, 3, paras 1.1–1.7.

and dates of birth of persons, and names and registered offices of corporations); the Suspicious Activity Reports and the relevant bank accounts; the circumstances in which the suspicious activities took place; whether the request for information is owed to the disclosure of an offence or to a request made by police authorities; and the link with the requested FIU's country.[45]

The requesting FIU, however, is expected to conduct a preliminary research into the suspected activities with a view to identify the suspect or the vital links between the suspect and other persons, companies and bank accounts prior to making the request to its counterpart FIU. This preliminary research facilitates the efficacious and rapid exchange of intelligence at FIU level especially in those circumstances that requests for information may be sent to a number of FIUs simultaneously.[46] All incoming requests for information from counterpart FIUs must be answered and handled instantly after having recorded the name and contact details of the person in charge and the reference number that the responding FIU has assigned to the case.[47]

The requested FIU must reply to its counterpart FIU either in the positive or in the negative within one week from receipt of the request for information or by transmitting an interim response. The requested FIU's response may be positive if the information requested matches the information that it directly accessed domestically, whereas the response may be negative either because the data within its jurisdiction do not match the particular request or because the requested FIU cannot provide a complete answer due to national legal restrictions.[48]

In those circumstances that the requested FIU must access external databases or it is necessary to contact third parties, such as financial institutions and other obliged entities, it is expected to provide a complete answer to its counterpart FIU within one month of the request being made. In practical terms, nothing prevents the requesting and the requested FIUs to engage in oral consultations during the aforementioned one-month period.[49] In those circumstances that a full reply cannot be given within one month, the requested FIU should provide the partially complete information it obtained to the requesting FIU or indicate the period of time it anticipates to deliver a complete response.[50]

FIUs are expected to establish the proper systemic conditions for the monitoring of request-related information and the tracing of new information that they may receive in regard to those Suspicious Activity Reports having constituted the subject of previous requests. In other words, human intelligence is expected to be intertwined with analytical software for the purpose of delivering smart money laundering and terrorism financing controls even if this entails the recirculation

45 Text to n 34, 3, para 1.8.
46 Text to n 34, 4, para 1.9.
47 Text to n 34, 4, paras 2.1–2.5.
48 Text to n 34, 4, para 2.6(a).
49 Text to n 34, 4, para 2.6(b).
50 Text to n 34, 4, para 2.6(c).

of unresolved Suspicious Activity Reports until the opportunity arises to resolve them by linking them with the appropriate persons and corporations.[51]

The requested FIU has the right to explicitly request its counterpart for feedback as to how it used the intelligence shared. When the requesting FIU is not in a position to provide such a reply, it must state the reasons for which it is unable to provide the feedback to its counterpart. However, knowledge and experience shared in understanding the reasons for which a negative response had to be given can prove to be an asset for future cooperation.[52] The important point to keep in mind is that the exchange of information must take place through the Egmont Secure Web (ESW) at FIU level.[53]

Confidentiality

FIUs are expected to manage[54] the information exchanged with respect to the right to confidentiality and for the specific purpose that the financial and personal data were requested and provided. The confidential management of the information exchanged is thus well founded upon the sound principle that FIUs must have in place a mechanism of strict controls, which not only guarantees the use of the information exchanged in an authorised manner and in conformity with national rules on privacy and data protection, but also prevents unauthorised third parties, such as administrative, investigative, prosecutorial and judicial authorities, from accessing and processing the information exchanged without the express consent of the FIU that disclosed the information.[55]

But there is more to be said about the issue of the secure and confidential handling of the sensitive information exchanged at FIU level, its compatibility with national provisions on privacy and data protection, and the core function of FIUs. It is important to keep in mind that FIUs must assess money laundering and terrorism financing trends and patterns through the use of sophisticated analytical software, provide feedback to reporting institutions and law enforcement authorities on recommended proactive targets, and cooperate with their counterparts.[56]

On the basis of the aforementioned findings, the following three additional issues should be addressed next. First, to understand what the confidential

51 Text to n 34, 4, para 2.7.

52 Text to n 34, 5, para 3.1.

53 Text to n 34, 5, para 3.3.

54 Text to n 34, 5, para 4.1.

55 The Egmont Group, Egmont Group Library: Egmont Documents, 'Information Paper on Financial Intelligence Units and the Egmont Group' (Egmont Group website 2009) 5 <http://www.egmontgroup.org/library/egmont-documents> accessed 28 February 2014.

56 The Egmont Group, Egmont Group Library: Egmont Documents, 'Interpretive Note Concerning the Egmont Definition of a Financial Intelligence Unit' (Egmont Group website 2009) 3, para 3 <http://www.egmontgroup.org/library/egmont-documents> accessed 28 February 2014.

exchange and use of intelligence entails. Second, to appreciate the importance of strengthening and promoting the protection of privacy and personal data by national measures, which must be proportionate to conventional obligations.[57] And, third, to verify where the intelligence exchanged is channelled to, and for what purposes.

The Confidential Exchange and Use of Intelligence

As already pointed out in the beginning of this section, the exchange of financial intelligence enables administrative, law enforcement and prosecutorial authorities in different jurisdictions to resolve money laundering,[58] corruption[59] and terrorism financing[60] cases. FIUs are thus empowered to share with their counterparts both publicly available information and sensitive information under the terms and conditions laid down by national authorities for the protection of the intelligence shared against misuse by unauthorised users.[61]

Therefore, setting aside the obligation of FIUs to function independently, but within the regulatory framework of their own jurisdiction, there is in place the following complementary safety valve for privacy and confidentiality: the consent of the FIU that disclosed the information must be sought in order for that information to be used for a different purpose than the one that was initially sought and provided.[62]

Proportionality

Indeed, the exchange of financial intelligence must take place in conformity with the laws of privacy and data protection of the requested FIU. The protection of the personal and financial data exchanged depends on the obligation imposed by the requested FIU to the requesting FIU. In the result, the requesting FIU must make use of the information received strictly within the processing parameters set by the requested FIU.

At the same time, it is equally imperative to stress that, although national authorities shoulder the burden of enforcing measures that strengthen the protection of privacy and personal data, they are under a conventional obligation to make these measures proportionate so as to not constitute legal impediments to

57 Text to nn 14–16.

58 Guy Dinmore, 'France to Extradite Kazakh Ex-banker' *Financial Times* (London, 10 January 2014) 4.

59 Philip Stephens, 'Riches and Risk: Welcome to the World of Tomorrow' *Financial Times* (London, 10 January 2014) 11.

60 Sam Jones, 'US Reveals Fears of "Virtual" bin Laden' *Financial Times* (London, 10 January 2014) 4.

61 Text to n 56, 3, para 4.

62 Text to n 55, 5.

the cross-border exchange of intelligence for the prevention of terrorism financing. In other words, national rules must not affect the full authority and ability of FIUs to exchange information with their counterparts.[63]

But the aforementioned requirements show two additional aspects of proportionality. The first aspect is well founded upon the international initiative of the Egmont Group to pool together the similar coercive measures of countries against the financing of terrorism. By virtue of any national law against the financing of terrorism, national FIUs are automatically granted full authority and ability to exchange intelligence with their counterparts. Moreover, in such compelling circumstances, national rules protecting privacy and personal data must be temporarily suspended in the interests of disrupting terrorism financing as a predicate offence to money laundering.[64]

The second aspect of proportionality has an operational rationale. The financial and counter-terrorism financing intelligence exchanged is protected by the national provisions on privacy and data protection, and must thus be used by the receiving FIU for the specific purpose that they were sought and provided.[65]

The Channelling of Financial Intelligence

Financial intelligence is channelled to national government agencies around the world in order to solve money laundering and terrorism financing cases, and deliver the proper reports, typologies and trends that enable law enforcement, intelligence and prosecutorial authorities to take the appropriate proactive and reactive actions to disrupt evolving money laundering and terrorism financing techniques.[66]

The information exchanged is therefore channelled to the competent national authorities of the requesting FIUs. What determines the competency of a traditional

---

63 The Egmont Group, Egmont Group Library: Egmont Documents, 'FIU Definition "Countering of Terrorism Financing" Complementary Interpretative Note' (Egmont Group website 2009) 1, paras 4–6 <http://www.egmontgroup.org/library/egmont-documents> accessed 28 February 2014.

64 FinCEN, US Department of the Treasury, 'Department of the Treasury 31 CFR Part 103 RIN 1506 – AB04: Financial Crimes Enforcement Network: Expansion of Special Information Sharing Procedures To Deter Money Laundering and Terrorist Activity' 74 Federal Register 219 (FinCEN website 2009) <http://www.edocket.access.gpo.gov/2009/pdf/E9-27447> accessed 28 February 2014.

65 The Egmont Group, Egmont Group Library: Egmont Documents, 'Principles for Information Exchange Between Financial Intelligence Units for Money Laundering and Terrorism Financing Cases, The Hague, 13 June 2001' (Egmont Group website 2009) 2, para 13 <http://www.egmontgroup.org/library/egmont-documents> accessed 28 February 2014.

66 The Egmont Group, Egmont Group Library: Egmont Documents, 'Statement of Purpose of the Egmont Group of Financial Intelligence Units, Guernsey, 23 June 2004' (Egmont Group website 2009) 1 <http://www.egmontgroup.org/library/egmont-documents> accessed 28 February 2014.

national agency, administrative, investigative, prosecutorial, judicial, hybrid or the joint competency of two or more of the aforementioned types of national agencies to obtain the intelligence received, is the national law of the requesting FIU. Yet it is important to appreciate that, in the result, it is the national law of the requesting FIU and the national law of the requested FIU that will impose strict controls and safeguards on the information shared in order to ensure that the intelligence cannot be further processed[67] in an unauthorised manner that would violate the right to privacy and data protection.[68]

So much is clear in regard to where financial intelligence is channelled to and for what (repressive) purposes. However, it is equally important to appreciate that, on the one hand, by virtue of Article 8 of the European Convention for the Protection of Human Rights and Fundamental Freedoms, public authorities do not interfere with the exercise of the person's right to private and family life, his income and correspondence. On the other hand, when national security, public safety and the economic wellbeing of a country are threatened, data protection laws cannot restrict the exchange of information because the main aim is to prevent disorder and crime, and protect health, morals and the rights and freedoms of others.

In legal and practical terms, it would be impossible if not anecdotal to enter upon a hypothetical discussion of the length of time that law enforcement, intelligence and counter-terrorism agencies around the world would be prepared to remain on alert, and to maintain active electronic files[69] of the leads[70] disclosed by Suspicious Activity Reports or of the intelligence they may have accessed through the exchange of information at FIU level. One may also assume that, in certain cases, it may be in the interests of national security and public safety[71] to not deactivate red flags from databases until the offences that are allegedly hidden behind can be prosecuted.

Case Study: The Hellenic FIU

Recommendation 26 of the FATF (2003 FATF Recommendations)

Responsible governments are expected to fulfil the following four fundamental obligations required in Recommendation 26 of the FATF (2003 FATF

67 Council Framework Decision (EC) 2008/977/JHA of 27 November 2008 on the protection of personal data processed in the framework of police and judicial cooperation in criminal matters [2008] OJ L350/60, Articles 12(1)–(2), 13 and 22.

68 Text to n 193 in chapter 2.

69 Text to n 67, Articles 4–5 and 9(1)–(2).

70 Text to n 6, 29–30, para 65.

71 Barry Rider, Regional Conference on Security and Terrorist Finance, Speech by Barry AK Rider 03/06, 'The Financial War Against Crime and Terror' 20 <http://www.bcra.gov.ar/eventos/ev140000_i.asp> accessed 28 February 2014.

Recommendations)[72] or Recommendation 29 of the FATF as adopted on 15 February 2012.[73] The first obligation is to grant full authority and ability to FIUs by enacting the appropriate national measures. The second is to ensure that FIUs are able to carry out their core function. The third is to provide FIUs with sufficient financial, human and technological resources. And, the fourth is to ensure that FIUs have in place an integrated, operational and securely protected IT database for the gathering, analysis and exchange of intelligence.

These basic conditions were laid down by the FATF with a view to conclusively establish the central position and role of FIUs in the implementation of the international anti-money laundering and counter-terrorism financing strategy. FIUs must therefore have at their disposal sufficient financial, human and IT resources in order to be able to analyse the information they gather from the Suspicious Activity Report Regime, let alone the information that they receive from their counterparts.[74] For this reason, countries are expected to first put their houses in order by establishing independent, sufficiently resourced and sophisticated FIUs, and, thereupon, to participate meaningfully in the international fight against money laundering, the financing of terrorism and proliferation.

The Problem

In February 2008, the FATF placed the Hellenic Republic (Greece) to an enhanced follow-up because the country had received an unusual number[75] of recommendations as partially compliant or non-compliant. In October 2008, the FATF Plenary reviewed the results of the high level mission that visited Greece in September 2008 (FATF/PLEN (2008) 46), and decided that Greece had to provide a full report in October 2009 on the actions taken to strengthen the effectiveness

---

72 FATF–GAFI, 'The 40 Recommendations' (FATF–GAFI website 2009) <http://www.fatf-gafi.org/document/28/0,3343,en_32250379_32236930_33658140_1_1_1_1,00.html#r26> accessed 28 February 2014.

73 FATF, 'International Standards on Combating Money Laundering and the Financing of Terrorism and Proliferation' *FATF* (The FATF Recommendations, February 2012) <http://www.fatf-gafi.org/media/fatf/documents/recommendations/pdfs/FATF_Recommendations.pdf> accessed 20 December 2013.

74 The Egmont Group, Egmont Group Library: Egmont Documents, 'Egmont Group of Financial Intelligence Units Principles for Information Exchange Between Financial Intelligence Units: Approved by the Egmont Group Heads of Financial Intelligence Unites, July 2013' (Egmont Group website 2013) 3–6 <http://www.egmontgroup.org/library/egmont-documents> accessed 24 December 2013.

75 First follow-up report: October 2007; second follow-up report: February 2008; third follow-up report: June 2008; and fourth follow-up report: October 2008.

of the Hellenic FIU. Consequently, in June 2009, Greece was placed on a fifth follow-up because of the serious weaknesses of the Hellenic FIU.[76]

In those compelling circumstances that the FATF warns governments that their FIUs do not satisfactorily comply with the requisite international standard (Recommendation 26), sufficient actions must be taken in remedying the identified deficiencies within a specific period of time. The FATF Mutual Evaluation Report (MER) of Greece, Sixth Follow-Up Report of 12 October 2009, revealed that Greece had failed to comply with Recommendation 26 of the FATF (2003 FATF Recommendations) and that the Greek government had not taken the necessary actions for remedying the deficiencies of its FIU.[77]

The newly established Hellenic FIU was granted extensive powers beyond its core function; it had limited human resources, and a dysfunctional IT system, which seriously impacted the processing of Suspicious Activity Reports.[78] In synopsis, serious concerns were raised in regard to the Greek government's unwillingness to provide sufficient human and IT resources to the FIU over a period of more than two years.

Lack of Proportionality

As the FATF pointed out, the Hellenic FIU was granted extensive law enforcement powers, which enabled it to freeze allegedly criminal and subversive assets for extended periods of time,[79] and to control the accounts of any government agency and enterprise in Greece.[80]

Naturally, the FATF could not make sense of the reasons for which the Greek lawmakers granted these extra powers to the national FIU. First, these powers were clearly disproportionate to the core function of the FIU.[81] Second, they were totally useless in the light of the FIU's limited human resources and the lack of an integrated, operational and securely protected IT database. Third, these extensive powers demonstrated the lack of proportionality[82] of the Greek anti-money laundering regulation in the light of the enactment of the Second Anti-Money Laundering Directive[83] by Law 2331/1995 and its amending Law 3424/2005.

76 FATF–GAFI, Financial Action Task Force Working Group on Evaluations and Implementation, 'Mutual Evaluation of Greece – 6th Follow-up Report' (OECD Headquarters, Paris, France, 12 October 2009) FATF/WGEI (2009) 38, 2, para 1.

77 Text to nn 8 and 23 in chapter 1.

78 Text to n 76, 18, para 81.

79 Text to n 76, 15, para 69.

80 Text to n 76, 15, para 69.

81 Text to nn 41 and 63.

82 Hellenic Criminal Bar Association, *Money Laundering: 'Clean' or Free Society?* (Ant N Sakkoulas Publishers 2007).

83 Directive 2001/97/EC of the European Parliament and of the Council of 4 December 2001 amending Council Directive 91/308/EEC on the prevention of the use of the financial system for the purpose of money laundering [2001] OJ L344/76.

Human Resources and Operational Independence

The FATF confirmed that the FIU's total number of 26 employees was insufficient to enable the unit to discharge its statutory obligations. Furthermore, the representatives seconded by the Ministry of Economy and Finance did not safeguard the FIU's[84] operational independence (The Egmont Group, Best Practices for the Exchange of Information Between Financial Intelligence Units).[85]

The serious concerns raised in regard to the lack of independence of the Hellenic FIU interconnected with the following complementary negative finding. The Suspicious Activity Reports were processed and controlled by the FIU's STR Analysis and Tax Controls Unit, which comprised of one head and 14 analysts, the majority of whom were full-time civil servants seconded by the Ministry of Economy and Finance. In practical terms, the core function of an independent FIU, the gathering, analysis and exchange of intelligence, was questionable in the light of the fact that the leads and raw intelligence of Suspicious Activity Reports were exclusively analysed by operators exclusively seconded by the Ministry of Economy and Finance.

Access to Financial, Administrative and Law Enforcement Intelligence

The FATF pointed out that the Greek authorities indicated that the Hellenic FIU had direct access to information from different registers, such as credit and debit scores (overall indebtedness of borrowers), company information, land ownership, passport and social security, tax, customs and excise, non-EU/UN sanction lists, politically exposed persons, criminal records, and other intelligence from law enforcement authorities.[86] However, the aforementioned indications were not verified by the FATF because it was impossible to evaluate the improvement of the FIU's IT resources in parallel to its ability to discharge its statutory duties to the requisite international standard of Recommendation 26 of the FATF.[87]

In the absence of an integrated, operational and secure database, which enables operators to rapidly gather, process and analyse Suspicious Activity Reports, it is evident that the Hellenic FIU did not have in place sufficient safeguards for the physical and electronic security of the intelligence. In practical terms, the Hellenic FIU did not have in place a secure system of different levels of access to financial and personal data by permitted users.

In summary, it is important to appreciate the following three crucial points in the context of the deficiencies concerning physical and electronic security. First, not all end users should have the same level of direct access to intelligence. Second, in the absence of a secure database, there does not exist the proper mechanism for the

84 Text to n 34.

85 Text to n 76, 16, para 73.

86 Text to n 76, 16, para 74.

87 Text to n 76, 16, para 74.

electronic recording of who, why and when is permitted to access the intelligence of the FIU.[88] Third, FIUs are data-processing entities, which are expected to discretely and confidentially investigate the financial affairs of the data subjects (suspects) in the interests of national security and public safety, but in conformity with international standards on the protection of the personal data processed.[89]

Reports, Typologies and Trends

The FATF concluded that the Hellenic FIU did not produce requisite statistical information, reports, typologies and trends.[90] The particular deficiency could not be rectified at the time because the FIU had to first establish an integrated, operational and securely protected database. The fact that the Hellenic FIU did not publish relevant information on its website[91] at the time of the evaluation because the website was under construction, complementarily indicated the genuine lack of its operational independence. Furthermore, reporting forms were available only for the financial sector.[92] At the same time, the FATF made reference to a few positive developments achieved in regard to a minor increase in the reporting of tax offences, a potential improvement of the quality of the Suspicious Activity Reports received in 2005 and 2006, and a corresponding increase of FIU cases that resulted in prosecutions.[93]

Against that background, it is also necessary to point out that the Greek government did not sufficiently concentrate its efforts to inform and engage private sector reporting entities, let alone to involve private sector stakeholders in a fruitful dialogue with a view to deliver a proportionate and risk-sensitive anti-money laundering and counter-terrorism financing strategy. Moreover, unsatisfactory compliance with Recommendations 12–13 of the FATF (2003 FATF Recommendations) is the second important reason for which the Hellenic FIU failed to explain the low level of reporting suspicious financial activities and the absence of published annual reports on its website.[94]

On this particular point, perhaps, a 'both to blame' clause should equally apply to the Greek government and the Hellenic FIU. On the one hand, the Greek government failed to implement meaningful and proportionate national measures that would have enabled private sector reporters to effectively discharge

88 Text to n 76, 17, paras 74–75.

89 Home Affairs Committee, *Justice and Home Affairs at European Union Level* (HC 2006–07, 76–I) paras 279–280.

90 Text to n 76, 17, para 76.

91 National Crime Agency (NCA), 'Suspicious Activity Reports (SARs) Annual Report 2013' (NCA website 2014) 31–40 <http://www.nationalcrimeagency.gov.uk/publications/94-sars-annual-report-2013/file> accessed 14 January 2014.

92 Text to n 76, 17, para 76.

93 Text to n 76, 17, para 78.

94 Text to n 76, 17, para 79.

their statutory duties. On the other hand, the Hellenic FIU was responsible for having failed[95] to provide sufficient feedback to private sector reporters and law enforcement agencies on sanitised cases and money laundering and terrorism financing typologies.[96]

Cooperation with Counterparts

The FATF reported that the Hellenic FIU was linked to the Egmont Secure Web and to FIU.NET, and that it had signed MOUs with a number of its counterparts. However, these findings could not sufficiently corroborate that the Hellenic FIU was able to cooperate and provide assistance to its counterparts in a rapid, constructive and effective manner in the light of having had a database that was not operational. As the FATF pointed out, the fact that the Hellenic FIU had made only 17 requests for information between January 2009 and July 2009, but had at the same received 57 requests from other FIUs, reflected its substandard performance.[97]

In Synopsis

The findings of the case study confirm the suggestions offered earlier in this chapter. The exchange of financial intelligence in a secured mode makes no sense at all if a national FIU is not operationally independent.

The main criteria for determining the operational independence of FIUs are the following. First, FIUs must not lack sufficient financial, human and IT resources. Second, FIUs must have in place an integrated, sophisticated, operational and securely protected database to be able to carry out their operations. And, third, FIUs must be granted sufficient and proportionate powers to be able to cooperate and exchange information in a rapid, constructive and effective manner. The important legal point to keep in mind is that the power and ability of FIUs to discharge their responsibilities should be conceptually equated with the confidential and electronically secured gathering, processing, retaining and exchange of financial intelligence and personal data.[98]

Indeed, it was unfortunate and disappointing that, at the time, the Greek government failed to work in collective partnership with the administrative, law enforcement, intelligence, judicial and private sector reporters to ensure that the Hellenic FIU would have been operationally independent. In the result, the Greek government rightly shouldered the burden[99] of the Hellenic FIU's unsatisfactory

95 Text to n 76, 17, para 79.

96 Text to n 76, 25, para 140.

97 Text to n 76, 17, para 80.

98 Text to n 76, 19, para 90.

99 FATF–GAFI, *Greece: Fourth Follow-up Report* (FATF/PLEN 2008, 46/REV 1) 2–5.

compliance with the FATF's Recommendations 12–13, 25–26 and 40 (2003 FATF Recommendations).[100]

In October 2011, however, the FATF found that Greece[101] took sufficient actions in remedying the aforementioned deficiencies and that all the Key Recommendations were at a level equivalent to compliant or largely compliant.[102] In March 2011, by Law 3932/2011, the Hellenic FIU (The Anti-Money Laundering, Counter-Terrorist Financing and Source of Funds Investigation Authority) was restructured into the following three individual units: the Financial Intelligence Unit (FIU), the Financial Sanctions Unit (FSU) and the Source of Funds Investigation Unit (SFIU).[103]

100 FATF–GAFI, 'Financial Action Task Force, Mutual Evaluation Interim Follow-Up Report, Anti-Money Laundering and Combating the Financing of Terrorism, Greece, 19 February 2010, Mutual Evaluation of Greece 7th Follow-Up Report' (FATF–GAFI website 2010) <http://www.fatf-gafu.org/dataoecd/23/22/44725108.pdf> accessed 15 November 2010.

101 Law 3691/2008 on Prevention and suppression of money laundering and terrorism financing and other provisions as amended by Law 3932/2011.

102 FATF–GAFI, 'Financial Action Task Force, Mutual Evaluation Tenth Follow-Up Report, Anti-Money Laundering and Combating the Financing of Terrorism, Greece, 28 October 2011, Third Mutual Evaluation of Greece: 10th Follow-Up Report' (FATF–GAFI website 2010) <http://www.fatf-gafi.org/media/fatf/documents/reports/mer/FoR%20Greece.pdf> accessed 15 December 2012.

103 Hellenic F.I.U, 'New Editable Reporting for Credit Institutions (doc/pdf/odt) in Electronic STR Submission – FATF: Mutual Evaluation 10th Follow-Up Report' (Hellenic F.I.U website 2009) <http://www.hellenic-fiu.gr/index.php?lang=en> accessed 10 December 2012.

compliance with the FATF's Recommendations [illegible]

recommendations).

Chapter 7

The Impact of the Retention of Personal Data on the Rights of Unconvicted Persons and the Effects of Financial Regulation on Businesses

Conceptual Distinctions

Delivering effective money laundering controls entails investigating beneath the apparently legitimate surface of transactions to verify the lawful provenance of the funds and the proper motivations of the natural and legal persons concerned. At the same time, the investigation of the financial affairs of those who have allegedly become concerned in the transmogrification of criminal proceeds or the financing of terrorism[1] must take place within the rule of law, with the utmost discretion and confidentiality,[2] and without controversially interfering with the suspect's right to privacy.[3]

The commonly held view is that, in the absence of criminal conduct, those persons and legal entities reported for having allegedly engaged in suspicious activity have nothing to hide from criminal and tax justice, and should thus not fear that the Suspicious Activity Report automatically constitutes evidence of the commission of economic crime.[4] This view is justifiable in the context of financial institutions discharging their statutory duties by generating reports when their clients deposit amounts in cash exceeding €15,000. Assuming that the large currency deposits are truly connected with a legitimate cash business, those who are reported as suspects have nothing to fear from the verification process managed by the national FIU.

Member States are entrusted with the tasks of delivering safe, stable and efficient business environments to all citizens and detecting and disrupting

1 Jeff Breinholt, Deputy Chief, Counterterrorism Section, Criminal Division, US Department of Justice, 'Reaching the White Collar Terrorist: Operational Challenges' (*US Department of Justice Office of Legal Education*, September 2004) 1 <http://www.imf.org,/external/np/leg/sem/2004/cdmfl/eng/breinh.pdf> accessed 28 February 2014.

2 Text to n 6 in chapter 6.

3 Article 8(1) of the ECHR.

4 Text to n 1, 6.

economic crime,[5] which can seriously undermine national security, public safety and economic wellbeing.[6] An effective and proportionate anti-money laundering strategy can strengthen tax justice,[7] redistributive tax policy,[8] accountability[9] and the good stewardship of public wealth[10] on condition that competent authorities operate under the rule of law and make lawful and proportionate use of the actionable intelligence deriving from the raw information submitted by reporting entities.[11]

The Tension

The pressing need to protect the reputation of Member States' financial marketplaces and the integrity of their financial systems triggers the exercise of the right of responsible governments to enact and enforce effective and proportionate anti-money laundering legislation with a view to strengthen and protect the rights and freedoms of others. Similarly, European Union citizens and those who have business interests in the European Union have the right to the protection of wealth and economic prosperity.

While Suspicious Activity Reports are not meant to be routinely retained in a national database for more than 10 years, including those Suspicious Activity Reports that were not justified, serious legal concerns arise in regard to the breach of the person's right to privacy under Articles 8(1) of the ECHR and Article 16(1) of the Lisbon Treaty of the right of everyone to the protection of personal data concerning him or her. Business agreements are made privately and are well founded on the sound principle of the freedom to contract, however, transactions,

---

5 Banking Services Retail Banking (BBR), 'Bank of Tokyo – Mitsubishi UFJ to Pay $250 Million for Money-Laundering Case Settlement' (BBR Staff Writer, 21 June 2013) <http://www.retailbanking.banking-business-review.com/news.bank-of-tokyo-mitsubishi-ufj-to-pay-250m-for-money-laundering-case-settlement-210613> accessed 20 August 2013.

6 Dave Shellock, 'Robust US Jobs Data Weigh on Treasury Prices and Lift Dollar' *Financial Times* (London, 9 January 2014) 27.

7 Martin Wolf, 'Failing Elites Threaten Our Future' *Financial Times* (London, 15 January 2014) 11.

8 Robin Harding, 'Inheritance Should Not be an Alternative to Hard Work' *Financial Times* (London, 8 January 2014), 11.

9 Suzie Neuwirth, 'BlackRock Backs Bolton against Italian Civil Suit' *CITY A.M.* (London, 13 January 2014) 4.

10 Nicholas Paphitis and Derek Gatopoulos, 'Greece to Review Arms Purchases and Bribe Scandal' *AP* (AP website, 3 January 2013) <http://news.yahoo.com/greece-review-arms-purchases-amid-bribe-scandal-172802102--finance.html> accessed 14 February 2013.

11 HM Treasury, 'Delivering Better Regulation Two Years On: HM Treasury's Simplification Plan December 2008' (HM Treasury website 2009) 6, paras 1.16–1.17 <http://www.hm-treasury.gov.uk/d/simplificationplan_101208.pdf> accessed 28 February 2014.

constituting mainly the financial traces of transacting parties and the legitimate proceeds of lawful business arrangements, are carried out through regulated credit and financial institutions.

These intermediary institutions are also private sector reporting entities, and are therefore statutorily obliged to monitor, filter and store the details of financial transactions. Furthermore, financial institutions are obliged to apply Know Your Customer (KYC) controls and due diligence measures in regard to their clients and their counterparts operating in third countries, and to disclose to competent authorities suspicious or unusual transactions even if their doing so results in the suspension of the banking contract.

New Legislative Proposals

The proposed new legal framework for the protection of personal data in the European Union is set out in COM (2012) 9 final,[12] which consists of two separate legislative proposals. A proposal for a Regulation of the European Parliament and of the Council on the protection of individuals in relation to the processing of their personal data and the free movement of such data.[13] And, a proposal for a Directive of the European Parliament and of the Council on the protection of individuals in relation to the processing of personal data by competent authorities for the purposes of prevention, investigation, detection or prosecution of criminal offences or the execution of criminal penalties, and the free movement of such data.[14]

The first legislative proposal, COM (2012) 11 final, is an important instrument in the context of General Data Protection Regulation,[15] but it is not directly relevant

---

12 Commission, 'Communication from the Commission to the European Parliament, the Council, the European Economic and Social Committee and the Committee of the Regions Safeguarding Privacy in a Connected World A European Data Protection Framework for the 21st Century' COM (2012) 9 final.

13 Commission, 'Proposal for a Regulation of the European Parliament and of the Council on the prevention of individuals with regard to the processing of personal data and on the free movement of such data (General Data Protection Regulation)' COM (2012) 11 final.

14 Commission, 'Proposal for a Directive of the European Parliament and of the Council on the protection of individuals with regard to the processing of personal data by competent authorities for the purposes of prevention, investigation, detection or prosecution of criminal offences or the execution of criminal penalties, and the free movement of such data' COM (2012) 10 final.

15 Article 4: genetic data, biometric data, data concerning health, main establishment, enterprise, group of undertakings, binding corporate rules, the child, and the supervisory authority. Article 5: general principles of personal data processing, principles of transparency and data minimisation, and the responsibility and liability of the controller. Article 6: criteria for lawful processing, balance of interest criterion and compliance with legal obligations. Article 7: conditions for consent as legal ground for lawful processing. Article

to the present analytical context because of its General Data Protection character. However, it is important to briefly set out the five main objectives that the European Union aims to achieve through the aforementioned legislative proposal.

First, to introduce harmonised core rules on the right to personal data protection for strict implementation by Member States. Second, to reduce the existing risks of legal fragmentation and uncertainty, which is owed to the implementation of the different national rules of Member States. Third, to facilitate the progressive development of the Internal Market's digital economy and to reduce the existing risks related to online activity. Fourth, to enable individuals to control their own data within a harmonised, transparent, secure and supervised regulatory framework for the processing of personal data and the free movement of such data. Fifth, to enable economic operators and public authorities to perform their functions with legal certainty on the basis of the principles of uniformity, subsidiarity and proportionality.[16]

The Centerpiece of Existing EU Legislation

Directive 95/46/EC[17] of 23 November 1995 is the European Union's General Data Protection Regulation for the protection of the fundamental right to data protection and the free flow of personal data between Member States. Framework Decision 2008/977/JHA[18] is a complementary instrument[19] to the aforementioned General Data Protection Directive, and applies only to cross-border data processing. However, due to the limited scope of its application, Member States are still in a position to implement mainly their own national laws as opposed to strictly implementing the instrument's provisions. In the result, it is not always possible

8: conditions for the lawful processing of personal data for children. Article 9: prohibition of processing of special categories of data. Article 11–15: transparency and modalities. Articles 16–18: rectification and erasure. Articles 19–20: right to object and profiling. Articles 21–29: restrictions and obligations. Articles 30–32: data security. Articles 33–34: data protection impact assessment and prior authorization. Articles 35–30: data protection officer and codes of conduct and certification. Articles 40–45: transfer of personal data to third countries or international organisations. Articles 46–50: independent supervisory authorities. Articles 51–54: duties and powers of supervisory authorities. Articles 55–63: cooperation and consistency. Articles 64–72: European Data Protection Board. Articles 73–79: remedies, liability and sanctions. Articles 80–85: specific data processing situations.

16 Text to n 13, 1–16.

17 Council Directive 95/46/EC of the European Parliament and of the Council of 24 October 1995 on the protection of individuals with regard to the processing of personal data and on the free movement of such data [1995] OJ L281/31.

18 Text to n 67 in chapter 6.

19 Commission, 'Proposal for a Regulation of the European Parliament and of the Council on the prevention of individuals with regard to the processing of personal data and on the free movement of such data (General Data Protection Regulation)' COM (2012) 11 final, 1.

to distinguish between domestic and cross-border processing of personal data, let alone that it is not always clear whether certain personal data may be exchanged at a later stage at the cross-border level.[20]

The Problem

Financial institutions are obliged to monitor and keep records of all transactions in the interests of tracing and reporting alleged offences. But when financial institutions do not have in place the proper safeguards to protect their clients' right to financial privacy,[21] they automatically expose their clients to the risk of unlawful disclosures of confidential financial information and trade secrets by insiders.

It is therefore important to appreciate that all clients, not only those who are reported for alleged wrongdoing, are exposed to this risk despite the fact that they engage in legitimate financial transactions involving funds that are not interconnected with money laundering or with the financing of terrorism. The other aspect of the problem that is addressed in this chapter concerns those persons who are reported and accused for wrongdoing, but are not convicted or are granted a discharge. The personal data of these affected persons is often retained and moved by competent authorities regardless of their acquittal.

The gathering and processing of actionable intelligence often controversially interferes with the unconvicted person's right to privacy due to the disproportionate or abusive practices of the data controllers. It is thus the disproportionate retention and movement of personal data, not financial intelligence per se, that has given rise to legal and philosophical concerns in regard to the so-called presumption of innocence.[22]

Stated differently, what we are actually dealing with may be the disproportionate, unfair and unacceptable operability of the cycle of intelligence, which may be owed to the overzealous implementation of a strategy to prevent and prosecute all crimes at the national and transnational levels. For it would be anecdotal to suggest that the law of personal data protection provides for the indefinite retention of personal data and the free movement of such sensitive data with a view to violate the human rights and the freedoms of innocent people.

The retention of fingerprints, cellular samples and DNA profiles by law enforcement authorities after the acquittal of accused persons or the discontinuance of proceedings against them has prompted serious legal concerns. The interference

20 Commission, 'Proposal for a Directive of the European Parliament and of the Council on the protection of individuals with regard to the processing of personal data by competent authorities for the purposes of prevention, investigation, detection or prosecution of criminal offences or the execution of criminal penalties, and the free movement of such data' COM (2012) 10 final, 3.

21 Text to nn 111–114 in chapter 3.

22 *Sheldrake v DPP and Attorney General's Reference* (No 4 of 2002) [2004] UKHL 43, [2005] 1 AC 264, [2004] 3 WLR 976, [2005] 1 All ER 237.

with the rights[23] of unconvicted persons is owed to the disproportionate and erroneous application of Article 8(2) of the ECHR. It is against that particular background that the next section aims to enquire deeper into the controversial interference with the unconvicted person's right to privacy.

The Impact of the Retention and Movement of Personal Data on the Rights of Unconvicted Persons

The retention of sensitive financial information and personal data on the ELMER database when the financial investigation of data subjects has verified that the initial self-induced suspicion was unfounded, is unfair, unnecessary and, above all, incompatible with the ECHR.[24] As we will have the opportunity to ascertain from sources of jurisprudence and authority, there are in place national statutes[25] and international instruments,[26] known as protect and enhance instruments, for the limitation of the excessive powers of the Police National Computer (PNC) data controllers being responsible for the retention of the personal information of data subjects and the deletion of such sensitive data from nominal records.

On the one hand, the State shoulders the heavy burden of establishing an effective mechanism, which rapidly gathers, processes and disseminates financial intelligence from different sources, such as reporters, law enforcement authorities, intelligence agencies, judicial authorities, tax authorities, the national FIU and foreign FIUs. On the other hand, as pressing these social and political needs may be, the State also shoulders the burden of striking a fair balance between public and private interests. Therefore, in the interests of elementary fairness, neither the police nor government agencies should be allowed to retain and process the fingerprints and the DNA samples of unconvicted persons.

---

23 Articles 7, 11, 16, 42 and 47 of the Charter on Fundamental Rights of the European Union; Article 1(1) of Directive 95/46/EC.

24 House of Lords, *European Union Committee 19th Report of Session 2008–09 Money Laundering and the Financing of Terrorism* (HL 2008–09, 132–I) 50, paras 180–181 (HL website 2009) <http://www.publications.parliament.uk/pa/ld200809/ldselect/ldeucom/132/132i.pdf> accessed 28 February 2014.

25 Sections 13, 40, 47 and 55 of the Data Protection Act adopted by the UK on 16 July 1998 to implement Directive 95/46/EC; sections 61, 63 and 64(1A) of Police and Criminal Evidence Act 1984 (the latter section substituted by section 82 of the Criminal Justice and Police Act 2001); and the Retention Guidelines for Nominal Records on the Police National Computer 2006, Appendix 2.

26 Articles 5–7 of the Council of Europe Convention of 1981 on the protection of individuals with regard to the automatic processing of personal data (the Data Protection Convention), which entered into force in the UK on 1 December 1987; Principles 2, 3 and 7 of Recommendation No R(87) 15; Principles 3–4 and 8 of Recommendation No R(92) 1; and paras 47 and 49–50 of the Explanatory Memorandum to the Recommendation as regards item 8 on the storage of samples and data of Recommendation No R(92) 1.

Of course, there is more to be said in regard to that heavy burden of striking a fair balance between public and private interests in a democratic society. Member States are not prevented from implementing national rules that reduce the risks of the abuse of personal data; the indefinite retention and the legally unjustified movement of such sensitive data; and the wide accessibility[27] of such data to different public authorities and private groups.

By virtue of Article 8(1) of the ECHR, private interests are guaranteed because every person has the right to respect for his private and family life, his home and correspondence.[28] However, by virtue of Article 8(2) of the ECHR, under compelling circumstances, but well within the limits of compatibility with the Convention, the equally guaranteed public interests may modestly, but not controversially, interfere with the person's exercise of the right to privacy for the protection of the rights and freedoms of others.[29]

The European Court of Justice has ruled that the protection of personal data in the Union is a right that is not absolute.[30] Similarly, the legislative proposal set out in COM (2012) 10 final[31] has clarified that the right to the protection of personal data must be treated in relation to its function in society. The Union's new legislative proposals[32] are therefore in line with Article 52(1) of the Charter on Fundamental Rights, which foresees that limitations may be imposed on the exercise of the right to data protection on condition that these limitations: are provided for by law, the limitations respect the rights and freedoms, and subject to their proportionality, they serve the need to protect the rights and freedoms of others (general public interest).

In the result, the right to protection of personal data is not absolute in those compelling circumstances that competent authorities must process and move personal data for the purposes of prevention, investigation or prosecution of criminal offences or the execution of criminal penalties.[33] However, it is equally crucial to appreciate that the retention and movement of the personal data of accused persons after the termination of criminal proceedings against them due to acquittal or discontinuance is unfair and illegal.

---

27 *S and Marper v the United Kingdom* App nos 30562/04 and 30566/04 (ECtHR, 4 December 2008) para 87.

28 European Commission, Freedom – Security and Justice – Justice and Home Affairs, Data Protection – The Law – Treaty on the European Union, 'European Convention for the Protection of Human Rights and Fundamental Freedoms, Article 8' (Europa website 2009) <http://www.ec.europa.eu/Justice_home/fsj/privacy/law/treaty_en.htm> accessed 28 February 2014.

29 Text to n 27.

30 Joined Cases C – 92/09 and 93/09 *Volker und Markus Schecke and Eifert* [2010] ECR I–0000.

31 Text to nn 2–3, 20.

32 Text to nn 12–13, 20.

33 Text to n 20.

In line therefore with Article 52(1) of the Charter on Fundamental Rights, the unconvicted person's right to the protection of personal data is absolute because the compelling circumstances to protect national security, public safety, the economic wellbeing of the country, the protection of health or morals, and the protection of the rights and freedoms of others no longer exist and thus do not justify the subsequent imposition of any limitations whatsoever. In the light of the accused person's acquittal or discontinuance of proceedings, competent authorities are no longer justified to retain and move the fingerprints, cellular samples and DNA profiles of the data subject. Consequently, the retention and moving of such data constitutes a substantial and controversial interference with the person's right to private life.[34]

But the interference with the fundamental right to private life[35] also interconnects with the negative effect[36] on the data subject's psychological integrity because the sensitive information retained in nominal records and the free movement of such information becomes fully and permanently available to third parties, let alone that the data subject loses total control over the personal data. Consequently, the affected person's fundamental right at stake is all the more important to the effective enjoyment of intimate rights.[37]

Of course, serious legal concerns arise in regard to the damage that unconvicted persons may suffer as a result of social stigmatisation. Accused but unconvicted persons are entitled to the presumption of their innocence. But after their fair trial, unconvicted persons are equally entitled to be treated in a way that evidences the restitution of their innocence and the elimination of suspicion of guilt. This is the legal therapy that the State is expected to offer to unconvicted persons, which must differ from that offered to convicted persons.[38] The State is expected to lay the foundations for the social reintegration of unconvicted persons. It is therefore important to appreciate that, when such sensitive personal information[39] is made public and in a way that persons are identifiable,[40] then it is only legally reasonable to characterise the interference as being neither modest nor compatible with the ECHR.[41]

The other central issue that should be addressed is whether the provision of Article 8(2) of the ECHR is applicable in those compelling circumstances that the

34 *S and Marper* (n 27), para 87.

35 Case 11/70 *Internationale Handelsgesellschaft mbH v Einfuhr and Vorratsstelle fur Getreide und Futtermittel* [1970] ECR I–1125, para 4.

36 *Connors v the United Kingdom* App no 66746/01 (ECtHR, 27 May 2004) para 82.

37 Consolidated Version of the Treaty on European Union (TEU) of 9 May 2008 [2008] OJ C115/13, Article 6(1).

38 *Asan Rushiti v Austria* App no 28389/95 (ECtHR, 21 March 2000) para 31.

39 Multiple aspects of the person's physical and social identity, such as gender identification, ethnic identity, name and sexual orientation, sexual life, and family links.

40 *S and Marper* (n 27), para 66.

41 *ASML Netherlands BV v Semiconductor Industry Services GmbH (SEMIS)* App no 283/05 (ECtHR, 28 September 2006) para 26.

State must prevent serious crime and protect the rights and freedoms of others. The second paragraph of Article 8 of the ECHR distinguishes between the general provision of law in the first paragraph in regard to the protection of the person's rights and freedoms, the so-called private interests; and the specific provision of law in regard to the prevention of crime and the protection of the rights and freedoms of others, the so-called public interests.

Moreover, Article 8(2) of the ECHR does not expressly provide that the protection of the rights of others must be achieved without respect to subsidiarity and proportionality[42] or by treating unconvicted persons in the same way that convicted persons are treated. The retention and movement of the decoded personal data of persons suspected but not convicted of offences after acquittal is the major cause of their unfair exposure to automated means of sensitive data access and processing by government departments and private groups.[43]

By way of summary, four main ideas lie behind this central issue. The first is that suspicion is legally unacceptable after the accused's acquittal. Beyond acquittal or discontinuance of criminal proceedings, the application of Article 8(2) is erroneous and contrary to the rule of law because unconvicted persons are entitled to the fundamental or justiciable classic right[44] of the presumption of their innocence after trial.

The second is that the retention and movement of the fingerprints, cellular samples and DNA profiles of unconvicted persons is not compatible with the ECHR because it controversially interferes with the fundamental right to private life of innocent persons. The expansion of the database by the retention and subsequent processing and movement of the personal data of unconvicted persons is unfair, disproportionate and does not offer any advantages[45] in the fight against serious crime and the financing of terrorism. After all, the database was established for the purposes of restricting convicted persons, investigating and prosecuting persons for criminal offences, and facilitating the execution of criminal penalties. Unconvicted persons are innocent persons and do not interconnect with any of the aforementioned three purposes.

The third is that suspects, accused and unconvicted persons have guaranteed rights and freedoms under the European Union's Justice and Home Affairs framework. The legal tension and the controversial and disproportionate interference with the unconvicted person's right to privacy is not owed to the ineffectiveness of financial regulation or to the unfair nature and character of the existing laws governing the retention and movement of personal data, but rather to

---

42 *Coster v the United Kingdom* App no 24876/94 (ECtHR, 28 January 2001) para 104.

43 *S and Marper* (n 27), paras 106, 110 and 125.

44 House of Lords, *European Union Committee 10th Report of Session 2007–08 The Treaty of Lisbon: An Impact Assessment* (HL 2007–08, 62–I), para 5.17 (HL website 2008) <http://www.parliament.th-stationery-office.co.uk/oa/Id200708/Idselect/Ideucom/62/6209.htm#a117> accessed 28 February 2014.

45 *LS, R (on application of) v South Yorkshire Police* [2004] UKHL 39, para 38.

the unfair and abusive practices of the data controllers. As we had the opportunity to review in this chapter, the time has come for the European Union to introduce harmonised core rules on the right to personal data protection that will reduce the existing risks of legal fragmentation and legal uncertainty.

The fourth and last is that England, Wales and Northern Ireland appear to be the only jurisdictions in the Council of Europe that allow the indefinite retention and movement of the personal data of suspects and unconvicted persons. The government's overzealous commitment to prevent and prosecute of all forms of serious criminal conduct should not be associated with the fallacious view that financial regulation and the law of financial intelligence are to blame for the negative impacts on the rights and freedoms of unconvicted persons.[46]

The Effects of Financial Regulation on Businesses

This section extends the discussion beyond the suggestions offered in chapters 3 and 4 that the current trend is corruption and that we are actually dealing with evolving transparency laws. It aims to deliver a critical analysis on how businesses are affected by financial regulation with a particular focus on the way that regulated entities have been statutorily transformed from entirely profit-making enterprises and institutions into reporters and good corporate citizens.[47] The effects of financial regulation on businesses derive from the peculiar social interaction of two major parties working in collective partnership to prevent and control crime and terror: the State representing the public sector, and financial institutions and enterprises representing the private sector.

On the one hand, the State shoulders the heavy burden of protecting national security, public safety, public and private wealth. The State must thus deliver prudential regulation and ensure that the measures it implements are effective and proportionate so as to prevent negative effects on the competitiveness of its financial marketplace and unnecessary interference with the free flow of trade.[48] On the other hand, financial institutions and other regulated enterprises shoulder the heavy burden of prudentially minding other people's money and disclosing alleged offences to competent authorities in order to discharge their statutory duties and maintain their immunity under the existing regulatory framework.

As we already had the opportunity to review in Chapter 5, the basic condition for minimising the risks of exposure to sanctions under the criminal and civil statutes is the confidential and rapid submission of well founded Suspicious

---

46 *S and Marper* (n 27), paras 47–48 and 67.

47 Text to n 175 in chapter 2, 10.

48 *Bank of Scotland v A Ltd* [2001] EWCA Civ 52, [2001] 1 WLR 751; *Amalgamated Metal Trading Ltd v City of London Police Financial Investigation Unit* [2003] EWHC 703 Comm, [2003] 1 WLR 2711; and *K Ltd v National Westminister Bank Plc* [2006] EWCA Civ 1039 (CA).

Activity Reports by reporters to national FIUs, which must take place in the process of the exercise of their financial and entrepreneurial duties. After all, the efficacy of anti-money laundering legislation partly depends on the quality of the controls supervisory authorities exercise upon financial institutions and regulated entities to verify that they sufficiently discharge their statutory duties.

The Main Effects

Financial intelligence can be used in court to prove the deliberate and dishonest choice of defendants or respondents to violate existing regulation for the record keeping of transactions in order to conceal unlawful conduct for profit or otherwise; forge documents in order to cheat the tax authorities; and transmogrify criminal property through bogus transactions that are not properly motivated.

Another aspect of the same effect on businesses is that the financial information gathered and processed by the national FIU is used to guide private sector reporters in regard to actions taken by regulators to prevent specific forms of disguised criminal conduct. In other words, there exists an open line of communication between efficient regulators and prudential businesses, which not only guides businesses on the latest repressive developments, but also constitutes a reliable source for important lessons to be learned from the wrongdoing and the sanctioning of those who engage in economic crime and the financing of terrorism.

A different but equally important effect is that of obliging businesses to prudentially mind their own financial resources and other people's money through the one-way statutory direction. More specifically, today's businesses are statutorily obliged to show zero tolerance towards exploring possibilities of intermingling criminal property with legitimate funds. Businesses are expected to report other entities or persons whose conduct triggers the suspicion of potential participation in arrangements to launder criminal proceeds potentially emanating from corruption, bribery, fraud,[49] tax evasion and insider dealing.[50]

But there is more to be said about certain additional effects that derive from the aforementioned impact on businesses. The first is that financial regulation has imposed on businesses the responsibility to postulate a new mental model for understanding what constitutes a law-abiding and transparent business conduct. Clearly, the prevailing norm is that of engaging in legitimate financial transactions involving funds that are not interconnected with money laundering or with the financing of terrorism but not failing to report self-induced suspicion.

The second is that the aforementioned international mental model, which is well founded upon transparency standards, anti-money laundering rules and anti-corruption measures, has boosted the evolution of traditional business models. Today's businesses can no longer afford to be unsuspicious of what is financially

49 *The Economist*, 'White-Collar Trials: Subcrime' (2009) 393 (8657) 84.

50 Andy Sharman and Sam Fleming, 'Morrison Suspends Treasurer after His Arrest in Insider Dealing Probe' *Financial Times* (London, 21 January 2014) 15.

taking place around them, for it would be socially irresponsible on their part to do so. Financial institutions and companies cannot simply mind their own business in the traditional meaning of the term by overlooking wrongdoing because they are expected to demonstrate social responsibility within a globalised business environment, which is closely and continuously monitored by international supervisory authorities and international standard-setting fora.

The third additional effect is that, in the light of the institutionalisation of self-induced suspicion, today's businesses are less susceptible to engagement in money laundering because they can no longer fallaciously presume that they do not risk being reported for alleged offences by other national and international competitors who are also obliged reporting entities. Financial regulation has therefore imposed the responsibility on businesses to be transparent and to adopt international business ethics that are inseparable from the broader notion of being continuously on alert and suspicious of others.

Against that background, two last propositions are offered. The first is that the mandatory engagement of credit and financial institutions in the reporting system affects businesses in a unique way. The statutory engagement links the reporters' performance with qualitative indicators. More specifically, internal and external compliance controls and regulatory impact assessments constitute the mirror reflections of the reporters' abilities to effectively distinguish between what is suspicious and worthy to report for the disruption of the criminal enterprise,[51] and what is plainly unusual but not indicative of alleged criminal conduct.

The second is that today's businesses have to shoulder the burden of the high costs of compliance. In the United Kingdom, approximately £40,000,000,000[52] is spent every year to comply with financial regulation and to contribute to the international efforts to combat organised crime[53] and terrorism.[54] The financial services employment in the United Kingdom has grown at its fastest rate since 2007 (10,000 staff were hired in the three months to December 2013) because financial institutions must meet the demands of the regulatory agenda[55] while rebuilding their balance sheets.

In conclusion, today's businesses enjoy their freedom to contract privately but their transactions, the financial traces of their private financial arrangements,

---

51 HM Treasury, 'Money Laundering Regulations 2007: Regulatory Impact Assessment 07/2007' 4, para 1.16.

52 Barry Rider, 'A Serious Problem' (2004) 11 JFC 4, 311.

53 Jane Wild and Vanessa Houlder, 'UK Reviews Tax on Bitcoin as Global Regulators Seek to Cash in' *Financial Times* (London, 20 January 2014) 1.

54 Sam Jones, Borzou Daraghi and Simeon Kerr, 'On the March Al-Qaeda Terror Affiliates are Active in More Countries than Ever' *Financial Times* (London, 20 January 2014) 7; Kathrin Hille, 'Islamists Boast of Volgograd Raid in Warning to Olympics' *Financial Times* (London, 21 January 2014) 8.

55 Brian Groom, Business and Employment Editor, 'Financial Sector Sees Jobs Boom' *Financial Times* (London, 20 January 2014) 3; Thomas Hale, 'Recruiters' Net Fees Rise as Confidence Gets to Work' *Financial Times* (London, 21 January 2014) 21.

take place through regulated financial intermediaries. As a result, the transactions of persons and companies cannot escape the enhanced due diligence measures mandatorily applied by financial institutions without offering proper justifications and revealing confidential financial information and trade secrets to financial institutions. It is therefore impossible for natural and legal persons to structure their business in a way that escapes money laundering or tax evasion controls by making use of tax havens, splitting taxable profits between jurisdictions, eroding tax revenues and out-trading competitors.[56] Furthermore, it is not feasible to conduct business in a way that can avoid the suspicion of financial intermediaries unless there is facilitation from within.

Today's professionals and enterprises seek to structure and conduct business in a way that neither triggers the self-induced suspicion of credit and financial institutions nor provokes the prolongation of potential financial investigations. Financial regulation has imposed the obligation on natural and legal persons to have in place the proper documentation evidencing the lawful provenance of the funds involved and their innocent and reasonable motivations, which may be put to the test at various stages by financial institutions and competent authorities.

The particular impact undoubtedly interferes with the right of businesses to privacy of financial information and trade secrecy. Nevertheless, those persons and corporations lacking the proper documentation and the proper motivations to evidence the legality of their transactions will risk exposure to delays arising from the internal controls of financial institutions or the money laundering controls of existing legislation.[57] After all, financial regulation does not aim to harm legitimate business interests or prevent healthy competition[58] in financial markets. On the contrary, financial regulation aims to promote and protect economic growth in a way that prevents and controls crime and terror.

Due to the technological advancements and the rapid digitalisation of economies, today's Internet, hardware and software companies have been transformed into channels for the transfer of user data to intelligence agencies. IT businesses take advantage of their privileged position to the extent that they abuse their storage powers by tracking what their clients buy, store and use for commercial purposes. As a result, this negative direct link between government surveillance and the abusive techniques of digital advertising companies demonstrates the substantial

56 Vanessa Houlder, 'Tech Groups Tax Crackdown Seen as Unviable' *Financial Times* (London, 21 January 2014) 3.

57 Angela Veng Mei Leong, 'Anti-Money Laundering Measures in the United Kingdom: A Review of Recent Legislation and FSA Risk-based Approach' (2007) 28 Comp Law 2, 35.

58 Text to n 56, 3 (case study showing how digital companies' revenues can move across tax regimes through structural changes).

and controversial interference with the person's rights to private life, privacy of communication, and financial information and trade privacy.[59]

Sadly, the scandal in the United States with regard to Internet metadata surveillance and computer security demonstrates that the challenges to privacy came from Washington (NSA) and Silicon Valley (storage of user data). The two-year inquiry to investigate the way governments make use of Internet data following the mass surveillance by the United States and its allies can be an asset for laying down laws to protect human rights online and ensure stability on the Internet.[60]

This divorce between accountability and power can be prevented in the Union if European policy-makers fully appreciate that, since power is concentrated in the hands of the governments of the creditor countries and their top companies holding unspent corporate cash,[61] the European Commission, the European Central Bank, and the International Monetary Fund, there are pressing needs to ensure that the measures to be introduced in the Union will not allow any room for the misuse of financial intelligence as it was revealed in the United States.

59 Richard Waters, 'Obama Drags Tech Companies Deeper into Mire Surveillance' *Financial Times* (London, 21 January 2014) 6.

60 Sam Jones and John Gapper, 'Expert Panel to Investigate Internet Governance' *Financial Times* (London, 23 January 2014) 9.

61 Anousha Sakoui, 'Concentrated $2.8tn Cash Pile Puts Global Recovery in the Hands of the Few' *Financial Times* (London, 22 January 2014) 1, 21.

Chapter 8
Conclusion

The starting point for reshaping anti-money laundering policy has always been, and, will always be, the understanding of the different techniques criminals use to introduce their ill-gotten gains into the legitimate financial system.[1] In the concluding chapter of his book on criminal finance, Dr Kris Hinterseer emphasised, amongst other things, the high speed which with information and electronic money can move from one jurisdiction to another.[2]

In 2009, Professor Iain Cameron of Uppsala University submitted in written evidence to the House of Lords Select Committee on the European Union, Sub-Committee F, that New York's InterBank System handled daily some 200,000 payments totalling $1,100,000,000,000.[3] The Director of UKFIU, SOCA, drew the Committee's attention to the fact that SOCA processed some 200,000 Suspicious Activity Reports in 2008, which accrued to the total figure of 1,500,000 Suspicious Activity Reports.[4]

By way of comparison, in 2013, Jennifer Shasky Calvery, Director of Financial Crimes Enforcement Network, US Department of the Treasury, stated before the US Senate Committee on Homeland Security and Government Affairs that, according to 2012 figures, the Bank of America processed $224,400,000,000,000 in wire transfers; PayPal processed some $145,000,000,000; Western Union remitted approximately $81,000,000,000; the Automated Clearing House Network processed some 21,000,000,000 transactions with a total value of $36,900,000,000; and Fedwire processed 132,000,000 large-scale wholesale transactions with a total value of $599,000,000,000,000.[5] Moreover, FinCEN's Director underlined that, according to the United Nations Office on Drugs and Crime (UNODC), in 2009, the amount of global criminal proceeds available for laundering through the legitimate financial system amounted to $1,600,000,000,000.

What can perhaps match the high speed of the movement of information, electronic and virtual money through different jurisdictions, is preventive thinking in regard to the increasing impact of two equally evolving parallel forces. On the hand, the technological advancements, the sophistication of financial instruments,

1 Robert Wardle, 'Money Laundering: A Prosecutor's Perspective' (1999) 3 JMLC 2, 125.

2 Text to n 3 in chapter 1, 387.

3 Text to n 74 in chapter 1, para 74.

4 Text to n 15 in chapter 1, 37.

5 Text to n 175 in chapter 2, 7.

and the rapid growth of the digital economy. On the other hand, the evolving sophistication of money laundering and asset cloaking techniques.[6]

European Union anti-money laundering legislation is well founded upon the 12 conceptual objectives reviewed in Chapter 1 and tested in Chapter 2 by reference to existing instruments and the forthcoming Fourth Anti-Money Laundering Directive in the light of COM (2013) 45 final. In their totality, these conceptual objectives enable Member States to prevent and control economic crime and the financing of terrorism from all possible repressive angles: serious criminality and organised crime groups, legal persons and legal arrangements used as vehicles by criminals; those public servants and officials abusing their positions of trust; private sector employees abusing their positions of trust from within financial institutions and enterprises; and NCCTs providing safe harbours to organised crime and terrorism and wilfully looking the other way when their government agencies and front companies[7] get involved in illicit financial activities.

We also had the opportunity to consider the four main justifications for the extension of the global anti-money laundering regime: the war on drugs, the war on organised crime, the war on the financing of terrorism, and the war on illicit enrichment currently evolving. The implementation of the international anti-money laundering and counter-terrorism financing standards aims to deliver effective, proportionate, risk-sensitive and, hopefully, cost-effective financial regulation in the future.

Responsible governments and prudential regulators deliver effective money laundering controls that disrupt the criminal enterprise and ensure that crime neither pays nor funds criminality and terror. The reporting and the exchange of information systems constitute the central, suspicious and vigilant eye of the global anti-money laundering regime. Without disclosures of alleged offences by private sector reporters and operationally independent FIUs to manage disclosures, the aforementioned central eye will become legally and operationally useless.

Effective money laundering controls also enable prosecutors to place under the reach of the law property that cannot be reasonably and truthfully explained by persons accused of laundering criminal proceeds. As long as the property remains unexplained in court by defendants and respondents, it cannot but represent the proceeds of crime, and, consequently, remain well within the reach of the law for recovery purposes. Today's prosecutors are not expected to establish the nexus

---

6 FATF–GAFI Financial Action Task Force on Money Laundering, 'Methodology for Assessing Compliance with the FATF 40 Recommendations and the FATF 9 Special Recommendations 27 February 2004 (Updated as of February 2009)' 3–74 (FATF website 2009) <http://www.fatf-gafi.org/dataoecd/16/54/40339628.pdf> accessed 28 February 2014.

7 US Department of the Treasury FinCEN, 'Advisory FIN-2009-A002 Issued: June 18, 2009 (Amended 18 December 2009) Subject: North Korea Government Agencies' and Front Companies' Involvement in Illicit Financial Activities' 1–3 (FinCEN website 2009) <http://www.fincen.gov/statutes_regs/Guidance/pdf/fin-2009-a002.pdf> accessed 28 February 2014.

between the wealth seized and a specific crime. If they were expected to establish the opposite, criminal assets would simply remain beyond the reach of the law.

At the same time, it is equally useful to bear in mind that the picture of the fabric of societies that is drawn by Article 8(2) of the ECHR is a blend of legal, social, political and economic interests at stake, such as national security, public safety, economic wellbeing, health and morals, and the rights and freedoms of citizens. From the perspective of the international initiatives taken to establish the global regulatory framework against money laundering and the financing of terrorism, chapters 1–4 emphasised a number of important legal issues, which may be summarised as follows.

Internationalism should be conceptually approached as the reflection of States' decentralised normative atrophy in contradistinction to international organisations' centralised standard-setting powers. There are two alternative justifications to consider for the explanation of this phenomenon. Either the normative powers of States were absorbed by the FATF as a result of States' volition to improve justice in the world economy or States allowed their normative powers to be absorbed by the FATF with a view to control the redistribution of global wealth through the FATF's standard-setting mechanism.

International cooperation against economic crime should be conceptually equated with the initiatives taken at the international level to combat the different forms of illicit enrichment in the light of evolving international standards on transparency. The current mental model postulated by States to understand the significance of promoting global economic wellbeing is partly interconnected with the concept of the prevention and control of money laundering as a substantive and acquisitive offence. Money laundering is internationally perceived as the main gate between the formal and the informal economies.

One cannot but confirm that the initiatives taken by the OECD, the Council of Europe and the United Nations constitute drastic blows against domestic and international bribery; public and private corruption; peculation of public wealth; and fraud. From a macroscopic perspective, the initiatives of the United Nations (the UNCAC and the UNTOC) and the Council of Europe (the Council of Europe 2005 Convention) to enhance international cooperation against money laundering, corruption, terrorist financing, organised crime, and trafficking in human beings and sexual exploitation, should be appreciated because they are well founded upon the following triptych: standard setting; monitoring compliance in parallel to evolving standards; technical cooperation for capacity building.

Intergovernmental cooperation to make financial systems hostile environments to transnational crime and terror aims, amongst other things, to minimise the risks of unintentionally reversing criminal trends from fully FATF-compliant jurisdictions to those jurisdictions that have partly adopted the international standards or are more vulnerable to the threats posed by organised crime and corruption due to geographical, social and political peculiarities.

The fact that today's objectives for the prosecutorial toll are hypertrophied, but remain well within the limits of proportionality with the ECHR for the purpose of prosecuting and sanctioning economic crime, is neither coincidental nor unexplainable. One of the most important purposes of anti-money laundering regulation is to maintain orderly, reputable, prudential and transparent financial markets within which individuals and corporations can create taxable wealth that can be reinvested. At the same time, two important factors should not escape critical assessment. With this proposition in mind, it should make better sense that, in the Third World Summit of Prosecutors General, Attorneys General and Chief Prosecutors, crime prevention and criminal justice policies were conceptually approached as the master key to sustainable economic and social development.

The central issue that Directive 2005/60/EC, Regulation (EC) 1889/2005 on controls of cash entering or leaving the Community, and Regulation (EC) 1781/2006 on information on the payer accompanying transfers of funds, have shifted responsibility to financial institutions and other obliged entities to disclose alleged offences to national FIUs involves two sets of important factors that merit to be taken into final consideration.

The first set of factors concerns the three legislative achievements of the European Union. First, the Third Anti-Money Laundering Directive consolidated the previous two Directives but introduced in the Union the FATF's 40 Recommendations on money laundering and the 9 Recommendations on terrorist financing. Second, due to the fact that Directive 2005/60/EC does not apply directly to natural and legal persons, it was used as the main instrument for the imposition of the obligation on Member States to harmonise their national rules on the basis of the FATF's 40 Recommendations on money laundering and the 9 Recommendations on terrorist financing.

Third, the Directive 2005/60/EC not only called upon Member States to statutorily oblige financial and other obliged entities to verify and record their clients' identities, continuously train their personnel to trace suspicious activities, qualitatively assess their employees' level of distinguishing between normal and anomalous activities, and report suspicious activities to competent authorities, which in legal terms, legalised the extroversion of self-induced suspicion and consolidated the starting point for financial intelligence, but also laid down six fundamental principles against money laundering that are briefly summarised in the second set of factors that follows next.

The second set of factors concerns six core principles incorporated into European Union anti-money laundering law. Uniform and broadened scope of application; application of CDD measures; risk-based approach; application of simplified CDD measures; application of enhanced CDD measures; and reliance on regulated third parties.

Anti-money laundering legislation applies to traders in goods or services when payments are made in cash in excess of €15,000 and to providers of trust and company services. Consequently, money laundering activity through traders and intermediaries remains under strict controls.[8] The intermediaries are thus obliged to

8 Directive 2005/60/EC, Preambular Text, para 9.

apply enhanced CDD measures by verifying and storing their clients' identification and maintaining records of ultimate beneficial owners. The particular principle appears to interfere with the individual's exercise of the right to information privacy in regard to the acquisition of trusts and companies, but the interference in this case is modest and proportionate because it does not aim to make the relevant information publicly available. The aim here is to enable reporters and competent authorities to assess whether the nature and the purpose of particular business relationships justifies suspicion and reporting.

There are four main compelling circumstances under which CDD measures are applied: when a business relationship is established; when an occasional transaction amounts to €15,000 or more (irrespective of whether the transaction is structured in a number of operations); when a professional suspects that the customer is engaging in money laundering or terrorist financing irrespective of the threshold amount involved; and when serious concerns arise in regard to the sufficiency of the client's identification data obtained in the first place.[9]

The Directive has imposed three obligations on trust and company service providers: to fully understand the ownership and control structure of their customers;[10] to gather information on the nature and propose of the business relationship; and to retain proof of the continuous monitoring of that relationship. All the data must be stored and must be rapidly accessed on the request of competent authorities.[11] Indeed, these obligations made the intermediaries' businesses transparent and accountable to regulators, but did not interfere with the efficient operation of businesses. The Directive's risk-based approach allowed regulated professionals and institutions to apply simplified CDD standards depending on the type of customer, business relationship, and transaction or product.[12]

It is only reasonable for simplified CDD measures to be applied when the customer is either a financial institution or an institution operating in a third country applying similar standards to the Directive.[13] Cooperation amongst financial institutions is particularly valuable because it essentially enables them to assess the conditions under which a customer may or may not qualify to become the subject of simplified CDD measures. The principle that financial institutions are obliged to develop risk-based policies is important because their tailor-made guidelines are useful for their personnel and can be reviewed by regulators and supervisory bodies.

The Directive provided that enhanced CDD measures must be applied when the customer is not physically present for identification purposes; cross-border banking transactions involve third countries' credit and financial institutions; and

9 Directive 2005/60/EC, Article 7.
10 Directive 2005/60/EC, Article 8(1)(b).
11 Directive 2005/60/EC, Article 8(1)(c)–(d).
12 Directive 2005/60/EC, Article 8(2).
13 Directive 2005/60/EC, Article 11(1)–(2), (5).

politically exposed persons are involved.[14] Especially in regard to the latter, the Directive required natural and legal persons to explain not only the source of the wealth, but also the source of the funds involved in a particular transaction or business relationship.

Persons and financial institutions covered by the Directive may rely on other regulated third parties having already applied the enhanced CDD measures laid down by the instrument. The central idea behind this principle is to simplify processes when circumstances permit the minimization of unnecessary delays, especially in the interests of delivering better services and minimising business costs.[15] Nevertheless, is useful to also bear in mind that reliance on this principle does not necessarily mean that regulated persons and financial institutions should not reconfirm that other regulated third parties have applied enhanced CDD measures at an earlier stage.

The creation of the proper conditions by anti-money laundering laws to trace, seize and restrain the proceeds of transnational crime, corruption and tax evasion is another dynamic legal issue addressed in chapters 2–3. Both the UNTOC and the UNCAC called upon national legislators to recognise that the civil law ought to be used as an effective weapon next to the criminal law for the purposes of tracing, seizing and restraining criminal and subversive assets. The findings have shown that corruption is a multifaceted and transnational phenomenon that can seriously harm the integrity of financial markets and the integrity of the anti-money laundering system.

The findings of Chapter 3 confirmed that the current trend is corruption. It stems from the inherent vice of those individuals who prostitute their personal and professional ethics. Facilitation from within institutions and enterprises is not an issue of parochial interest because it concerns the collaboration of insiders with wrongdoers, including serious and organised criminals, peculators of public wealth, and fraudsters.

The idea that the tax law should be used as an effective weapon to tax unaccountable wealth when it is legally possible and as a tool for restructuring it was detailed in Chapter 4. Just like the prosecutorial toll was widened for the sound reasons already reviewed, there are pressing needs to uniformly widen the tax base in a judicious and proportionate way that promotes sustainable economic and social development. Setting aside that there is in place an effective toolbox for combating unaccountable wealth parked in offshore jurisdictions,[16] there are four sets of crucial factors that should be kept in mind.

The first set of factors concerns the international tax revolution taking place presently. The idea that the financial system should be reformed interconnects with the concept of using the global anti-money laundering regime to press those

14 Directive 2005/60/EC, Article 13(2)–(4).

15 Directive 2005/60/EC, Article 14.

16 Tom Mitchell and Paul J Davies, 'Prominent Chinese Anti-Corruption Activist Tried in Secret' *Financial Times* (London, 23 January 2014) 6.

parasitical storage tanks of mobile unaccountable wealth to return expatriated capital, including tax-evading money, to those economies in which reinvestment opportunities can contribute to economic development. The issue in question is dynamic enough to enable developed countries to deliver more effective tools to developing and poor countries that must minimise illicit outflows of public wealth and foreign aid.

The second set of factors concerns the idea that the tightening of money laundering, corruption and tax evasion controls cannot but result in the more efficacious tracing, freezing and confiscature of unaccountable wealth. Indeed, the tax issue is so dynamic[17] that it sufficiently enables us to fix our eyes on transparency laws.

The third set of factors concerns the significance of the conventional obligation of State Parties to the UNCAC to implement rules that enable judicial authorities to freeze and confiscate property in the hands of those public servants and officials who cannot reasonably and truthfully explain how they acquired it. While the primary objectives are to facilitate the administration of justice and to combat the peculation of public wealth by statutorily imposing the obligation on alleged wrongdoers to explain the source of their wealth beyond their official emoluments, it is important to appreciate once more that the possession of unexplained wealth by public servants and officials ought to lead to rapid civil forfeiture and sanctioning before the wealth is siphoned off to offshore centres or transferred to untouchable third parties from the social and professional circles of the offenders.

The fourth set of factors concerns the presumption of corruption in the absence of satisfactory explanations for the possession of significant amounts of wealth. Admittedly, the scope of its application should be broadened so as to cover all persons accused of possession of unexplained wealth. This approach can meaningfully facilitate the administration of justice and can contribute to the reduction of the deficit of pragmatism that civil law jurisdictions appear to have in contradistinction to common law jurisdictions, especially in regard to the efficacious implementation of international anti-corruption and transparency laws. It is important to appreciate with the pragmatic eye of the common law this unique tracing remedy, which promotes the implementation of uniform criminal and civil law measures and ensures that unexplained wealth remains well within the reach of the law.

The central issues addressed in chapters 1–4 reached the peak point of the critical analysis offered in Chapter 5 in that the wealth of information gathered from private sector reporters has given rise to a domain of intelligence pregnant with commercial, financial and personal data that can be used by different law enforcement, intelligence and prosecutorial authorities around the world to prosecute and prevent crime and terror. Indeed, this proposition reinforces the view

17 Vanessa Houlder, 'More Taxpayers Seek Judicial Review of Revenue Decisions' *Financial Times* (London, 23 January 2014) 2.

that Suspicious Activity Reports constitute the starting point for the investigation of the financial affairs of suspects.

In regard to the expectation on the part of defendants or respondents to offer to courts reasonable, truthful and innocent explanations on the sources of the wealth in their hands, there are four sets of crucial factors that need to be taken into consideration. The first set of factors concerns the reporters' task. Their task is peculiar and complex because they are statutorily obliged to act as if they are the eyes and ears of law enforcement and prosecutorial authorities. Yet they are criminally liable if they wantonly or for reasons of wilful blindness fail to disclose unusual or suspicious activities that colourfully sketch money laundering conspiracies.

But the state of mind of professionals handling other people's money is not left totally uncontrolled. There are safeguards in place that work for the mutual benefit of those who report suspected criminal conduct and those who are being reported for alleged wrongdoing. In order for bank employees to confidently report their self-induced suspicion to competent authorities, other compliance professionals filter self-induced suspicion and make the final choice for disclosure.

In legal and procedural terms, the aforementioned process constitutes the safety valve for the filtering of self-induced suspicion. In those cases that it is decided to disclose offences, Suspicious Activity Reports preliminarily sketch the skeleton of the alleged class of offence. Thereupon, the financial investigation is triggered, and depending on the force of the financial intelligence gathered and processed, which constitutes an additional safety valve in favour of the suspect, prosecutors shoulder the burden of proving in court that the property traced in the hands of the accused represents the proceeds of criminal conduct.

The second set of factors concerns the judicial treatment of circumstantial evidence. Circumstantial evidence in regard to the particular way in which the alleged criminal property was handled, may, in the majority of criminal cases, point towards the one-way direction of the accused person's guilt. This constitutes the added value of financial intelligence and its inferential force in courts. However, it should be kept in mind that the prosecutor's work is difficult and challenging because it is extremely difficult to always prove beyond reasonable doubt that the accused's conduct is worthy of sanctioning for what may essentially be a thought crime.

It is for all these law-centric reasons that the judicial review of money laundering aims to ascertain whether the defendant actually passed the boundaries of the conspiratory plan by acting in pursuance of the conspiracy agreement knowingly or by having reasonable grounds to suspect the laundering of criminal property. Of course, this neither means that the defendant's innocence is not presumed nor that it does not rank at the top of the barometer of innocence at the commencement of the trial. It simply means that the more the defendant or the respondent fails to explain, to the satisfaction of the court, that the property in his hands is not unexplainable, that barometer of innocence will increasingly fall down to the bottom where guilt will be established.

The third set of factors concerns the crucial finding that the prosecution does not have to particularise the specific offence that generated the primary source of criminal property. However, this does not mean that the prosecution does not shoulder the burden of proving the class of crime committed. In the absence of proof as to the derivative source of the property handled, possessed or acquired by the accused, the prosecutor's force will be either strengthened or weakened by the objective force of the circumstantial evidence of the case.

The issue in question is exceptionally dynamic because the inference that the jury will draw must pass the criminal standard of proof on the balance of probabilities. Furthermore, where the jury is permitted to infer from circumstances that the particulars of the case sufficiently complete the elements of the defendant's guilt, at that particular point, the defendant has the chance to break the walls of his right to remain silent during the proceedings, and offer to the court truthful explanations that will lead to his acquittal or to the establishment of his guilt.

The fourth set of factors concerns the need to separate myths from realities in regard to the burden of proof. The current system requires that prosecutors shoulder the burden of proving guilt in money laundering conspiracies. At the same time, it is equally important to appreciate that the defendant shoulders the evidential burden. Circumstantial evidence can reposition the probabilities upon which juries decide whether the property in the defendant's hands represents the fruits of criminal conduct. It does not therefore make sense to equate two different standards: the evidential burden and the reversal of the burden of proof.

The aforementioned two standards are well balanced both in criminal and civil proceedings. In regard to the alleged weaker position of the defence in criminal trials, two additional points should be kept in mind. First, no innocent person will suffer any damage or will lead himself to self-incrimination if he truthfully explains that his knowledge and intent was not blameworthy. Second, the explanations that courts expect defendants to offer are meant to protect and enhance the interests of the defendants themselves, not the interests of the prosecution.

It would be erroneous to presume that judges and prosecutors are satisfied every time that a defendant is found guilty of money laundering offences. However, it should be borne in mind that, once these explanations are offered by the defendant to the court, they must be completely reasonable and innocent so as to drastically weaken the force of the evidence of the case, which very often properly draws the overall picture of the defendant's guilt.

As detailed in Chapter 6, to think in financial intelligence law is to clearly recognise that the starting point for financial intelligence is the submission of Suspicious Activity Reports. At the same time, there are other good reasons for which Chapter 6 enriched further the majority of the central issues discussed in chapters 1–5 as opposed to having recycled them. There are five sets of factors worthy of appreciation that are briefly summarised as follows.

The first set of factors concerns what the law of financial intelligence does. It governs the central gathering, analysis and exchange of financial information and personal data for the purposes of ensuring that organised crime and terror are effectively prevented and deterred. Furthermore, financial intelligence creates the proper conditions for the competent authorities to take away from criminals their ill-gotten gains before they introduce them into the legitimate economies.

The second set of factors has to do with the fact that Suspicious Activity Reports do not constitute evidence of crime. They provide the leads that enable FIUs, law enforcement and intelligence authorities to prevent and detect crime and terror. However, not all Suspicious Activity Reports will be well founded or will enable law enforcement and prosecutorial authorities to gather sufficient inculpatory evidence against suspects simply because not all suspects are guilty. Not all suspects will fail to offer reasonable explanations to competent authorities when they are requested to do so.

The third set of factors concerns how the investigation of the financial affairs of suspects is expected to progress. It must not interfere with the person's private life and it must be proportionate to the very purpose it originally aimed to achieve. It is therefore reminded that proportionality is well founded upon two sound principles. First, confidentiality and discretion must be fully respected at the stage of submitting a Suspicious Activity Report and during the process of investigating the financial affairs of the suspect. Second, the sensitive data available to the reporter and the information gathered and processed by the FIU must be securely stored and protected.

The fourth set of factors, as detailed in chapters 1–3 and 5, concerns the critical function of FIUs. Financial Intelligence Units manage and control the Suspicious Activity Reports submitted to them. They are also responsible for the gathering, processing and exchange of information from different sources, such as law enforcement, intelligence agencies, prosecutorial authorities, foreign counterparts, commercial databases, government databases, and publicly available information.

While FIUs are expected to confidentially handle the information they exchange in a secure mode, they also shoulder the heavy burdens of complying with national laws on privacy and data protection, providing censored feedback to reporters, producing money laundering trends and typologies, and recommending to law enforcement authorities the appropriate actions to be taken. The important legal point to keep in mind is that, when the information exchanged involves two FIUs, two different national laws will ultimately impose the strict controls and the necessary safeguards on the information shared in order to preclude the use and subsequent movement of that information in an unauthorised manner: the national law of the requesting FIU and the national law of the requested FIU.

The fifth and last set of factors concerns the fact that the law of intelligence requires FIUs to gather, process, store and exchange financial intelligence and personal data in a qualitative, confidential and secure mode that enables them to discharge their statutory duties and minimises the risks of interference with the person's fundamental right to information privacy and financial information privacy.

The case study of the Hellenic FIU demonstrated that, when governments do not allocate sufficient financial, human and IT resources to their FIUs, and do not effectively engage law enforcement, intelligence, prosecutorial and judicial authorities, and private sector stakeholders, not only do they fail to ensure that their FIUs achieve full operational independence, but they also fail to secure compliance with the FATF's standards (Recommendations 12–13, 25–26 and 40). It is disappointing that the Greek Government did not succeed in getting its house in order at the time.[18] Of course, these disappointing results[19] should be evaluated parallel to Greece's chronic poor governance.

Chapter 7 emphasised two significant topics: the impact of the retention of personal data on the rights of unconvicted persons with a particular focus on the United Kingdom, and the effects of financial regulation on businesses. In regard to the first topic, it is underlined that the findings demonstrated incompatibility with the ECHR. There are two sets of important legal factors that should interest academics, legal practitioners, prosecutors, judges, legislators and law enforcement personnel.

The first set of factors concerns the secrecy and confidentiality under which the investigation of the alleged money laundering offender ought to take place for the purpose of gathering sufficient inculpatory evidence. During that stage, the suspect is totally unaware of the fact that the competent authorities investigate his financial affairs with a view to link him to the wrongdoing. Yet the suspect is entitled to the presumption of innocence until the diametrically contrary is proved in court. Indeed, one of the major strengths of delivering effective money laundering controls is that the financial personal data gathered and processed by FIUs and law enforcement authorities will be used in court by the prosecution against the accused. However, it is imperative to underline that, beyond acquittal

18 FATF–GAFI, 'Mutual Evaluation Interim Follow-Up Report Anti-Money Laundering and Combating the Financing of Terrorism GREECE 19 February 2010' 20–22 (FATF website 2010) <http://www.fatf-gafi.org/dataoecd/23/22/44725108.pdf> accessed 21 June 2010.

19 The FATF's Mutual Evaluation Interim Follow-up Report is particularly revealing in regard to the following additional dysfunctionalities of the Greek Anti-Money Laundering System: lack of guidance to financial institutions and DFNB's on the rapid seizure of assets of listed entities for compliance measures taken under UN Resolutions; lack of a system of sanctions for failure to follow freezing requests; lack of publicly known processes for de-listing and unfreezing funds; lack of procedures in place for the allowance of basic living expenses and fees in accordance with UNSCR 1452; lack of appropriate procedures through which natural or legal persons whose funds were frozen to challenge the imposition of that measure in court; the inability of the Greek authorities to freeze terrorist assets without first prosecuting the offences and opening a criminal investigation with a view to prosecute the persons involved; lack of civil procedure measures to protect the rights of good faith third party owners of property that may have been involved in terrorist financing; and the application of Article 22 of the Law of 2008 (Recommendation 6 on PEPs) only to Community and international PEPs as opposed to also covering those persons falling under the same category but residing in Greece.

or discontinuance of proceedings, the inculpatory evidence submitted to the court against accused persons is legally useless.

The second and last set of factors is legally more substantive because it concerns the erroneous application of Article 8(2) of the ECHR. The heart of the problem is that Article 8(2) of the ECHR cannot prevent unconvicted persons from being entitled to the presumption of their innocence, let alone that it does not constitute the sufficient legal basis for the legitimisation of the indiscriminate and indefinite retention of the fingerprints, cellular samples and DNA profiles of persons suspected, accused, but not convicted of criminal offences.

The legitimate social needs to fight economically motivated crime and terrorist financing do not entitle any financial regulator to misinterpret the law governing the retention and subsequent movement of the personal data of unconvicted persons. The unconvicted person's fundamental right to information privacy is inviolable and absolute. This fundamental right can be suspended only when the accused is convicted through the retention of his personal data for a specified period of time in order for law enforcement authorities to continuously monitor his movements and propensity, if any, to commit crimes in the future. The indefinite retention and free movement of the personal data of unconvicted persons interferes with their right to private life, their right to freedom of expression under Article 10 of the ECHR, and socially stigmatises them. This is unfair, discriminatory and totally incompatible with the ECHR.

On the second hot topic of the effects of financial regulation on businesses, three crucial observations should be kept in mind. First, in today's globalised financial system, it is almost impossible to escape money laundering controls. All transactions are monitored to such an extent that neither the structuring of bogus transactions nor the technocratic conducting of business can suffice to copy what commercial people do, ordinary and unsuspicious transactions which, above all, reflect their transactional profile.

Second, financial regulation does not interfere with the person's right to privacy and financial information privacy at the stage of agreeing upon the details of successful and legitimate business deals. The realisation of transactions through financial institutions acting as intermediaries and agents of their clients, inevitably, leaves traces that in today's regulated financial system are recorded, verified and monitored. Moreover, today's businesses cannot escape the simplified or enhanced CDD measures applied by financial institutions and other regulated entities.

Suspicion is triggered when reporting entities trace unusual or suspicious activities by professionals who are expected to pursue their financial affairs properly and with a commercial mind. Those who are innocent and do not cheat the tax authorities have no reason to fear that the recording or the reporting of the details of their transactions can affect their innocence or their businesses, on the condition that financial institutions have in place the proper safeguards to protect the right to financial privacy of their clients. Indeed, in the absence of such safeguards, the clients of financial institutions are automatically exposed to the risk of unlawful disclosures of confidential financial information and trade secrets by insiders.

Third, financial regulation has imposed the obligation on natural and legal persons to have in place the appropriate documentation that evidences both the lawful sources of the funds involved and their reasonable and innocent motivations, which will be put to the test by financial institutions and competent authorities at various stages, especially if the transaction in question has a cross-border character. The particular impact of financial regulation on businesses may be characterised as overloading financial institutions and businesses with the maintenance of records of the documentation evidencing the legal sources of the funds handled and acquired through their transactions.

On the other hand, this may be interpreted as an alternative way of shifting responsibility to businesses and financial institutions to become more transparent, and, of course, fully accountable to financial regulators, tax authorities and their shareholders. Last but not least, the fact that compliance with anti-money laundering regulation is obligatory and involves knowing in advance the type of conduct that is criminalised, those who conduct business should have developed by now a more suspicious culture in regard to handling property that their clients may not be in a position to reasonably explain. Perhaps, the obligation to suspect and demand additional explanations from clients and associates as to the provenance of the funds involved, will contribute to the isolation of wrongdoers in the long term.

Finally, it would be appropriate to modestly offer to the reader four key observations that look into the future of financial regulation. Let us recall that, in 2008, the Director of Public Prosecutions, Sir Ken MacDonald QC, warned us that we should first imagine the world that we are about to create prior to building it. Indeed, it would be academically improper not to acknowledge that the issue of the Security State preoccupies us.

On the one hand, there stands freedom, which encompasses the fundamental rights and freedoms of all citizens, and, on the other hand, there stands State surveillance, ready, willing and able to serve the insecurities of the Security State[20] with the aid of financial regulation. And, the more surveillance expands, the more it is expected to upset the balance between the freedom of individuals and the powers of the State. Of course, it would be useful to recall that citizens and the State are united by the rule of law. Both States and their citizens are expected to mutually uphold it. It can therefore be deduced that neither security nor proportionate surveillance, which protects and enhances security at times of insecurity, can attack the rule of law, for such an attack would negatively affect both the State and its citizens.

Financial regulation cannot bring irreversible social changes to the extreme extent that science fiction films such as *The Matrix* or *The Hunger Games* have presented to us fantastic conspiracy scenarios for entertainment purposes. Even if we are prepared to accept that anti-money laundering legislation is draconian, the

20 Text to n 59 in chapter 7.

fact that it is draconian is owed to trends of justified insecurity, such as the 9/11 terrorist attacks, the Madrid bombings and the London bombings.

With the above general observation in mind, it would be proper to predict the kind of model that will dominate the legal regime in the European Union. The Union's anti-money laundering regime shows zero tolerance towards economic crime and terror. It has become as restrictive and as punitive as it can get in imposing legislation that traces and sanctions money launderers and financiers of terrorism. Phillip R. Wood was more pessimistic when he made a similar prediction with the only exception that he was not convinced that the European Union has reached that maximum restrictive and punitive level suggested by this author. Of course, to predict whether financial regulation will become more restrictive and punitive in the foreseeable future involves taking the risk of predicting how financial transactions will be carried out in the next decade, and the new ways that criminal and terrorist minds will invent to harm financial systems and public safety.

This is as impossible as it would have been to predict the financial crisis that took place in 2008. In all modesty, this author predicts that financial regulation, in its present form, will be used by the rich-world coalition and exporting States of transparency norms, such as, the United States Canada, Germany and the United Kingdom, to convince recalcitrant governments to make progress in adopting transparency laws and to exchange financial intelligence and to contribute towards the redistribution of global wealth.

Professor Barry Rider rightly predicted that, by 2013, legal systems would impose obligations on those persons who possess significant amounts of wealth to publicly justify its true sources. In 2014, this research work reconfirms not only Professor Barry Rider's prediction, but also the dynamism of his forward thinking. In the next decade, global transparency laws will absorb the existing international instruments against economically motivated crime such as money laundering, corruption, bribery and tax evasion, in broader international instruments.

As a result, European Union financial regulation will be amended to keep up with evolving transparency standards. We will see more strengthened civil and tax law regimes and the main gaps between the civil law and the common law will have to be bridged with a view to effectively trace and attack unaccountable mobile wealth wherever it might be placed and, as such, the traditional offshore banking system will be reformed in the interests of promoting tax justice.

Last but not least, a prediction is offered in regard to the retention of fingerprints, cellular samples and DNA profiles of all persons. Today's forensic laboratories can analyse a single drop of blood from crime scenes and provide law enforcement authorities with sufficient information that can lead to the identification of suspects. But as *The Economist*[21] rightly pointed out in 2009, analysts work with a snapshot of a person's entire genome, and, for the time being, the brain must fill certain gaps that could lead to errors in some cases.

---

21 *The Economist*, 'Human Identity: An Elusive Illusion' (2009) 393 (8662) 138–139.

At the same time, one can only expect that technology will enable forensic laboratories in the foreseeable future to work with a person's entire genome. It would therefore appear permissible to predict that, in the next decade, in the light of technological advancements expected to be made in DNA analysis, we will experience the first legislative steps to be taken at the international level for the proactive retention of the DNA profiles of all persons in the interests of the prevention and control of serious crimes, including economic crime. It should therefore not come as a surprise to us if the European Union's legislator will pursue the necessary adaptations, which will inevitably affect the data protection law and financial regulation.

Bibliography

EU Legislation

Commission, 'An area of Freedom, security and justice serving the citizen' (Communication) COM (2009) 0262 final.
Commission, 'Commission Recommendation on procedural safeguards for vulnerable persons suspected or accused in criminal proceedings' COM (2013) 8178/2.
Commission, 'Commission Recommendation on the right to legal aid for suspects or accused persons in criminal proceedings' COM (2013) 8179/2.
Commission, 'Communication from the Commission to the Council and the European Parliament on Preventing and Combating Corporate and Financial Malpractice' COM (2004) 611 final.
Commission, 'Communication from the Commission to the European Parliament, the Council, the European Economic and Social Committee and the Committee of the Regions Delivering an area of freedom, security and justice for Europe's citizens Action Pan Implementing the Stockholm Programme' COM (2010) 171 final.
Commission, 'Communication from the Commission to the European Parliament and the Council, The EU Internal Security Strategy in Action: Five steps towards a more secure Europe' (COM) 2010 673 final.
Commission, 'Communication from the Commission to the European Parliament, the Council, the European Economic and Social Committee and the Committee of the Regions' COM (2010) 716 final.
Commission, 'Communication from the Commission to the European Parliament, the Council, the European Economic and Social Committee and the Committee of the Regions On the protection of the financial interests of the European Union by criminal law and by administrative investigations' COM (2011) 293 final.
Commission, 'Communication from the Commission to the European Parliament, the Council, the European Economic and Social Committee, and the Committee of the Regions and the Court of Auditors on the Commission Anti-Fraud Strategy' COM (2011) 376 final.
Commission, 'Communication from the Commission to the European Parliament and the Council: An Action Plan to strengthen the fight against tax fraud and tax evasion' COM (2012) 722 final.
Commission, 'Communication from the Commission to the European Parliament, the Council and the National Parliaments on the review of the proposal for a Council Regulation on the establishment of the European Public Prosecutor's

Office with regard to the principle of subsidiarity, in accordance with Protocol No 2' (Communication) COM (2013) 851 final.
Commission, 'Establishing an EU Anti-corruption reporting mechanism for periodic assessment ("EU Anti-corruption Report")' (Communication) COM (2011) 3673 final.
Commission, 'Proposal for a Directive of the European Parliament and of the Council on the protection of individuals with regard to the processing of personal data by competent authorities for the purposes of prevention, investigation, detection or prosecution of criminal offences or the execution of criminal penalties, and the free movement of such data' COM (2012) 10 final.
Commission, 'Proposal for a Directive of the European Parliament and of the Council on the fight against fraud to the Union's financial interests by means of criminal law' COM (2012) 363 final.
Commission, 'Proposal for a Directive of the European Parliament and of the Council on the freezing and confiscation of proceeds of crime in the European Union' COM (2012) 85 final.
Commission, 'Proposal for a Directive of the European Parliament and of the Council on the strengthening of certain aspects of the presumption of innocence and of the right to be present at trial in criminal proceedings' COM (2013) 821/2.
Commission, 'Proposal for a Directive of the European Parliament and of the Council on procedural safeguards for children suspected or accused in criminal proceedings' COM (2013) 822/2.
Commission, 'Proposal for a Directive of the European Parliament and of the Council on provisional legal aid for suspects or accused persons deprived of liberty and legal aid in European arrest warrant proceedings' COM (2013) 824.
Commission, 'Proposal for a Directive of the European Parliament and of the Council on the prevention of the use of the financial system for the purpose of money laundering and terrorist financing' COM (2013) 45 final.
Commission, 'Proposal for a Regulation of the European Parliament and of the Council on the protection of individuals with regard to the processing of personal data and on the free movement of such data (General Protection Regulation)' COM (2012) 11 final.
Commission, 'Proposal for a Regulation of the European Parliament and of the Council on electronic identification and trust services for electronic transactions in the internal market' COM (2012) 238/2.
Commission, 'Regulation of the European Parliament and of the Council amending Regulation (EC) No 1073/1999 concerning investigations conducted by the European Anti – Fraud Office (OLAF) and repealing Regulation (EURATOM) No 1074/1999' COM (2011) 135 final.
Commission Directive 2003/6/EC of the European Parliament and of the Council of 28 January 2003 on insider dealing and market manipulation (market abuse) [2003] OJ L96/16.

Commission Directive 2004/72/EC of 29 April 2004 implementing Directive 2003/6/EC of the European Parliament and of the Council as regards accepted market practices, the definition of inside information in relation to derivatives on commodities, the drawing up of lists of insiders, the notification of managers' transactions and the notification of suspicious transactions [2004] OJ L162/70.

Commission Directive 2005/60/EC of the European Parliament and of the Council of 26 October 2005 on the prevention of the use of the financial system for the purpose of money laundering and terrorist activity [2005] OJ L309/15.

Commission of the European Communities, SEC (2006) 1792 of 19 December 2006 Commission Staff Working Document, 'The application of Directive 91/309/EEC on the prevention of the use of the financial system for the purpose of money laundering in relation to the identification of clients in non-face transactions and possible implications for electronic commerce'.

Commission of the European Communities, SEC (2009) 939 final of 20 June 2009 Commission Staff Working Paper, 'Compliance with the anti-money laundering directive by cross-border banking groups at group level'.

Council Decision (EC) 2000/642/JHA concerning arrangements for cooperation between financial intelligence units for the Member States in respect of exchanging information [2000] OJ L271/14.

Council Decision 2007/845/JHA of 6 December 2007 concerning cooperation between Asset Recovery Offices of the Member States in the field of tracing and identification of proceeds from, or other property related to, crime [2007] OJ L332/103.

Council Directive 91/308/EC of 10 June 1991 on prevention of the use of the financial system for the purpose of money laundering [1991] OJ L166/77.

Council Framework 2001/500/JHA of 26 June 2001 on money laundering, the identification, tracing, freezing, seizing and confiscation of instrumentalities and the proceeds of crime [2001] OJ L182/1.

Council Framework Decision 2003/577/JHA of 22 July 2003 on the execution in the European Union of orders freezing property or evidence.

Council Framework Decision 2005/212/JHA of 24 February 2005 on Confiscation of Crime-Related Proceeds, Instrumentalities and Property [2005] OJ L668/49.

Council Framework Decision 2006/783/JHA of 6 October 2006 on the application of the principle of mutual recognition to confiscation orders [2006] OJ L328/59.

Council Framework Decision 2008/919/JHA of 28 November 2008 amending Framework Decision 2002/475/JHA on combating terrorism [2008] OJ L330/21.

Council Regulation (EC) 1781/2006 of the European Parliament and of the Council of 15 November 2006 on information on the payer accompanying transfer of funds [2006] OJ L345/1.

Council Regulation (EC) 1889/2005 of the European Parliament and of the Council of 26 October 2005 on control of cash entering or leaving the Community [2005] OJ L209/9.

Council Regulation (EC) 2580/2001 of 27 December 2001 on specific restrictive measures directed against certain persons and entities with a view to combating terrorism [2001] OJ L344/70.

Council Regulation (EC) 881/2002 of 27 May 2002 imposing certain specific restrictive measures directed against certain persons and entities associated with Usama bin Laden, the Al-Qaida network and Taliban, and repealing Council Regulation (EC) 467/2001 prohibiting the export of certain goods and services to Afghanistan, strengthening the fight ban and extending the freeze of funds and other financial resources in respect of the Taliban of Afghanistan [2002] OJ L139/9.

Directive 2001/97/EC of the European Parliament and of the Council of 4 December 2001 amending Council Directive 91/308/EC of 10 June 1991 on prevention of the use of the financial system for the purpose of money laundering – Commission Declaration [2001] OJ L344/76.

Directive 2001/97/EC of the European Parliament and of the Council of 4 December 2001 amending Council Directive 91/308/EEC on the prevention of the use of the financial system for the purpose of money laundering [2001] OJ L344/76.

Directive 2006/70/EC of the European Commission of 1 August 2006 laying down implementing measures for Directive 2005/60/EC of the European Parliament and of the Council as regards the definition of 'politically exposed person' and the technical criteria for simplified customer due diligence procedures and for exemption on grounds of financial activity conducted on an occasional or very limited basis [2006] OJ L214/29.

Directive 2007/64/EC of the European Parliament and of the Council of 13 November 2007 on payment services in the internal market amending Directives 97/7/EC, 2002/65/EC, 2005/60/EC and 2006/48/EC and repealing Directive 97/5/EC [2007] OJ L319/1.

Directive 2010/64/EU of the European Parliament and of the Council of 20 October 2010 on the right to interpretation and translation in criminal proceedings [2010] OJ L280/1.

Directive 2012/13/EU of the European Parliament and of the Council of 22 May 2012 on the right to information in criminal proceedings [2012] OJ L142/1.

Directive 2013/48/EU of the European Parliament and of the Council of 22 October 2013 on the right of access to a lawyer in criminal proceedings and in European arrest warrant proceedings, and on the right to have a third party informed upon deprivation of liberty and to communicate with third persons and with consular authorities while deprived of liberty [2013] OJ L294/1.

Books

Argyroiliopoulos, H, *Private and Public Corruption as a Crime of Unfair Competition* (Nomiki Bibliothiki Publishers, Athens 2006).

Baker, RW, *Capitalism's Achilles Heel: Dirty Money and How to Renew the Free-Market System* (John Wiley & Sons, Inc, New Jersey 2005).

Bannock, G, RE Baxter and E Davis, *The Penguin Dictionary of Economics* (4th edn, Penguin Group, London 1987).

Bennett, T, *Money Laundering Compliance* (2nd edn, Tottel Publishing, West Sussex 2007).

Dimitrainas, GN, *Laundering Dirty Money: Issues of Application of Law 2331/1995* (Nomiki Bibliothiki SA, Athens 2002).

Gilmore, WC, *Dirty Money: The Evolution of Money Laundering Counter-Measures* (2nd edn, Council of Europe Publishing, Strasbourg 1999).

Heaton, DT, 'Commercial Law – Text and Seminar Work-book' in E Perakis (trans), *Elements of English Legal Terminology* (NOMIKI BIBLIOTHIKI S.A. Publishers, Athens 1992).

Hellenic Criminal Bar Association, *Money Laundering: 'Clean' or Free Society?* (Ant N Sakkoulas Publishers, Athens 2007).

Hinterseer, K, 'Criminal Finance: The Political Economy of Money Laundering in a Comparative Legal Context' in B Rider (ed.), *Studies in Comparative Corporate and Financial Law, vol 15, IALS, University of London* (Kluwer 2002) 1.

Huber, D, *A Decade Which Made History: The Council of Europe 1989–1999* (Council of Europe Publishing, Strasbourg 1999).

James, H, *The Creation and Destruction of Value: The Globalisation Cycle* (Harvard University Press, Cambridge, MA 2009).

Kaiser, G, 'The Penal Control of Serious Economic Criminality' in L Kotsalis (tr), *Penal Series of University of Athens* (Ant N Sakkoulas Publishers, Athens 1983).

Kotzias, N, *Political System and Identity: Globalisation and the Case of the United Kingdom* (1st edn, Kastanioti Publishers, Athens 2008)

Kourakis, NE (ed.) and D Ziouvas, *Economic Crimes* Vol I (3rd edn, Ant N Sakkoulas Publishers, Athens 2007).

Lemay, JAL and PM Zall (eds), *Benjamin Franklin's Autobiography: An Authoritative Text Backgrounds Criticism* (1st edn, WW Norton & Company, Inc, Ontario 1986).

Leong, AVM, *The Disruption of International Organised Crime: An Analysis of Legal and Non-Legal Strategies* (Ashgate Publishing Ltd, Surrey 2008).

Levi, M, 'Criminal Asset-Stripping: Confiscating the Proceeds of Crime in England and Wales' in A Edwards and P Gill (eds), *Transnational Organised Crime: Perspectives on Global Security* (Routledge, Oxon 2003).

Levi, M, *Regulating Fraud, White Collar Crime and the Criminal Process* (Tavistock Publications, London 1987).

Millington, T and M Sutherland Williams, *The Proceeds of Crime: Law and Practice of Restraint, Confiscation, Condemnation and Forfeiture* (2nd edn, Oxford University Press, Oxford 2007).

Mitsilegas, V, *Money Laundering Counter-Measures in the European Union: A New Paradigm of Security Governance Versus Fundamental Legal Principles* (Kluwer Law International, The Hague 2003).

Muller, WH, CH Kälin and JG Goldsworth (eds), *Anti-Money Laundering: International Law and Practice* (John Wiley & Sons, Ltd, West Sussex 2007).

Naylor, RT, *Hot Money and the Politics of Debt* (Unwin Hyman Limited, London 1987).

Naylor, RT, *Patriots and Profiteers: On Economic Warfare, Embargoes Busting, and State-Sponsored Crime* (McClelland & Stewart Inc, Toronto 1999).

Nicoll, W and TC Salmon, *Understanding the European Communities* (1st edn, Philip Allan, Hertfordshire 1990).

Noonan, TJ Jr, *Bribes* (Macmillan, New York 1984).

Nugent, N, *Politics and Governance in the European Union* (5th edn, Savalas Publishers, Athens 2003).

Plano, JC and R Olton, *The International Relations Dictionary* (4th edn, Clio Press Ltd, Oxford 1988).

Reuter, P, *Disorganised Crime: The Economics of the Visible Hand* (MIT Press, Cambridge, MA 1983).

Rider, B (ed.), *Corruption: The Enemy Within* (Kluwer Law International, The Hague 1997).

Rider, B and M Ashe, *Money Laundering Control* (Sweet and Maxwell, Dublin 1996).

Rider, B, M Ashe and C Abrams, *Guide to Financial Service Regulation* (C.C.H. Editions Ltd, Bicester 1989).

Rider, B, A Kern and L Linklater, *Market Abuse and Insider Dealing* (2nd edn, Tottel Publishing Ltd, West Sussex 2009).

Roukounas, E, *International Law I* (3rd edn, Ant N Sakkoulas Publishers, Athens 2004).

Spirakos, DK, *The Critical Function of the Notion of Legal Good* (Ant N Sakkoulas Publishers, Athens 1996).

Stessens, G, *Money Laundering: A New International Law Enforcement Model* (CUP, Cambridge 2000).

Tsiridis, PP, *The New Law for Money Laundering: Law 3691/2008* (Nomiki Bibliothiki Publishers, Athens 2009).

Vassou, P, *Assessing Transnational Organised Crime: Results of a Pilot Survey of 40 Selected Organised Criminal Groups in 16 Countries* (Nathanson Centre for the Study of Organised Crime and Corruption, York University, Toronto 2005).

Young, OR, *International Cooperation: Building Regimes for Natural Resources and the Environment* (1st edn, Cornell University Press, New York 1989).

Journal Articles

Alexander, K, 'Multi-National Efforts to Combat Financial Crime and the Financial Action Task Force' (2000) 2 JIFM 5.

Alexander, RCH, 'Insider Dealing and Money Laundering in the EU: Law and Regulation' (2009) 34 ELR 2.

Alldridge, P, 'Reforming Bribery: Law Commission Consultation Paper 185: (1) Bribery Reform and the Law – Again' [2008] Crim Law Review 9.

Baker, E, 'From Past Imperfect to Future Imperfect? A Longitudinal Study of the Third Pillar' (2009) 34 ELR 1.

Barbas, N, 'Tax Competition as a Consequence of the Economic Globalization' [2009] Business and Company Law 155.

Beare, ME, 'The Devil Made Me Do It: Business Partners in Crime' (2007) 14 JFC 1.

Bell, ER, 'Prosecuting the Money Launderers Who Act for Organised Crime' (1999) 3 JMLC 2.

Bertezzolo, G, 'The European Union Facing the Global Arena: Standard Setting Bodies and Financial Regulation' (2009) 34 ELR 2.

Brown, G and T Evans, 'The Impact: The Breadth and Depth of the Anti-Money Laundering Provisions Requiring Reporting of Suspicious Activities' (2008) 23 JIBLR 5.

Carr, I, 'Corruption in Africa: Is the African Union Convention on Combating Corruption the Answer?' [2007] JBL Mar.

Chaikin, D, 'Commercial Corruption and Money Laundering: A Preliminary Analysis' (2008) 15 JFC 3.

Demetis, DS and IO Angell, 'The Risk-based Approach to AML: Representation, Paradox, and the 3rd Directive' (2007) 10 JMLC 4.

Engdahl, O, 'The Role of Money in Economic Crime' (2008) 48 BJC 2.

Fagan, N and L Thompson, 'Corporate Responsibility and Group Redress Mechanisms' (2009) 10 BLI 1.

Gallant, MM, 'Tax and Terrorism: A New Partnership?' (2009) 14 JFC 4.

Gbandi, M Kaiafa, 'The Penal Confrontation of Laundering Dirty Money: Between International, European and National Legislation' [2007] Penal Chronicles NZ.

Harvey, J, 'The Search for Crime Money – Debunking the Myth: Facts versus Imagery' (2009) 12 JMLC 2.

Hodge, N, 'A Taxing Issue: With Huge Amounts of Money being Lost by Developing Countries through Tax Avoidance and Evasion, a New G20 Communiqué Aims to Reverse the Trend – but Many Feel it Does Not Go Far Enough'. (2009) 63 International Bar News 4.

Ioannides, ES, 'Country Spotlight: Greece Anti-Corruption Developments in Greece' [2009] IBA Anti-Corruption Committee Newsletter 1.

Johnstone, P and G Brown, 'International Controls of Corruption: Recent Responses from the USA and the UK' (2004) 11 JFC 3.

Kennedy, A, 'Dead Fish across Trail: Illustrations of Money Laundering Methods' (2005) 8 JMLC 4.
Kennedy, A, 'Winning the Information Wars: Collecting, Sharing and Analysing Information in Asset Recovery Investigations' (2007) 14 JFC 4.
Leong, AVM, 'Anti-Money Laundering Measures in the United Kingdom: A Review of Recent Legislation and FSA's Risk-based Approach' (2007) 28 Comp Law 2.
Leong, AVM, 'Chasing Dirty Money: Domestic and International Measures against Money Laundering' (2007) 10 JMLC 2.
Magliveras, K, 'Defeating the Money Launderer – the International and European Network' [1992] JBL 3 (Mar).
Margolis, A, 'Follow the Money: Recovering Ill-gotten Gains' [2009] International Bar News October 2009.
Mitsilegas, V and B Gilmore, 'The EU Legislative Framework against Money Laundering and Terrorist Finance: A Critical Analysis in the Light of Evolving Global Standards' (2007) 56 ICLQ 1.
Musikali, LM, 'Why Criminal Sanctions still Matter in Corporate Governance' (2009) 20 ICCLR 4.
Nardo, M, 'Building Synergies between Theory and Practice: Countering Financial Crime on a Systemic Approach' (2006) 13 JFC 3.
Osborne, D, 'Transparency and Accountability Reconsidered' (2004) 11 JFC 3.
Picciotto, S, 'Constitutionalizing Multilevel Governance?' (2008) 6 IJCL (3/4).
Rider, B, 'A Bold Step?' (2009) 30 Comp Law 1, 2.
Rider, B, 'A Serious Problem' (2004) 11 JFC 4.
Rider, B, 'A Murkey World' (2003) 24 Comp Law.
Rider, B, 'An Insider Paradox?' (2008) 29 Comp Law 1.
Rider, B, 'Corruption: The Enemy Within' (1998) 13 JIBL 9.
Rider, B, 'Financial Regulation and Supervision after 11th September, 2001' (2003) 10 JFC 4.
Rider, B, 'Here We Go Again!' (2008) 15 JFC 3.
Rider, B, 'In Pursuit of Fees!' (2007) 10 JMLC 4.
Rider, B, 'Taking Money Launderers to the Cleaners: Part 1' [1996] PCB 2.
Rider, B, 'Taking Money Launderers to the Cleaners: Part 2' [1996] PCB 3.
Rider, B, 'Taking Money Launderers to the Cleaners: Part 3' [1996] PCB 4.
Rodmell, G, 'Corruption – Economic Crime or Economic Reality?' (2007) 28 Comp Law 9.
Rossbacher, HH, 'The Business of Corruption, or is the Business of Business Corruption?' (2006) 13 JFC 2.
Schafer, A, 'Resolving Deadlock: Why International Organisations Introduce Soft Law' (2006) 12 ELJ 2.
Schwartz, J, 'Rights and Powers: Protecting the Legitimate Interests of Taxpayers' [2009] BTR 3.
Shehu, A, 'International Initiatives against Corruption and Money Laundering: An Overview' (2005) 12 JFC 13.

Simser, J, 'Money Laundering and Asset Cloaking Techniques' (2008) 11 JMLC 1.

Simser, J, 'Tax Evasion and Avoidance Typologies' (2008) 11 JMLC 2.

Stefanou, C and H Xanthaki, 'Greece: Money Laundering' (1999) 3 JMLC 2.

Stolowy, N, 'Transparency and Prevention for Corporate Bankruptcy: A US–France Comparison' [2009] JBL 6.

Tellechea, AF, 'Economic Crimes in Capital Markets' (2008) 15 JFC 2.

Van Dyne, PC and M Levi, 'Drugs and Money: Managing the Drug Trade and Crime – Money in Europe' (2007) 47 BJC 4.

Viogaert, J, 'Fighting Economic Crime – Action taken in the European Union' (2001) 9 JFC 1.

Wardle, R, 'Money Laundering: A Prosecutor's Perspective' (1999) 3 JMLC 2.

Wood, PR, 'Predictions for the Future of Financial Law and Lawyers' (2008) 9 BLI 3.

Young, SNM, 'Why Civil Actions against Corruption?' (2009) 16 JFC 2.

Websites and Blogs

Basel Committee on Banking Supervision, 'Revisions to the Basel II Market Risk Framework' (Bank for International Settlements website 2009) <http://www.bis.org/publ/bcbs148.pdf?noframes=1>.

Breinholt, Jeff, Deputy Chief, Counterterrorism Section, Criminal Division, US Department of Justice, September, 2004, 'Reaching the White Collar Terrorist: Operational Challenges' <http://www.imf.org./extermal/np/leg/sem/2004/cdmfl/eng/breinh.pdf>.

British Bankers' Association, 'Annual Report 2008/09' (BBA website 2009) <http://www.bba.org.uk/content/1/c6/01/66/53/BBA%20Annual%20Review%202009.pdf>.

CIA, 'Speeches & Testimony > Appendix A: Chronology of Nuclear Smuggling Incidents > The Continuing Threat from Weapons of Mass Destruction' (CIA website 2009) <https://www.cia.gov/news-information/speeches-testimony/1996/go_appendixa_032796.html>.

COE, 'Background Information' (COE website 2009) <http://www.coe.int/t/dghl/monitoring/moneyval/about/background_m>.

COE, 'Committee of Experts on the Evaluation of Anti-Money Laundering Measures and the Financing of Terrorism – MONEYVAL' (COE website 2009) <http://coe.int/t//dghl/monitoring/moneyval/>.

COE, 'Complete List of the Council of Europe's Treaties' (COE website 2009) <http://www.conventions.coe.int/Treaty/Commun/ListeTreaties.asp?CM=8&CL=ENG>.

COE, 'Council of Europe Treaties' (COE website 2009) <http://www.conventions.coe.int/>.

COE, 'Explanatory Report to the Convention on Laundering, Search, Seizure and Confiscation of the Proceeds from Crime (CETS 141)' (COE website 2009) <http://conventions.coe.int/Treaty/en/Reports/Html/141.htm>.

COE, 'Explanatory Report to the Convention on Laundering, Search, Seizure and Confiscation of the Proceeds from Crime and on the Financing of Terrorism (CETS 198)' (COE website 2009) <http://conventions.coe.int/Treaty/EN/Reports/Html/198.htm>.

COE, 'Human Rights and Legal Affairs' (COE website 2009) <http://www.coe.int/t/e/legal_affairs/legal_co-operation/Transnationalcriminal_justice/>.

COE, 'Special File: Financial Investigations and Confiscation of Proceeds from Crime' (COE website 2009) <http://www.coe.int/t/dghl/cooperation/economiccrime/SpecialFiles/FI_en.asp>.

COE, 'Technical Cooperation against Economic Crime Activity Report 2008' (COE website 2009) <http://www.coe.int/t/dghl/cooperation/economiccrime/ECD%202008%20actrep2008m%20Provisional%2021%20jan%2009.pdf>.

COE Action against Economic Crime, 'Judicial Cooperation' (COE website 2009) <http://www.coe.int/t/dghl/cooperation/economiccrime/JudicialCooperation/default_en.asp>.

COE Action against Economic Crime, 'Organised Crime' (COE website 2009) <http://www.coe.int/t/dhl/cooperation/economiccrime/organisedcrime/default_en.as>.

COE Action against Economic Crime, 'Standards and Initiatives of Other International Organisations and Mechanisms' (COE website 2009) <http://www.coe.int/t/dghl/cooperation/economiccrime/Money/Laundering/default_en.asp>.

COE Committee of Ministers, 'Rec (2000) 10E of 11 May 2000 on Codes of Conduct for Public Officials' with further link to CM (2000) 61 of 20 April 2000 (COE website 2009) <https://wcd.coe.int/ViewDoc.jsp?id=353945&Site=CM&BackColorInternet=9999CC&BackColorIntranet=FFBB55&BackColorLogged=FFAC75>.

COE Committee of Ministers, 'Rec (2001) 11E of 19 September 2001 Concerning Twenty Guiding Principles on the Fight against Organised Crime' (COE website 2009) <https://wcd.coe.int/com.intranet.InstraServlet?command=com.instranet.CmdBlobGet&InstranetImage=62085&SecMode=1&DocId=212804&Usage=4>.

COE Committee of Ministers, 'Rec (2003) 4 of the Committee of Ministers to Member States on Common Rules against Corruption in the Funding of Political Parties and Electoral Campaigns' (COE website 2009) <http://wcd.coe.int/ViewDoc.jsp?id=2183&Site=CM&BackColorInternet=9999CC&BackColorIntranet=FFBB&BackColorLogged=FFAC75>.

COE, Economic Crime Division Directorate General of Human Rights and Legal Affairs, 'The Role of Technical Assistance in Development of Anti-Money Laundering and Counter-Terrorist Financing Systems. Lessons Learnt from TA Projects Implemented by the Council of Europe, 2003–2007' (COE website

2009) <http://coe.int/dghl/cooperation/economiccrime/MoneyLaundering/Report%20lessons%20learnt%20fin.pdf>.

COE, Economic Crime Division Directorate General of Human Rights and Legal Affairs, 'Technical Cooperation against Economic Crime Activity Report 2007' (COE website 2009) <http://www.coe.int/t/dghl/cooperation/economiccrime/ECD2007%20actrep2007k%PROVISIONAL%20_29%jan%2008_en.pdf>.

Congressional Research Service, 'Tax Cuts on Repatriation Earnings as Economic Stimulus: An Economic Analysis' (CRS Report for US Congress Prepared for Members and Committees of Congress) <http://www.levin.senate.gov/newsroom/supporting/2009/CRS.RepatriationAnalysis.013009.pdf>.

CRA International, 'Final Report: Evaluation of the Economic Impacts of the Financial Services Action Plan, March 2009' (European Commission website 2009) <http://ec.europa.eu/internal_market/finances/docs/actionplan/index/090707_economic_impact_en.pdf#xml=http://158.167.146.104:7001/www/xmlread.jsp?ServerSpec=158.167.146.104:9000&K2DocKey=http%3A%2F%2Fec.europa.eu%2Finternal_market%2Ffinances%2Fdocs%2Factionplan%2Findex%2F090707_economic_impact_en.pdf%40EUROPACORE_eceu_x&QuetyText=impact+of+third+anti+money+laundering+directive>.

DG Internal Market and Services, Unit F2 'Company Law, Corporate Governance, Financial Crime', 'EU AML Info-letter: Countries with Deficient AML/CFT Regimes' (Europa website 2009) <http://ec.europa.eu/internal_market/company/docs/financial-crime/aml-news-200709_en.pdf>.

E/08–09/F70 ML 'Written evidence by the Crown Prosecution Society (CPS) Submission by the Director of Public Prosecutions to the Sub-Committee F (Home Affairs) of the House of Lords Select Committee on the European Union in Response to the Call for Evidence for the Inquiry into Money Laundering and the Financing of Terrorism' HL (2008–09) 10 February 2009, 132–II, Mr Jeremy Rawlins, Head of Proceeds of Crime Delivery Unit, Mr Mike Kennedy, Chief Operating Officer, <http://www.parliament.uk/documents/upload/F070DirectorPublicProsecutionsCPS120209.pdf>.

Egmont Group, 'Benefits of Egmont Group Membership' (Egmont Group website 2009) <http://www.egmontgroup.org/files/library_egmont_docs/egmont_membership_benefit.pdf>.

Egmont Group, 'Best Practices for the Exchange of Information Between Financial Intelligence Units 11/04' (2004) (Egmont Group website 2009) <http://www.egmontgroup.org/bestpractices.pdf>.

Egmont Group, 'Best Practices for the Exchange of Information Between Financial Intelligence Units' (Egmont Group Library: Egmont Documents) (Egmont Group website 2009) <http://www.egmontgroup.org/library/egmont-documents>.

Egmont Group, 'FIU Definition "Countering of Terrorism Financing" Complementary Interpretative Note' (Egmont Group Library: Egmont Documents) (Egmont Group website 2009) <http://www.egmontgroup.org/library/egmont-documents>.

Egmont Group, 'Information Paper on Financial Intelligence Units and the Egmont Group' (Egmont Group Library: Egmont Documents) (Egmont Group website 2009) <http://www.egmontgroup.org/library/egmont-documents>.

Egmont Group, 'Interpretive Note Concerning the Egmont Definition of a Financial Intelligence Unit' (Egmont Group Library: Egmont Documents) (Egmont Group website 2009) <http://www.egmontgroup.org/library/egmont-documents>.

Egmont Group, 'Principles for Information Exchange Between Financial Intelligence Units for Money Laundering and Terrorism Financing Cases The Hague, 13 June 2001' (Egmont Group Library: Egmont Documents) (Egmont Group website 2009) <http://www.egmontgroup.org/library/egmont-documents>.

Egmont Group, 'Statement of Purpose of the Egmont Group of Financial Intelligence Units Guernsey, 23rd June 2004' (Egmont Group Library: Egmont Documents) (Egmont Group website 2009) <http://www.egmontgroup.org/library/egmont-documents>.

Egmont Group Financial Intelligence Units of the World 'Operational Units Meeting the Egmont Definition Status as of June 2009 06/09' (2009) (the Egmont Group website 2009) <http://www.egmontgroup.org/list_of_fius.pdf>.

European Commission, 'Consultations: Internal Market, Call for Evidence: Review of Directive 2003/6/EC on Insider Dealing and Market Manipulation 4/09' (Europa website 2009) <http://europa.eu/internal_market/consultations/docs/2009/market_abuse/call_for_evidence.pdf>.

European Commission, 'Treaties Office Database: Summary of Treaty' (Europa website 2009) <http://ec.europa.eu/world/agreements/prepareCreateTreatiesWorkspace/treatiesGeneralData.do?step=0&redirect=true&treatyId=5461>.

EUROPA – Press Releases Reference: IP/04/832 Date: 30/06/2004 'Money Laundering: Commission Proposes to Update and Improve Directive' (Europa website 2009) <http://europa.eu/rapid/pressReleasesAction.do?reference=IP/04/832…>.

EUROPA – Press Releases Reference: IP/04/1164 Date: 25/06/2009, 'European Commission Launches Strategy to Prevent Financial and Corporate Malpractice' (Europa website 2009) <http://europa.eu/rapid/pressReleasesAction.do?reference=IP/04/11…>.

EUROPA – Press Releases Reference: IP/05/682 Date: 07/06/2005 'Adoption of Anti-Money Laundering Directive Will Strike a Blow against Crime and Terrorism' (Europa website 2009) <http://europa.eu/rapid/pressReleasesAction.do?reference=IP/05/682…>.

EUROPA – Press Releases Reference: IP/07/832 Date: 14/06/2007 'Customs/New Rules to Combat Money Laundering and Terrorist Financing: Persons Entering or Leaving the EU Have to Declare Cash Movements' (Europa website 2009) <http://europa.eu/rapid/pressReleasesAction.do?Reference=IP/07/8332…>.

EUROPOL, 'Financial & Property Crimes 1/06' (Europol website 2006) <http://www.Europol.europa.eu/publications/Serious_Crime_Overviews/overviewFCPC.pdf>.

EUROPOL, 'OCTA 2006: EU Organised Crime Threat Assessment 2006' (Europol website 2009) <http://www.Europol.europa.eu/publications/European_Organised_Crime_Threat_Assessment_(OCTA)/OCTA2008.pdf>.

EUROPOL, 'OCTA 2008: EU Organised Crime Threat Assessment' (Europol website 2009) <http://www.Europol.europa.eu/publications/European_Organised_Crime_Threat_Assessment_(OCTA)/OCTA2008.pdf>.

EUROPOL European Law Enforcement Cooperation, 'Annual Report 1998' <http://www.Europol.europa.eu/index.asp?page=publar1998>.

EUROPOL European Law Enforcement Cooperation, 'Annual Report 1999' <http://www.Europol.europa.eu/index.asp?page=publar1999>.

EUROPOL European Law Enforcement Cooperation, 'Annual Report 2000' <http://www.Europol.europa.eu/index.asp?page=publar2000>.

EUROPOL European Law Enforcement Cooperation, 'Annual Report 2001' <http://www.Europol.europa.eu/index.asp?page=publar2001>.

EUROPOL European Law Enforcement Cooperation, 'Annual Report 2002' <http://www.Europol.europa.eu/index.asp?page=publar2002>.

EUROPOL European Law Enforcement Cooperation, 'Annual Report 2003' <http://www.Europol.europa.eu/index.asp?page=publar2003>.

EUROPOL European Law Enforcement Cooperation, 'Annual Report 2004' <http://www.Europol.europa.eu/index.asp?page=publar2004>.

EUROPOL European Law Enforcement Cooperation, 'Annual Report 2005' <http://www.Europol.europa.eu/index.asp?page=publar2005>.

FATF–GAFI, 'Financial Action Task Force, Mutual Evaluation Interim Follow-up Report, Anti-Money Laundering and Combating the Financing of Terrorism, Greece, 19 February 2010, Mutual Evaluation of Greece 7th Follow-up Report' (FATF website 2010) <http://www.fatf-gafi.org/dataoecd/23/22/44725108.pdf>.

FATF–GAFI, Financial Action Task Force Working Group on Evaluations and Implementation, 'Mutual Evaluation of Greece – 6th Follow-up Report' (12 October 2009, OECD Headquarters, Paris, France) FATF/WGEI (2009) 38.

FATF–GAFI, 'The 40 Recommendations' (FATF–GAFI website 2009) <http://www.fatfgafi.org/document/28/0,3343,en_32250379_32236930_33658140_1_1_1_1,00.html#r26>.

FATF–GAFI Financial Action Task Force 'Mutual Evaluation Interim Follow-up Report Anti-Money Laundering and Combating the Financing of Terrorism Greece 19 February 2010' (FATF website 2010) <http://www.fatf-gafi.org/dataoecd/23/22/44725108.pdf>.

FATF–GAFI Financial Action Task Force on Money Laundering, 'Methodology for Assessing Compliance with the FATF 40 Recommendations and the FATF 9 Special Recommendations 27 February 2004 (updated as of February 2009)' (FATF website 2009) <http://www.fatf-gafi.org/dataoecd/16/54/40339628.pdf>.

Financial Transactions and Reports Analysis Centre of Canada, 'FINTRAC – 2008 Annual Report – Financial Intelligence' (FINTRAC website 2008) <http://www.fintrac-canafe.gc.ca/publications/ar/2008/41-eng.asp>.

FinCEN, 'Advisories/Bulletins/Fact Sheets' (FinCEN website 2009) <http://www.fincen.gov/news_room/advisory/index.html>.

FinCEN, 'Department of the Treasury 31 CFR Part 103 RIN 1506-AB04: Financial Crimes Enforcement Network: Expansion of Special Information Sharing Procedures To Deter Money Laundering and Terrorist Activity' (2009) 74 Federal Register 219, (FinCEN website 2009) <http://edocket.access.gpo.gov/2009/pdf/E9–27447.pdf>.

FinCEN, 'Department of the Treasury, Advisory FIN-2009-A002 Issued: June 18, 2009 (Amended 18 December 2009) Subject: North Korea Government Agencies' and Front Companies' Involvement in Illicit Financial Activities' (FinCEN website 2009) <http://www.fincen.gov/statutes_regs/Guidance/pdf/fin-2009-a002.pdf>.

FinCEN, 'Financial Institutions Outreach Initiative: Report on Outreach to Large Depository Institutions, October 2009' (FinCEN website 2009) <http://www.fincen.gov/news_room/rp/reports/pdf/Bank_Report.pdf>.

FinCEN, 'The SAR Activity Review: Trends Tips & Issues Issue 16' (Published under the auspices of the BSA Advisory Group, October 2009, FinCEN website 2009) <http://www.fincen.gov/news_room/rp/files/sar_tti_16.pdf>.

FinCEN United States Department of the Treasury, 'FinCEN Advisory: Guidance to Financial Institutions Based on Anti-Money Laundering and Counter-Terrorist Financing Risks Posed by Iran, Uzbekistan, Turkmenistan, Pakistan, and Sao Tome and Principe 07/09' (FinCEN website 2009) <http://www.fincen.gov/statutes_regs/guidance/html/fin-2009-a004.html>.

FinCEN United States Department of the Treasury Advisory, 'Withdrawal of Advisory FIN-2008-A003 regarding the area of Cyprus administered by Turkish Cypriots (northern part of Cyprus) 07/09' (FinCEN website 2009) <http://www.fincen.gov/statutes_regs/guidance/pdf/fin-2009-a005.pdf>.

Freedom, Security and Justice, European Commission > Justice and Home affairs > Data Protection > The law > Treaty on the European Union, 'European Convention for the Protection of Human Rights and Fundamental Freedoms, Article 8' (Europa website 2009) <http://www.ec.europa.eu/Justice_home/fsj/privacy/law/treaty_en.htm>.

Freis, JJ, Jr, Director, FinCEN, US Department of Treasury, 'Global Markets and Global Vulnerabilities: Fighting Transnational Crime Through Financial Intelligence. Remarks Delivered at the Academic Session on Global Initiatives to Avoid the Mis(use) of the Financial System for Illegal Purposes of the Committee on International Monetary Law of the International Law Association – (MOCOMILA) Salamanca, Spain 04/08' (2008) <http://www.fincen.gov/news_room/speech/pdf/20080425.pdf>.

Freis, JJ, Jr, 'Prepared Remarks of James H. Freis, Jr., Director, Financial Crimes Enforcement Network, U.S. Department of the Treasury Delivered at the ABA/

ABA Money Laundering Network' (Speech at ABA/ABA Money Laundering Enforcement Conference, Washington DC, 13 October 2009, FinCEN website 2009) <http://www.fincen.gov/news_room/speech/pdf/20091013.pdf>.

GOPAC – Global Organisation of Parliamentarians Against Corruption, 'GOPAC Anti-Money Laundering Initiative: A Proposal 08/06' (GOPAC website 2009) <http://www.gopacnetwork.org/Docs/Global/AML_PROPOSAL_FINAL_en.pdf>.

GRECO – Group of States Against Corruption, see especially, CoE, 'GRECO's 43rd Plenary Meeting (GRECO 43, Strasbourg, 29 June – 2 July 2009)' (COE website 2009) <http://www.coe.int/t/dghl/monitoring/greco/default_en.asp>.

HM Treasury, 'Delivering Better Regulation Two Years On: HM Treasury's Simplification Plan December 2008' (HM Treasury website 2009) <http://www.hm-treasury.gov.uk/d/simplificationplan_101208.pdf>.

HM Treasury, 'The Financial Challenge to Crime and Terrorism 02/2007' (HM Treasury website 2009) <http://www.hm-treasury.gov.uk/d/financialchallenge_crime_280207.pdf>.

House of Lords European Union Committee 10th Report of Session 2007–08 'The Treaty of Lisbon: An Impact Assessment' HL (2007–08) 62–I, II (House of Lords website 2008) <http://www.parliament.the-stationeryoffice.co.uk/oa/ld200708/ldeucom/62/6209.htm#a117>.

House of Lords European Union Committee 19th Report of Session 2008–09, 'Money Laundering and the Financing of Terrorism' HL (2008–09) 132–I (House of Lords website 2009) <http://www.publications.parliament.uk/pa/ld200809/ldselect/ldeucom/132/132i.pdf>.

ICC Commercial Crime Services Annual Lecture by Professor Barry Rider, Director of the Institute for Advanced Legal Studies, Skinners' Hall, 'Organised Crime and Terrorism: Tracking and Attacking the Assets of Economic Crime and Terrorism 06/02' (2002) <http://www.iccwbo.org/iccbjfh/index.html>.

IMF, 'Code of Good Practices on Fiscal Transparency (2007)' (IMF website 2009) <http://www.imf.org/external/np/fad/trans/code.htm>.

IMF, 'Guide on Resource Revenue Transparency: 2007 Revised Edition' (IMF website 2009) <http://www.imf.org/external/np/fad/trans/guide.htm>.

IMF, 'Manual on Fiscal Transparency: 2007 Revised Edition' (IMF website 2009) <http://www.imf.org/external/np/fad/trans/manual.htm>.

International Association of Prosecutors, 'Responses to the Consultation Paper on the Review of the OECD Anti-Bribery Instruments' (OECD website 2009) <http://www.oecd.org/dataoecd/8/8/40498974.pdf>.

International Association of Prosecutors, 'Third Word Summit of Prosecutors General, Attorneys General and Chief Prosecutors (Bucharest, Romania, 24–25 March 2009) Report' (IAP website 2009) <http://www.iap-association.org/ressources/Bucharest_Summit_final_report_09.pdf>.

International Chamber of Commerce (ICC Commission on Anti-Corruption) 'Responses to the Consultation Paper on the Review of the OECD Anti-Bribery Instruments' (OECD website 2009) <http://www.oecd.org/dataoecd

/7/27/40498870.pdf> Responses to the Consultation Paper on the Review of the OECD Anti-Bribery Instruments.

INTERPOL, 'About Corruption: Conventions regarding Anti-Corruption' (Interpol website 2009) <http://www.interpol.int/Public/Corruption/Conventions/default.asp>.

Jesus College, Cambridge, 'The 27th Cambridge International Symposium on Economic Crime: The Enemy Within – Internal Threats to the Stability and Integrity of Financial Institutions 08/09' (2009) Commentary by Professor Barry AK Rider, Symposium Director and Co-Chairman.

McCafferty, Kenney Qui Tam Lawyers, 'US Treasury Moves to Thwart Offshore Tax Evasion with Further Implementation of New Law' Kenney McCafferty Blog (31 October 2013) <http://blog.tax-fraud.net/2p=533>.

OECD, '14/01/2008 – The OECD Working Group on Bribery Invites Public Comment on its Consultation Paper: Review of the OECD Instruments on Combating Bribery of Foreign Public Officials in International Business Transactions Ten Years after Adoption' (OECD website 2009) <http://www.oecd.org/dataoecd/18/25/39882963.pdf>.

OECD, 'Key OECD Anti-Corruption Documents' (OECD website 2009) <http://www.oecd.org/document/42/0,3343,en_2649_37447_41799402_1_1_1_1,00.html>.

OECD, 'The OECD Fights Corruption' (OECD website 2006) <http://www.oecd.org/dataoecd/36/51/37418910.pdf>.

OECD Centre for Tax Policy and Administration, 'Countering Offshore Tax Evasion: Some Questions and Answers on the Project 11 September 2009' (OECD website 2009) <http://www.oecd.org/dataoecd/32/45/42356522.pdf>.

OECD Centre for Tax Policy and Administration, 'OECD Global Forum Consolidates Tax Evasion Revolution in Advance of Pittsburgh' (OECD website 2009) <http://www.oecd.org/document/43/0,3343,en_2649_33767_436015>.

OECD Centre for Tax Policy and Administration, 'Overview of the OECD's Work on Countering International Tax Evasion: A Background Information Brief 11 September 2009' (OECD website 2009) <http://www.oecd.org/dataoecd/32/45/42356522.pdf>.

OECD Centre for Tax Policy and Administration, 'Summary of the Meeting of the Global Forum on Transparency and Exchange of Information for Tax Purposes Held in Mexico on 1–2 September 2009' (OECD website 2009) <http://www.oecd.org/dataoecd/44/39/43610626.pdf>.

OECD Centre for Tax Policy and Administration, 'Tax Co-operation 2009: Towards a Level Playing Field – 2009 Assessment by the Global Forum on Transparency and Exchange of Information' (OECD website 2009) <http://www.oecd/org/document/23/0,3343,en_2649_33767_435556>.

OECD Directorate for Financial and Enterprise Affairs, 'Guidelines for Multinational Enterprises' (OECD website 2009) <http://www.oecd.org/department/0,3355,en_2649_34889_1_1_1_1_1,00.html>.

OECD Directorate for Financial and Enterprise Affairs, 'Steps Taken by State Parties to Implement and Enforce the OECD Convention on Combating Bribery of Foreign Public Officials in International Business Transactions' (OECD website 2009) <http://www.oecd.org/document/44/0,3343,en_2649_34859_36433004_1_1_1_1,00.html>.

OECD Directorate for Financial, Fiscal and Enterprise Affairs Committee on International Investment and Multinational Enterprises, 'Working Group on Bribery in International Business Transactions (CIME) Convention on Combating Bribery of Foreign Public Officials in International Business Transactions and Related Documents' (OECD website 2009) <http://www.oecd.org/dataoecd/4/18/38028044.pdf>.

Press communiqué by Holger Matt, President of the ECBA (Personal – ECBA member email correspondence 22 June 2009) <http://www.ecba.org>.

Report from the European Union Committee on Money Laundering and the Financing of Terrorism, 'Volume I Report, Chapter 2: The Fora for International Cooperation' HL (19th Report of Session 2008–09) <http://www.publications.parliament.uk/[a/Id200809/Idselect/Ideucom/132/132i.pdf>.

Report to the Committee on Foreign Relations United States Senate by Senator John Kerry and Senator Hank Brown 12/92, 'The BCCI Affair' US 102d Congress 2d Session Senate Print 102 – 140 (1992) <http://www.fas.org/irp/congress/1992_rpt/bcci/01exec.htm>.

SOCA, 'Review of the Suspicious Activity Reports Regime (The SARs Review) Sir Stephen Lander March 2006' (SOCA website 2009) <http://www.soca.gov.uk/downloads/SOCAtheSARsReview_Final_Web.pdf>.

SOCA, 'The Suspicious Activity Reports Regime Annual Report 2008' (SOCA website 2009) <http://www.soca.gov.uk/assessPublications/downloads/SAR-Annual-Report-08-pn.pdf>.

Stanley Foundation, The, '22nd UN of the Next Decade Conference 1987: The United Nations and the Future of Internationalism 06/87' (The Stanley Foundation, Iowa 1987).

Sub-Committee F – Home Affairs Money Laundering and the Financing of Terrorism, 'Corrected oral evidence given by Mr James Robertson, Head of Financial Crime Team, HM Treasury, Mr Stephen Webb, Acting Director of Policing Policy and Operations, Home Office, Ms Gaynor Ithell, Head of Proscription and Terrorist Financing, Office of Security and Counter Terrorism, Pursue, Home Office, and Mr Christopher Yvon, Deputy Head, International Organisations Department, Foreign and Commonwealth Office' HL (2008–09), 11 March 2009, 132–II <http://www.publications.parliament.uk/pa/ld200809/ldselect/ldeucom/999/euf110309ev2.pdf>.

Sub-Committee F – Home Affairs Money Laundering and the Financing of Terrorism, 'Corrected oral evidence given by Mr Stephen Webb, Acting Director of Policing and Policy Operations, Home Office, Mr Mike Kennedy, Chief Operating Officer, Mr Jeremy Rawlins, Head of Proceeds of Crime Delivery Unit, Crown Prosecution Service and Mr David Thomas, Director,

UKFIU, Serious Organised Crime Agency' HL (2008–09) 18 March 2009, 132–II <http://www.publications.parliament.uk/pa/Id200809/Idselect/Ideucom/999/euf180309ev3.pdf>.

Sub-Committee F – Home Affairs Money Laundering and the Financing of Terrorism, 'Corrected oral evidence given by The Commission: Mr Philippe Pellé, Deputy Head, Company Law, Corporate Governance and Financial Crime; Mrs Agnete Philipson and Mr Mariano Fernandez Salas, Directorate General for the Internal Market and Services (DG MARKET), Mr Jakub Boratynski, Head of Unit on Organised Crime, Mr Sebastiano Tine, Head of Head of Financial Crime Sector, and Mr Mickael Roudaut, Directorate General for Justice, freedom and Security (DG JLS)' HL (2008–09) 25 March 2009, 132–II <http://www.publications.parliament.uk/pa/Id200809/Idselect/Ideucom/999/euf250309ev5.pdf>.

Sub-Committee F – Home Affairs Money Laundering and the Financing of Terrorism, 'Corrected oral evidence given by Sir James Sassoon, former President of the Financial Action Task Force' HL (2008–09) 22 April 2009, 132–II <http://www.publications.Parliament.uk/pa/Id200809/Idselect/Ideucom/999/euf220409ev7.pdf>.

Sub-Committee F – Home Affairs Money Laundering and the Financing of Terrorism, 'Corrected oral evidence given by Ms Mieneke de Ruiter, General Secretariat of the Council, Professor Gilles de Kerchove, EU Counter-Terrorism Co-ordinator, and Mr Hans G Nilsson, Head of JHA Counsellors, Permanent Representation of Sweden to the European Union' HL (2008–09) 25 April 2009, 132–II <http://www.publications.parliament.uk/pa/id200809/Idselect/Ideucom/999/euf250309ev4.pdf>.

Sub-Committee F – Home Affairs Money Laundering and the Financing of Terrorism, 'Corrected oral evidence given by Ian Pearson, MP Economic Secretary to the Treasury, Mr Allan Campbell, Parliamentary Under Secretary of State, Home Office, Mr James Robertson, Head of Financial Crime Team, HM Treasury and Mr Stephen Webb, Acting Director of Policing Policy and Operations, Home Office' HL (2008–09) 29 April 2009, 132–II <http://www.publications.parliament.uk/pa/Id200809/Idselect/Ideucom/999/euf290409ev8.pdf>.

Sub-Committee F – Home Affairs Money Laundering and the Financing of Terrorism, 'Corrected oral evidence given by Mr Sean McGovern, General Counsel, Ms Louise Shield, Head of Communications, and Mr Andy Wragg, Senior Manager, International Regulatory Affairs Team, Lloyd's' HL (2008–09) 13 May 2009, 132–II <http://www.publications.parliament.uk/pa/ld200809/ldselect/ldeucom/999/euf130509ev9.pdf>.

Sub-Committee F – Home Affairs Money Laundering and the Financing of Terrorism, 'Inquiry into EU and International Cooperation to Counter Money Laundering and the Financing of Terrorism: Submission of the Financial Action Task Force Secretariat E/08–09/F99 ML' HL (2008–09) 25 April 2009, 132–II

<http://www.parliament.uk/documents/upload(F099)FATFwrittenevidence.pdf>.

Sub-Committee F – Home Affairs Money Laundering and the Financing of Terrorism, 'Inquiry into Money Laundering and the Financing of Terrorism – Memorandum by HM Treasury' HL (2008–09) 30 January 2009, 132–II, Annex A: The Kadi Case and the ECJ Judgement <http://www.parliament.uk/documents/upload/(F050)Treasury2memo300109.pdf>.

T-CY – Convention Committee on Cybercrime, see especially, COE, 'Convention Committee on Cybercrime (T-CY)' (COE website 2009) <http://www.coe.int/t/dghl/cooperation/economiccrime/cybercrime/T-CY/default_en.asp>.

The White House President George W. Bush, 'The United States and the European Union Initiative to Enhance Transatlantic Economic Integration and Growth ANNEX' <http://www.iasplus.com/usa/0506useupressrelease.pdf>.

The World Bank – Committee on Payment and Settlement Systems, 'General Principles for International Remittance Services 02/07' (2007) <http://www.bis.org/publ/cpss76.pdf>.

TJN, 'The Vatican Speaks Out on Tax Havens' (Tax Justice Network website 2008) <http://www.taxjustice.blogspot.com/2008/12/vatican-speaks-out-on-tax-hav>.

United States Department on the Treasury Financial Crimes Enforcement Network Advisory, 'FATF – VII Report on Money Laundering Typologies' (FinCEN website 2009) <http://www.fincen.gov/news_room/rp/advisory/pdf/advissu4.pdf>.

UNODC (United Nations Office on Drugs and Crime), 'Legislative Guide for the Implementation of the United Nations Convention against Corruption' (United Nations Office on Drugs and Crime Division for Treaty Affairs website 2006) <http://www.unodc.org/pdf/corruption/CoC_LegislativeGuide.pdf>.

UNODC, 'Objectives of the Global Programme against Money Laundering, Proceeds of Crime and the Financing of Terrorism' (UN website 2009) <http://www.unodc.org/unodc/en/money-laundering/programme-objectives.html>.

UNODC, 'Technical Guide to the United Nations Convention against Corruption' (Division for Treaty Affairs of UNODC and the Justice, Protection and Ethics Unit of UNICRI) (UNODC website 2009) <http://www.unicri.it/wwk/publications/books/docs/Technical_Guide_UNCAC.pdf>.

UNODC treaties, 'Crime-related Treaties' (UNODC website 2009) <http://www.unodc.org/uncode.org/unodc/en/treaties/index.html>.

US Department of Justice, 'FY 2008 Performance Budget Drug Enforcement Administration Congressional Budget Submission' <http://www.usdoj.gov/jmd/2008justification/Pdf/35_dea.pdf>.

US Department of Justice, 'Overview of the Law Enforcement Strategy to Combat International Organised Crime 4/08' (US Department of Justice website 2009) <http://www.usdoj.gov/criminal/icitap/press/room/2008/apr/04-23-08combat-intl-crime-overview.pdf>.

US Department of the Treasury, From the Office of Public Affairs: RR-2452 of 18 May 1998, 'U.S. Customs Service Takes Down Major Drug Traffickers, Corrupt Banks and Bankers in Largest Drug Money Laundering Case Ever' <http://www.treasury.gov/press/releases/rr2452.htm>.

Ward, John, 'Papandreou Accused of Greek Debt "Lifebelt" Fraud', *The Slog* (London, 1 June 2011) <http://hat4uk.wordpress.com/2011/06/01/papandreou/accused-of-greek-debt-lifebelt-fraud/> accessed 24 December 2013.

Written evidence submitted on 30 January 2009 to Sub-Committee F – Home Affairs on Money Laundering and the Financing of Terrorism, 'Written evidence submitted 30 January 2009 by Professor Iain Cameron, Professor in Public International Law, Uppsala University E/08–09/F47 ML' HL (2008–09) 25 April 2009, 132–II <http://www.parliament.uk/documents/upload/F047ProfessorCameron300109.pdf>.

Newspaper Articles

Baker, RW and J Nordin, 'How Dirty Money Thwarts Capitalism's True Course' *Financial Times* (11 October 2005) <http://www.gfip.org/index.php?option=com_content& task= view?id>.

Barker, A, 'Brussels Takes Aim at Industrial Espionage' *Financial Times* (Brussels, 28 November 2013) <http://www.ft.com/cms/s/0/b7fb43ae-57af-11e3-86d1-00144feabdc0.html#axzz2od3CtdCK>.

Braithwaite, T and K Scannell, 'JPMorgan Admits Madoff Errors' *Financial Times* (London, 8 January 2014) 15.

Dinmore, G, 'France to Extradite Kazakh Ex-banker' *Financial Times* (London, 10 January 2014) 4.

Groom, B, 'Financial Sector Sees Jobs Boom' *Financial Times* (London, 20 January 2014) 3.

Hale, T, 'Recruiters' Net Fees Rise as Confidence Gets to Work' *Financial Times* (London, 21 January 2014) 21.

Harding, R, 'Inheritance Should Not be an Alternative to Hard Work' *Financial Times* (London, 8 January 2014) 11.

Hille, K, 'Islamists Boast of Volgograd Raid in Warning to Olympics' *Financial Times* (London, 21 January 2014) 8.

Houlder, V, 'Tech Groups Tax Crackdown Seen as Unviable' *Financial Times* (London, 21 January 2014) 3.

Houlder, V, 'More Taxpayers Seek Judicial Review of Revenue Decisions' *Financial Times* (London, 23 January 2014) 2.

Jones, S, 'US Reveals Fears of "Virtual" bin Laden' *Financial Times* (London, 10 January 2014) 4.

Jones, S, Borzou Daraghi and Simeon Kerr, 'On the March Al-Qaeda Terror Affiliates are Active in More Countries than Ever' *Financial Times* (London, 20 January 2014) 7.

Jones, S and J Gapper, 'Expert Panel to Investigate Internet Governance' *Financial Times* (London, 23 January 2014) 9.
Mitchell, T and PJ Davies, 'Prominent Chinese Anti-Corruption Activist Tried in Secret' *Financial Times* (London, 23 January 2014) 6.
Neuwirth, S, 'BlackRock Backs Bolton against Italian Civil Suit' CITY AM (London, 13 January 2014) 4.
Rembelou, A, 'For the First Time Bank Accounts Open in Switzerland: In the Nails of … Ex Wives 4.450 clients of UBS in USA' *Kosmos Toy Ependiti* (Athens, Weekend Newspaper 29–30 August 2009) 15.
Sakoui, A, 'Concentrated $2.8tn Cash Pile Puts Global Recovery in the Hands of the Few' *Financial Times* (London, 22 January 2014) 1, 21.
Sharman, A and S Fleming, 'Morrison Suspends Treasurer after His Arrest in Insider Dealing Probe' *Financial Times* (London, 21 January 2014) 15.
Shellock, D, 'Robust US Jobs Data Weigh on Treasury Prices and Lift Dollar' *Financial Times* (London, 9 January 2014) 27.
Stephens, P, 'Riches and Risk: Welcome to the World of Tomorrow' *Financial Times* (London, 10 January 2014) 11.
The Economist, 'A Survey of Illegal Drugs' (2001) 360, 8232.
The Economist, 'Buttonwood Too Big for its Gucci Boots: The Causes of the Overexpansion of the Finance Industry' (2009) 392 8648.
The Economist, 'Buttonwood: Be Thankful They Don't Take it All' (2009) 392, 8647.
The Economist, 'Extending Freedom of Information – Uncovering the Next Scandal' (2009) 391, 8634.
The Economist, 'Foiling Terrorist Attacks: Home-grown Bombers' (2009) 393, 8651.
The Economist, 'Foreign Aid: Trap or Treat' (2009) 393, 8662.
The Economist, 'French Corruption Scandals: Peering into the Murk' (2009) 393 8655.
The Economist, 'Human Identity: An Elusive Illusion' (2009) 393, 8662.
The Economist, 'Making Fiscal Policy Credible: Bind Games' (2009) 392, 8648.
The Economist, 'Municipal Corruption in Canada' (2009) 391, 8637.
The Economist, 'Order in the Jungle' (2008) 386, 8571.
The Economist, 'Overhauling Financial Regulation: The Regulatory Rumble Begins' (2009) 391, 8633.
The Economist, 'Ralf Dahrendorf Definer and Defender of Liberty' (2009) 391, 8637.
The Economist, 'Software that Spots Hidden Networks: Electronic Ties that Bind' (2009) 391, 8637.
The Economist, 'Spain's Political Scandals: The Problem with Don Vito's Friends' (2009) 393, 8655.
The Economist, 'The G20 Meetings: What Next?' (2009) 392, 8648.
The Economist, 'The Galleon Affair – All at Sea' (2009) 393, 8654.

The Economist, 'The Global Crackdown on Corporate Bribery: Ungreasing the Wheels' (2009) 393, 8658.

The Economist, 'The Madoff Affair' (2009) 392, 8638.

The Economist, 'The New Supreme Court: Separation of Powers' (2009) 393, 8651.

The Economist, 'White-Collar Trials: Subcrime' (2009) 393, 8657.

Waters, R, 'Obama Drags Tech Companies Deeper into Mire Surveillance' *Financial Times* (London, 21 January 2014) 6.

Wild, J and V Houlder, 'UK Reviews Tax on Bitcoin as Global Regulators Seek to Cash in' *Financial Times* (London, 20 January 2014) 1.

Wolf, M, 'Failing Elites Threaten Our Future' *Financial Times* (London, 15 January 2014) 11.

Index